Wavelength

Pre-Intermediate • Coursebook

Kathy
Burke

Julia
Brooks

Contents

Skills	Wavelength pages
Listening: asking questions Reading: part-time courses Writing and speaking: *Finding the right course* questionnaire	*Day to day English* **Could you . . . ?** Requests, offers and answers Pron: linking and sentence stress
Speaking: talking about money Reading and listening: *Easy come easy go* Writing and speaking: *Are you the same as you used to be?* questionnaire	*Conversations* **Really? I think . . .** Giving opinions: agreeing and disagreeing *So* and *neither* Pron: sentence stress
Listening: *It's your life, Monica Gordon* Reading and speaking: The image makers Listening and speaking: First memories Writing and speaking: *My early years* questionnaire	*Skills* **Reading, listening, speaking** *I love a good read. . .* Word play: dealing with unknown words (nouns, verbs, adjectives), guessing meaning from context, remembering new words, using dictionaries
Listening and speaking: types of films Listening and reading: The director and the actress Speaking: Past experiences questionnaire	*Do you remember?* **Units 1–4** 1 *Money makes the world go round* 2 *You used to buy me flowers* 3 *Wanted!*
Listening: Rules and regulations Writing and speaking: *Do you have to wear a tie?* Reading and speaking: A great opportunity Writing: a letter to a friend	*Conversations* **Really? Are you?** Echo questions to show interest Listening and pron: intonation in echo questions Speaking: The echo game
Speaking and listening: *What's it like?* Speaking: *Where is it?* Listening and speaking: *What's the weather like?* Listening and speaking: *The shortest holiday I've ever had!*	*Day to day English* **Can you tell me . . . ?** Indirect questions to ask for information Giving directions
Reading and listening: *The cruel heart* filmscript Speaking: Reputations	*Skills* **Speaking, listening, reading** TV adverts and consumers
Reading and speaking: *Are you an optimist or a pessimist?* questionnaire Listening and speaking: *What'll you do if. . .?* Reading and writing: making a story more interesting by adding adjectives and adverbs	*Do you remember?* **Units 5–8** 1 *Do you have a choice?* 2 *What are you going to do with the money?* 3 *What do you think will happen?*

Skills	Wavelength pages
Listening and speaking: rooms in a house Listening, speaking and writing: My favourite things Reading, speaking and writing: designing rooms for a TV drama	*Conversations* **Could I speak to . . . ?** On the phone Pron: stress and intonation *Can you repeat that?:* altering sentence stress to ask for information again
Reading and listening: Jenny's relationships Listening: Mandy's relationships Listening and writing: Shades of anger Listening and speaking: Chat show interviews	*Skills* **Reading, writing, speaking** Jealousy and revenge
Listening and speaking: *In the beginning there was nothing* Listening and speaking: *If I didn't have my . . .* Writing and speaking: Pet hates Writing and speaking: *If things were different . . .*	*Day to day English* **I think you should . . .** Giving advice about a problem at work: *If I were you, I'd . . .* Pron: sentence stress *Help me, please!*
Reading: *It's in the stars* Listening: The driving lesson Listening: *No particular place to go* (song)	*Do you remember?* **Units 9–12** 1 *How long have they lived there?* 2 *Where were you?* 3 *If I were a . . .*
Listening and speaking: *Look out! He's going to . . .* Reading, writing and speaking: a week at Club Torso	*Day to day English* **There's a problem . . .** Making complaints
Writing and listening: Criminals and crimes Reading and speaking: *Reginald Kramer says he's innocent!* Writing: a newspaper article	*Skills* **Listening, speaking, reading, writing** *Guilty or not guilty?* Past Continuous for background in narratives Linkers and time expressions: *because, so, and, but, suddenly, finally, after, before, when, during*
Listening and speaking: at a party Listening, writing and speaking: family photographs	*Conversations* **What do you call . . . ?** Miming Talking round words Using *stuff* and *thing / things*
Speaking, listening and writing: Strangers on a train Reading: *It's a small world!* Speaking: telling stories about coincidences	*Do you remember?* **Units 13–16** 1 Defining Relative Clauses + *one / ones* 2 The Passive 3 Reported Speech

Finding out about people

Pronunciation: word stress and intonation
Present Simple or Present Continuous?
Frequency Adverbs: *hardly ever, always*
Part-time courses
Day to day English: *Could you . . . ?*

Asking the right questions

1 a) Read the questions in A and match them to the answers in B.

Example: 1 = e)

A
1 What's your name?
2 Where are you from?
3 What's your favourite subject?
4 What are you studying?
5 Do you like school?
6 Where do you work?
7 What job would you like to do?
8 Are you married?
9 Do you have any children?
10 What do you do?

B
a) I'd like to be a famous violinist – that's my dream.
b) I love music and Miss Stevens, my teacher, is great.
c) In the Engineering Department of OCI.
d) I'm a waiter, but I want to go to university.
e) I'm David Jefferson, but my friends call me Dave.
f) It's all right usually, but I've got exams at the moment.
g) Yes, a son and a daughter. They're both at university now.
h) I'm doing an advanced computing course.
i) Italy.
j) Yes, I am. My husband, Tom, works for OCI too.

b) In pairs. Look at the photographs of Dave, Sue, Jackie and Danilo and answer the questions.

1 Which answers in Exercise 1a) do you think each person gave?
2 Which questions aren't suitable for Jackie?

2 a) 🔊 1 Dave and Sue are doing a part-time evening course in advanced computing. It's the coffee break on the first evening. Listen. Which questions in Exercise 1a) does Sue ask Dave?

b) 🔊 1 Listen again. What are Dave's answers? Make some notes.

Pronunciation: word stress and intonation

3 a) 🔊 2 Listen. How many syllables do these words have?

Example: children 2

1 subject ☐
2 university ☐
3 engineering ☐
4 studying ☐
5 married ☐
6 department ☐

Dave

Sue

Jackie

Danilo

b) 🔊2 Read the Language Box. Listen again. Underline the stressed syllables in the words in Exercise 3a).

Example: <u>chil</u>dren

Word stress

In words of two or more syllables, one syllable always has more stress than the other(s):

<u>ques</u>tion, <u>ans</u>wer, com<u>pu</u>ter, pronunci<u>a</u>tion.

c) 🔊3 Listen to two of Sue's questions and Dave's answers again. Which question goes up ↗ at the end? Which question goes down ↘ ? Do Dave's answers go up ↗ or down ↘ at the end? Fill in the boxes.

Sue's questions	Dave's answers
1 ☐	☐
2 ☐	☐

d) Read the Language Box and fill in the boxes with up ↗ or down ↘.

Intonation

Our voices usually go ☐ at the end of *Yes / No* questions:
Do you have any children?

But they go ☐ at the end of *Wh-* questions:
What do you do?

Our voices also go ☐ at the end of sentences:
I'm a maths teacher.

e) 🔊4 Listen and repeat questions (1–5) in Exercise 1a). Do they go up ↗ or down ↘ at the end? Which are the stressed words / syllables?

f) Go round the class and ask questions from Exercise 1a) to find out about each other.

Which course do you want to do?

4 Read these adverts about part-time courses. Then in pairs, talk about which courses you think are interesting, useful or boring.

① Are you afraid to go out at night?
LEARN AIKIDO

- 𝛑 Feel safe
- 𝛑 Get fit
- 𝛑 Be confident
- 𝛑 Defend yourself

We have a course for you!
All levels – beginners to advanced.

②
Current affairs –
what's behind those headlines?

Do you know what's happening in the world at the moment?

This course gives you all the information and the chance to discuss it in small, friendly groups.

③
Bring out the writer in you

Learn how to write articles, short stories, novels and TV scripts.

Our professional team of writers can teach you everything you need to know. Don't delay! Start writing today! Fill in the form and send it to us.

④ Information technology Evening Courses

No computer skills? No problem! Come to our introductory courses:
- word processing
- e-mail
- the Internet
- databases

⑤

"I'm doing business in Japanese, thanks to the **Easy Language System.***"*

Learn a language in two weeks
We offer intensive courses in the following:
Arabic • Chinese • Portuguese • English • French
Spanish • German • Italian • Japanese

⑥
GUITAR & VIOLIN LESSONS
I'm a patient, experienced professional musician and I'm looking for students – beginners welcome! Lessons at students' homes.

⑦
FILM STUDIES
This course is for anyone who loves film. We will look at the work of Hitchcock, Fellini, Amoldóvar, Godard, Kieślowski and Tarantino.

⑧
Art & design diploma
We offer part-time diploma courses in:
- film and video
- fashion design
- interior design
- photography

Sue

Sue's an engineer and she works for an American company, OCI. At the moment she's managing a project in London. She loves working abroad and she'd like to work in South America or Asia one day. She hardly ever meets people that aren't connected with her job. She wants to meet new people, use her mind and discuss ideas. She's looking for an interesting evening course where she can do these things.

Jackie

Jackie loves music and wants to work in the music industry when she leaves school. She plays the violin very well and has lessons once a week. Now she wants to learn to play  the guitar or the piano. She isn't going out or getting much exercise at the moment because she's studying for her exams. She isn't happy about this because she's usually quite an active person.

Danilo

Danilo is from Italy but he's living in London at the moment. He's working as a waiter in an Italian restaurant. He'd like to go to university in England and he's trying to find out about courses. He likes travelling and he's interested in talking to people from different countries. In his free time he goes to the cinema a lot – one day he'd like to work in the film industry.

5 **a)** In pairs. Read about Sue, Jackie and Danilo. They're interested in doing part-time courses. Look back at page 7 and choose two courses for each person.

b) In groups of four. Say which courses you chose and why.

Present Simple or Present Continuous?

6 **a)** Read these two sentences about Sue. Which sentence is in the Present Simple and which sentence is in the Present Continuous? Fill in the gaps in the Language Box with *Present Simple* or *Present Continuous*.

1 Sue's an engineer and she works for an American company, OCI.
2 At the moment she's managing a project in London.

Present Simple or Present Continuous?

We use the .... to talk about general habits and lifestyles, and things that happen over a long time and are permanent:
She works for an American company.

We use the .... to talk about things which are happening now and around now – things that are temporary:
At the moment she's managing a project in London.

---

b) Read about Sue, Jackie and Danilo again and underline the sentences about what they are doing at the moment.

Example: <u>At the moment she's managing a project in London.</u>

c) What are you and your friends doing at the moment? Are these sentences true for you? If not, change them. Then, in pairs, compare your sentences.

1 I'm studying English for my job.
2 I'm working very hard at the moment.
3 The student next to me is doing other courses too.
4 All my friends are looking for jobs at the moment.

How often do you do that?

7 a) Do the words and phrases in the Word Box go before the verb or at the end of the sentence? Read the Language Box. Then write the sentence *I go to the gym* and add the words and phrases in the correct place.

Frequency Adverbs and phrases

Frequency Adverbs (*always, never, hardly ever,* etc.) usually come **before** the main verb but **after** the verb *be*. Longer phrases (*once a week*) usually come at the end of the sentence.

---

always ✓	once a week ✓	usually	every day
once a day	five times a year	hardly ever	often never
every Sunday	sometimes	all the time	twice a week

Examples: I **always** go to the gym.
I go to the gym **once a week**.

b) Now use the words and phrases from the Word Box in Exercise 7a) and make these sentences true for you. Then, in pairs, compare your sentences.

Example: 1 I **hardly ever** get up before 9 a.m.

1 I get up before 9 a.m.
2 I read the newspaper.
3 I'm tired at the weekend.
4 I go on holiday in August.
5 I go to nightclubs.

8 a) These questions are from the questionnaire on the right. Put the words in the correct order.

Example: 1 you / time / lot / free / have / Do / a / of ?
Do you have a lot of free time?

2 you / What / in / are / interested ?
3 films / talking / like / Do / about / you ?
4 doing / you / moment / the / Are / a / course / at ?
5 foreign / speak / often / you / a / language / do / How ?

b) 🔘🔘5 Listen and check. Then write the questions in the questionnaire.

c) Look at the questionnaire. One of the answers (a–c) for each question is grammatically wrong. Find it and correct it.

d) Now do the questionnaire for yourself. Write your own answer if answers (a–c) aren't right for you.

9 a) In pairs. You're going to find part-time courses for students. Write four more questions for the questionnaire.

b) Make new pairs. Ask each other your questions. Then look at the adverts in Exercise 4 (on page 7) and choose a course for your partner.

Finding the right course

▶ **1** Do you have a lot of free time? ....

 a) No, not really. I work very long hours.
 b) Yes, I do.
 c) No, I ~~haven't~~. I'm really busy these days
 No, I **don't**. I'm really busy these days.

▶ **2** ....

 a) Languages and the cinema.
 b) Current affairs. I take an evening course at the moment.
 c) I like discussing ideas and using my mind.

▶ **3** ....

 a) Yes, sometimes.
 b) No, I don't like. I'm not really interested in films.
 c) Not really.

▶ **4** ....

 a) No, I'm not. I'm too busy.
 b) Yes, I do.
 c) Yes, I'm doing photography at the moment. It's really interesting.

▶ **5** ....

 a) Every day in my job.
 b) Hardly ever. Only when I go abroad – about once a year.
 c) No, never.

Grammar reference
The Present: Present Simple and Present Continuous: page 102

The new temp

1 a) Steve is a temp and it's his first day at Maxi Publishing. Look at the photographs. Do you think he likes his new job?

b) 🔘6 Listen and fill in the gaps in the speech bubbles. Then read the Language Box and answer the questions.

① .... you .... 300 copies of this?

Yes, of ....

Requests and answers

Requests	Yes answers
A: Would you mind making me a copy of this?	B: No, not at all.
A: Could you make me a copy of this?	B: Yes, of course. All right.
A: Can you make me a copy of this?	B: Yes / Yeah, sure. OK. No problem.

Look!
• If we refuse (say *No*), we usually give a reason:
(I'm) Sorry, | I'm busy at the moment.
I'm afraid |

---

1 Which request and answer is the most polite?
2 Which request is the most informal?
3 Which *Yes* answer looks like *No?*

Pronunciation: linking and sentence stress

2 a) 🔘7 Listen to the requests from Exercise 1b) again. How do we pronounce *can you*, *could you* and *would you*?

1 Could you make three hundred copies of this?
2 Could you post these letters?
3 Could you get me a ham sandwich?
4 Would you mind taking this to Room 101?
5 Can you help me with the photocopier?

b) 🔘7 Underline the stressed words / syllables in each request. Then listen again and repeat.

Example: Could you make <u>three</u> hundred <u>copies</u> of <u>this</u>?

② Are you the new temp? .... you .... these letters? And .... you .... me a ham sandwich?

.... right.

3 a) In pairs. Look at the list of action points on the right. Take it in turns to be the boss and the temp. **Boss:** Ask your temp to do three of these jobs. **Temp:** If you refuse, give a reason.

Example: BOSS: Could you confirm my meeting with Mr Johnson on Tuesday?

TEMP: Yes, of course. / Sorry, I'm helping Mr Jones in Accounts.

b) Now both of you are temps. Take it in turns to ask each other for help. Answer *Yes* or *No*. If you refuse, give a reason.

Example: TEMP A: Sorry, can you help me? I'm going crazy! Can you order fifty sandwiches for the 12:00 meeting?

TEMP B: Yeah, sure. / Sorry, I . . .

Action points

• Confirm my meeting with Mr Johnson on Tuesday.
• Water my plants.
• Make 300 copies of the letter on my desk.
• Order fifty sandwiches for the 12:00 meeting tomorrow.
• Phone Mr Takahashi about my trip to Japan.
• Cancel my doctor's appointment.

1

(3) Sorry, I can see you're busy but, ... you .... this to Room 101? It's urgent!

No, ... at all.

(4) ...., I'm really busy.

Excuse me. .... you .... me with the photocopier? It's not working.

(5) Yeah, ...

Sorry, ... you .... me with the photocopier?

Can I help you?

4 8 Nina in photograph 5 feels sorry for Steve and offers to help him. Listen and match her offers in A and Steve's answers in B. Then read the Language Box.

Example: 1 = b)

A Offers

1 Would you like me to post those letters for you?
2 I'll get his sandwich.
3 Shall I get you something?
4 I'll take it.

B Answers

a) Oh, thanks a lot.
b) Yes, please. That's really nice of you.
c) Oh, don't worry. I'll do it.
d) No, it's OK. Thanks anyway.

Offers and answers

Offers	Yes / No answers
A: Would you like me to copy this? **A**: Shall I copy this?	**B**: Yes, please. That's really / very nice of you. **B**: No, it's all right / OK. Thank you / Thanks anyway.
Offers: 'll (will) + infinitive	**Yes / No answers**
A: I'll get his sandwich. **A**: I'll take it.	**B**: Thanks a lot. **B**: Thank you very much. **B**: Don't worry. I'll do it. **B**: That's OK / all right.

Pronunciation: sentence stress

5 **a)** 9 Listen to the offers in Exercise 4 again. Underline the stressed words / syllables.

1 Would you like me to post those letters for you?
2 I'll get his sandwich.
3 Shall I get you something?
4 I'll take it.

b) 9 Listen again and repeat.

Make my day!

6 In groups of three, look at page 131.

2 Money matters

Money
Past Simple: money verbs
Used to / didn't use to
Comparative Adjectives
Conversations: *Really? I think . . .*

Talking about money

1 In pairs. Read these English sayings about money and talk about the questions below.

"Money can't buy you happiness."
"Money talks."
"Money doesn't grow on trees."

1 Do you have the same or different sayings in your country?
2 Do you use them? When?
3 Can you translate them into English?

Past Simple: money verbs

2 a) The Past Simple irregular verbs in the Word Box are all connected with money. Write the infinitives. Then check your answers in the Irregular verb list on page 143.

| paid   cost   made   lost   spent   won   lent |

b) Now look at these Past Simple regular verbs. Write the infinitives.

| earned   rented   borrowed   invested   shopped   saved |
| wasted   inherited   gambled   refunded   owed   tipped |

Pronunciation: *-ed* endings

3 a) 🔊 10 Listen to the Past Simple endings of the regular verbs in Exercise 2b) and fill in the table. Then read the Language Box.

/d/	/t/	/ɪd/
earned	....	....
....	....	....
....	....	....
....	....	....
....	....	....

Regular verbs: *-ed* endings

We only pronounce the full *-ed* /ɪd/ ending when the infinitive of the verb ends with the sound /d/ or /t/:
refun**d**ed, was**t**ed

b) 🔊 11 Listen and check. Then listen again and repeat.

Easy come, easy go

4 a) Look at the picture. Bob and Rita are a young married couple. Read the end of the letter (on page 13) that Rita wrote to her brother, Derek. Then answer the questions.

1 Why are Bob and Rita unhappy?
2 Why is Rita writing to Derek?
3 Who do you think Sandra is?

b) In pairs. What do you think happened before Rita wrote the letter? Try to answer the questions.

1 Why is Uncle Jason's money finished?
2 Bob and Rita didn't listen to Sandra. What do you think Sandra said?
3 Why do you think their "friend" borrowed money from them, and then disappeared?

5 a) What really happened to Bob and Rita? Read their story and find out.

b) Are these sentences true (T) or false (F)? Fill in the boxes and correct the false sentences.

Example: Bob and Rita had very good jobs at the start of the story. ☐F☐
No, they didn't have very good jobs.

1 They were too tired to go out a lot when they worked. ☐

2 Bob's uncle was broke when he died. ☐

3 Bob and Rita rented a really nice apartment in Las Vegas. ☐

4 They were popular in the restaurants because they were generous to the staff. ☐

5 Bob and Rita hardly ever won money in the casino. ☐

c) 🔘🔘 12 Listen to the story. Then make two lists:

1 how money comes.
2 how money goes.

Examples: 1 you earn it
2 you spend it

P.O. Box 261
Las Vegas

Dear Derek,

Uncle Jason's money is finished. Bob and I are completely broke and we're so miserable. A friend of ours owes us a lot of money, but unfortunately he disappeared two days after he borrowed it from us. We have no idea where he is! We're stuck in Las Vegas now – staying in a camp site. Why didn't we listen to Sandra? The flight from Las Vegas to London costs £800. Can you lend us the money, please? I hate to ask you, but . . . we promise to work hard and pay you back. We just want to come home!

    Love,

    Rita

PS Love to Sandra and the kids.

Bob and Rita didn't like their jobs and they didn't earn big salaries. They were often broke at the end of the month so they couldn't afford to go out or buy nice things. Then Bob's wealthy Uncle Jason died and Bob inherited a lot of money. Suddenly everything changed . . .

JEFF: Art! That's the thing! Invest in art! You can make millions!

TEDDY: Uncle Bob, can I have a computer?

DEREK: Spend the money! Have a good time!

SANDRA: Don't listen to your brother or Jeff! Save your money! Put it in the bank! Don't waste it on stupid things.

Bob and Rita decided to get away. They sold their small flat for £40,000 and left their boring jobs. They were young and rich and they wanted to live like rich people. They wanted to see the world! They bought first-class tickets to Las Vegas and rented a luxury apartment. They ate in the best restaurants and the waiters and waitresses loved them because they always tipped well. They shopped in the most expensive stores and bought expensive clothes. They gambled in the casinos every night. They usually lost, but they didn't care – they were rich!

CROUPIER: I really think you should leave now, madam.

RITA: Just one more game. I'm feeling lucky. I know we can win.

BOB: Yeah, it's only money. We can afford it.

ADAM: My dear Bob, I have a little business idea. We could make a lot of money from it. Are you interested?

BOB: Yeah! It sounds great!

ADAM: Well, we'll both have to invest some money . . . just to get it started, of course.

BOB: No problem! How much do you need?

He used to . . . but he doesn't now

6 a) In pairs. Look at Andrew and Tom ten years ago and now. How is each man different now?

Example: Ten years ago Andrew was a rich businessman in New York City. Now he lives a simple life in the country.

b) Match four sentences to each man (two positive and two negative).

Example: 1 = Andrew

1 He used to earn a lot of money.
2 He used to have good eyesight.
3 He used to eat meat.
4 He used to spend a lot of time on his own.
5 He didn't use to wear nice clothes.
6 He didn't use to have a quiet lifestyle.
7 He didn't use to be bald.
8 He didn't use to have short hair.

c) Fill in the gaps with *Andrew* or *Tom*.

1 **A:** Did .... use to wear glasses?
  B: No, he didn't, but he does now.
2 **A:** Did .... use to be poor?
  B: No, he didn't, but he is now.
3 **A:** Did .... use to have a lot of money?
  B: No, he didn't, but he does now.
4 **A:** Did .... use to be famous?
  B: No, he didn't, but he is now.

d) 🔘 13 Listen and check.

e) Read the sentences about Andrew and Tom again and fill in the gaps in the Language Box.

Used to / didn't use to + infinitive

Positive sentences

Subject		Infinitive
I / You / We / They / He / She	....	eat meat. be famous.

Negative sentences

Subject		Infinitive
I / You / We / They / He / She	....	eat meat. be famous.

Yes / No questions   **Short answers**

A: Did you .... eat meat?   **B:** Yes, I **did**.
A: Did she .... be famous?   **B:** No, she **didn't**.

Look!
We use *used to / didn't use to* for:
• something that happened regularly in the past but doesn't happen any more (past habits that are now finished).
• something which was true in the past but isn't true any more (past states which are now finished).

f) Use the words and phrases in the Word Box and make three more sentences (two positive and one negative) about each man.

a vegetarian /ˌvedʒəˈteəriən/   a tiny flat
a glamorous /ˈglæmərəs/ lifestyle   fat
expensive restaurants   a moustache /məˈstɑːʃ/

① Andrew ten years ago.

Andrew now.

② Tom ten years ago.

Tom now.

Are you the same as you used to be?

	You	Your partner
1 Are you richer than you used to be?		
2 Are you happier than you used to be?		
3 Are you more careful with money than you used to be?		
4 Is life in your country more expensive than it used to be?		
5 Is money more important to you than it used to be?		
6 ....?		
7 ....?		
8 ....?		
9 ....?		
10 ....?		

Comparative Adjectives

7 a) Read the Language Box. Then read the questionnaire and underline the Comparative Adjectives.

> ### Comparative Adjectives
>
> We use Comparative Adjectives to compare two people, places or things:
> - One or two syllable adjectives, add *-er*: rich → richer
> - Short adjectives ending in *e*, add *-r*: nice → nicer
> - Two syllable adjectives ending with *-y*, change *y* to *i* and add *-er*: happy → happier
> - Most other adjectives use *more*: expensive → more expensive
> - We can also use *not as* + adjective + *as* to compare things:
>   Tom isn't as thin as he used to be. **OR** He's fatter than he used to be.
> - Some adjectives are irregular: good → better

b) Write the comparative forms of these adjectives.

> | difficult | poor | attractive | nice | bad |
> |---|---|---|---|---|
> | cheap | adventurous | easy | interesting | stressful |

c) Read the questionnaire again and write five more questions. Then fill in the questionnaire for yourself.

d) In pairs. Take it in turns to ask the questions and fill in the questionnaire for your partner.

> **Grammar reference**
>
> The Past: Past Simple; *used to / didn't use to* + infinitive: page 103
> Comparative Adjectives: page 107

① ② ③

Giving opinions: agreeing and disagreeing

1 **a)** 🔊 14 Look at the photographs and listen to three conversations (a–c). Which of the photographs (1–3) are the people talking about?

b) 🔊 14 Look at the expressions for agreeing and disagreeing. Listen to the conversations again and tick (✓) the ones you hear.

1 Absolutely! ☐   7 Really? (I think . . .) ☐
2 I agree (with you). ☐   8 Yeah / Yes. ☐
3 Perhaps. ☐   9 Yeah / Yes, but . . . ☐
4 Neither do I. ☐   10 You're joking! ☐
5 I don't think so. ☐   11 I don't agree / I disagree (with him). ☐
6 So do I. ☐   12 Maybe. ☐

c) In pairs. Where do you think the expressions for agreeing and disagreeing from Exercise 1b) go? Fill in the table.

yes, yes, yes   *no, no, no*

Strong agreement	Strong disagreement
....	....

Not sure

....
....

Agreement	Disagreement
I agree (with you).	Really? (I think . . .)
....	....
....	....
....	....

d) Fill in the gaps with expressions from Exercise 1c).

CONVERSATION A
A: Oh! She looks awful. She's too thin. Why do they all look like sticks?
B: I think she's really attractive but I don't like the dress.
C: .... It looks like something out of *Star Wars*. What a waste of money!
A: ....

CONVERSATION B
A: He's OK. I like him.
B: .... I think he's a bit rude.
C: .... He just says what he thinks. I like that.
A: .... And he was really helpful to me with that report.

CONVERSATION C
A: So, what did you think of that?
B: I thought it was quite interesting – experimental.
C: .... I hated it. I thought it was awful.
A: Oh, ... I didn't understand it. What was it all about?

Pronunciation: sentence stress

2 a) [oo] 15 Listen to these expressions for agreeing and disagreeing. Underline the stressed words / syllables.

Example: <u>Real</u>ly? I think he's a bit <u>rude</u>.

1 Neither do I.   4 Yeah. So do I.
2 Absolutely!   5 You're joking!
3 I don't think so.   6 I agree.

b) [oo] 15 Listen again and repeat.

So and *neither*

3 a) Look at the photographs. Then fill in the gaps in the Language Box with *so* or *neither*.

> ### Agreeing: *so* and *neither*
>
> We use .... when we agree with a positive sentence.
> We use .... when we agree with a negative sentence.
> **Look!**
> • I like him. **So** do I. **NOT** So I ~~do~~.
> • I don't like him. **Neither** do I. **NOT** Neither I ~~do~~.

b) These people are all giving their opinions about different places. Use the expressions in the Word Box and agree with each sentence. Then, in pairs, practise saying the sentences and agreeing.

> So did I.   Neither do I.   So do I.   Neither did I.

Example: A: I loved the museums.
                  B: So did I.

1 I really liked the pubs.
2 I love the buildings.
3 I didn't think the hotel was very nice.
4 I hate the noise and the traffic.
5 I thought the people were lovely.
6 I don't like the weather.

c) [oo] 16 Listen to more opinions. Use the expressions in Exercise 3b) to agree with them.

You're joking!

4 a) Write five sentences about things you like or don't like. Give your true opinions. Use the ideas in the Word Box to help you.

> a type of music   a person you all know
> a type of food   a place you all know
> a famous /ˈfeɪməs/ person you all know
> a sport   modern art   smoking

Examples: I think the food in the college café is great.
                    I think smoking is a disgusting habit.

b) In groups. Take it in turns to give your opinions and agree or disagree. If you disagree, say why.

Example: A: I think the food in the college café is great.
                  B: So do I.
                  C: You're joking! I think it's awful! It . . .

3 It's your life!

Biographies
Past Simple
First memories: *remember doing*
Skills: *I love a good read . . .*

It's your life, Monica Gordon

1 a) Larry Langford is interviewing Monica Gordon on the TV programme *It's your life*. In pairs. The pictures (a–f) give the answers to the questions (1–6). Match the questions to the pictures. What do you think the answers are?

Example: 1 = d)

1 What did you do when you left school?
2 Where did you get married?
3 Who looked after you when you were a child?
4 Where were you born?
5 Why did you get divorced?
6 Did you have a happy childhood?

b) [oo] 17 Listen and check. *(Stop the tape after each question for a check).*

2 In pairs. Which three questions from Exercise 1a) *Oil 12 (A)* would you like to answer? Take it in turns to ask *3,4 (B)* and answer the questions you chose. *5,6 (C)*

2nd Listening

3 a) [oo] 18 Listen to the next part of the TV programme and fill in the gaps in the questions.

1 Why .... your business?
2 Why .... to Scotland?
3 When .... there?

b) [oo] 18 Look at Monica's answers to the questions in Exercise 3a). There is one mistake in each answer. Listen again. Correct the mistakes.

1 Well, we needed a change. We wanted something more exciting.
2 Oh, it's so beautiful and wild. Life in the USA was too expensive and dangerous.
3 We moved in 1982 and our first baby was born in 1993.

Millionaire's daughter joins hippie commune

...and she could afford very large bell bottom... ...always happy looking at the... ...man in th...

Past Simple

4 a) Fill in the table with the infinitive and Past Simple of the regular and irregular verbs in the Word Box.

> die ✓   become ✓   can   come   start   join   leave
> live   look after   love   meet   miss   move
> need   run away   see   get   talk   want

Regular verbs		Irregular verbs	
Infinitive	**Past Simple**	**Infinitive**	**Past Simple**
die	died	become	became

b) Larry talked to his assistant to check his information about Monica. Fill in the gaps with the Past Simple of the verbs in brackets.

1 (like)

LARRY: .... she .... California?

ASSISTANT: Yes, she .... but she .... school. She only ....
one teacher, Mrs Moore. Oh . . . and she .... art.

2 (be)

LARRY: .... her parents around a lot when she was a child?

ASSISTANT: No, they .... They .... always busy.

LARRY: .... she happy with her first husband, Brian?

ASSISTANT: No, she .... He .... interested in her. He .... only
interested in politics.

3 (can)

LARRY: .... she play any musical instruments?

ASSISTANT: No, she .... – but she .... paint.

LARRY: .... she paint very well?

ASSISTANT: Yes, she ....

Pronunciation: -ed endings and linking

5 a) Do the Past Simple endings of the regular verbs in Exercise 4a)
have the sound /d/, /t/ or /ɪd/? Make three lists.

b) 19 Listen and check.

19

6 a) 🔘20 Read and listen to these sentences. Then listen again and repeat. Why do you think some of the words are linked (‿)? What happens to the "h" sound in *her*?

1 I really loved her.   3 You joined a commune.
2 She looked after me.   4 We moved in 1992.

b) Fill in the gaps in the Language Box with *consonant* or *vowel*.

c) How do we say these sentences? Which sounds are linked?

1 We lived in Latin America.   3 I really liked her.
2 We needed a change.   4 We wanted a family.

d) 🔘21 Listen and check. Then listen again and repeat.

> ### Linking
>
> When a word begins with a
> .... sound, the
> .... sound at the end
> of the word before links onto it.
>
> **Look!**
> • The beginning "h" sound in *him*
>   and *her* is very soft when it
>   comes after words ending in
>   consonant sounds:
>   I loved her.

The image makers

7 a) Look at the photograph and read the biography of a new pop star, BK James. Why do you think BK's agent is unhappy about his biography?

b) Write questions for these answers about BK James.

Example: 1 Where was BK James brought up?

1 In Sunnybridge.
2 His father was a bank manager and his mother was a doctor.
3 Yes, he did and he passed all his exams.
4 He played sports and helped old people.
5 No, never.
6 He went to university and studied economics.
7 When he was twenty-two years old.
8 At birthday parties and weddings.
9 His childhood sweetheart, Nancy.
10 Yes, one son called Bobby.

c) In pairs. You work for a public relations company and you are promoting BK James as a wild new star. Your company wants you to change his life story and make his past more exciting! Use the questions you wrote in Exercise 7b) to help you and make a new life story for BK. Make notes on your ideas.

Example: He was brought up in the slums of New York. His father was a gambler. He left home when BK was a baby…

d) Make pairs with a different student. Ask each other questions about BK's new "life stories".

BK James was born Benedict Kenneth James. He was brought up in a small town called Sunnybridge. His father was a bank manager and his mother was a doctor. They're both retired now. They lived in a pretty, suburban neighbourhood and he had a very happy childhood.

He did well at school and passed all his exams. When he was a teenager, he played sports with his friends and helped old people in his free time. He never got into trouble.

When he left school he went to university and studied economics. When he was twenty-one years old, he started working for a bank. A year later he joined his first band, *The Sugar Pops*. They played at birthday parties and weddings. He married his childhood sweetheart, Nancy, four years ago. They still live in their home town. They have a young son called Bobby.

BK James' single, "Tell you why" comes out on June 5th

First memories: *remember doing*

8 a) 🔊 22 Listen to three people answering the question "What's your first memory?". Listen again and fill in the gaps. Then read the Language Box.

1 I remember .... my bike when I was about six.
2 I remember .... and ....
3 I remember .... the ice cream and .... "School's really fun!".

Remember + infinitive + -ing

Nancy said:
I remember falling off my bike when I was about six.
(She fell off her bike when she was about six. Now she looks back and remembers it.)

b) Write one or two sentences about your first memory. Then go round the class and ask four other students about their memories. Does anyone have a similar memory to you?

9 a) Read the questionnaire and fill in the gaps in the questions. Then write two more questions (9 and 10). Use the Past Simple.

b) In groups of four. Ask and answer the questions. Make notes about the other students' answers.

c) Choose one of the students in your group and write a short paragraph about his / her early years. End your paragraph with the question *Who is it?*.

d) Make new groups of four. Put your descriptions on the table. Take it in turns to pick up a description and read it out. The other students guess who each description is about.

Grammar reference
Past Simple: page 103

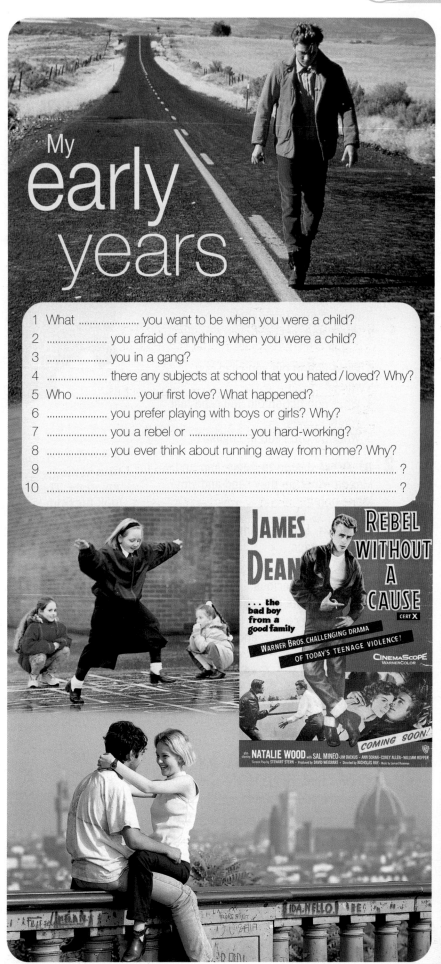

My **early years**

1 What .... you want to be when you were a child?
2 .... you afraid of anything when you were a child?
3 .... you in a gang?
4 .... there any subjects at school that you hated / loved? Why?
5 Who .... your first love? What happened?
6 .... you prefer playing with boys or girls? Why?
7 .... you a rebel or .... you hard-working?
8 .... you ever think about running away from home? Why?
9 .... ?
10 .... ?

JAMES DEAN

REBEL WITHOUT A CAUSE CERT X

... the bad boy from a good family

WARNER BROS. CHALLENGING DRAMA OF TODAY'S TEENAGE VIOLENCE!

CINEMASCOPE WARNERCOLOR

also starring NATALIE WOOD *with* SAL MINEO · JIM BACKUS · ANN DORAN · COREY ALLEN · WILLIAM HOPPER

COMING SOON!

I love a good read . . .

1 a) In pairs. Look at the people and the book covers (a–e). Match them to the types of books in the Word Box.

> science fiction /ˈsaɪəns ˈfɪkʃən/
> thriller /ˈθrɪlə/   love story
> biography /baɪˈɒgrəfi/
> detective /dɪˈtektɪv/ story

b) In groups. Talk about these questions.

1 What types of books do you read in your own language?
2 When and where do you usually read?
3 What fiction did you read last week?
4 What non-fiction did you read last week?
5 What do you read in English?

2 a) 🎧 23 Listen to Denis, Ann and Magda. What do they read and why? Make notes.

b) 🎧 24 Listen to Ann again and fill in the gaps.

Denis: I don't like books that are too "............" and serious.
Ann: I read lots of ....
Magda: They're .... It's easy to .... them .... and .... them ....

3 a) Read the extract from *The Thirty-Nine Steps*, on the right, as quickly as you can. What type of book do you think it's from?

b) Read the extract again and answer the questions. Then, in pairs, compare your answers.

1 Why isn't Richard happy with his life in London?
2 What was his job in Africa?
3 Why does Richard think his neighbour is crazy?
4 Do you think Richard will help his neighbour?

1 It was three o'clock on an afternoon in May. I, Richard Hannay, was a single man in the great city of London but I was bored. The city didn't interest me any more. This was my first visit to Britain since my childhood. My father took me from Scotland to Africa at the age of six.

5 When I was a young man I worked as an engineer. My salary was good and I had a comfortable life, but for years I dreamed of going back to Britain. But now that I was here, nothing was as good as I hoped – I was bored with the old buildings, the theatre, the people and I had no friend to go about with.

That evening I had a meal in a restaurant and went to the theatre. As I
10 walked back to my flat, I made a promise to myself. "I'll stay for one more day and if nothing interesting happens, I'll take the next boat back to Africa."

I was just putting my key in the door when a man ran up to me. I was surprised. It was a neighbour – the man who lived on the top floor.

"Can I speak to you?" he said. "Can I come in for a minute?" He sounded
15 worried.

I opened the door and we went inside. Immediately he ran into the bedroom, looked all round it and ran back again. "Is the door locked?" he asked.

"Of course it is."

20 "I'm sorry about this," he said, "but my life is very difficult at the moment. Will you do something for me?"

"I'll listen to you," I said. "I can't promise more than that."

He poured himself a drink of my whisky. "Forgive me," he said. "I'm very worried. You see, at this moment I am a dead man."

25 I sat down in an armchair and lit my pipe. "What does it feel like?" I asked. I thought he was probably crazy.

He smiled. "No, I'm not crazy," he said, "but I'm in bad trouble and I need your help. Will you help me?"

from *The Thirty-Nine Steps* by John Buchan (Penguin Readers)

5 a) 🔊 25 In groups. Listen to Hans(1), Maria(2), Stelios(3) and Magda(4) talking about how they remember new words. Make some notes about each person's ideas.

b) In groups. Talk about these questions.

1 Have you tried any of the ideas in Exercise 5a)? Did they work for you?
2 Which of the ideas sound good to you?
3 Do you have any other ideas?

6 When you write words in groups you can use a word map. Fill in the word map with words from the Word Box.

> heavy ✓ read ✓ author ✓ short chapter
> look up cover page long title light

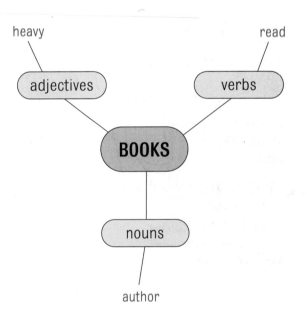

Word play

4 a) In pairs. Were there any words in the extract that you didn't understand? What did you do? What do you usually do when you're reading and you see a word you don't know? Do you:

1 look it up in the dictionary?   4 ignore it?
2 try to guess the meaning?   5 ask the teacher?
3 stop reading?

b) Look at the extract in Exercise 3a) again and find the word *worried* (line 15). Is *worried* a noun, a verb, or an adjective? Can you guess the meaning of *worried*?

c) In pairs. Compare your answers. Then do the same for the other words in green in the extract.

7 a) Read this extract from the *Longman Active Study Dictionary*. It shows how to pronounce the word and where the stress is. (The sign ' comes before the stressed syllable.) Practise saying the word. Do you use your dictionary to help you with pronunciation? (See the Guide to pronunciation, page 143)

salary /ˈsæləri/ *n* [C] money that you receive every month as payment from the organization you work for: *She earns a good salary.*

b) Is *salary* a countable or an uncountable noun? Which two things in the dictionary extract tell you this?

Hooray for Hollywood!

At the cinema
Interested or *interesting*?
Past Simple or Present Perfect?
Superlative Adjectives
Do you remember? Units 1–4

This film's really interesting.

1 This film's really ....

2 This film's really ....

3 This film's really ....

4 This film's really ....

At the cinema

1 In pairs. What kinds of films do you like? Why? Talk about the films in the Word Box.

> thrillers   action films   romantic films
> comedies   horror films   science fiction films
> dramas   westerns

Example: I hate science fiction films. They . . .

Interested or *interesting*?

2 **a)** Look at the picture. Where are the people? What do they think of the film? Use the adjectives in the Word Box and fill in the gaps.

> interesting ✓   frightening   depressing
> boring   exciting

b) 👀 26 Listen to two people coming out of the cinema and read their conversation. Then fill in the Language Box with *-ed* or *-ing*.

A: Great film, eh? I thought it was really interesting.

B: Really? I hated it! I was so bored I wanted to walk out halfway through.

Interested *or* interesting?

We use the .... form to say how we feel.
We use the .... form to describe the thing or person that gives us the feeling.

The director and the actress

3 a) 🎧27 Mike, a Hollywood film director, is interviewing Lara, an actress, for a part in a new film. Listen to the beginning of the interview and answer the questions.

1 Why does Lara want to work with Mike?
2 Why did she go to Hollywood?
3 Do you think she's a famous actress?

b) 🎧28 Now listen and read about Lara's acting experience. Was your answer to question 3 in Exercise 3a) correct?

MIKE: What kind of work have you done?

LARA: Well, I've been quite lucky. I've worked with some great directors – Cameron, Tarantino. I haven't had any problems finding film work. I've also done TV and radio work, some modelling and I've done some commercials. I did that ad for Tropical Cola last spring. Did you see it?

MIKE: So, that was you!

LARA: Yeah! I loved working in Hawaii. Anyway, my first big film was *Titanic*. That was fabulous!

MIKE: Yeah, great film. What part did you play?

LARA: I was one of the Irish immigrants. You know in the dancing scene.

MIKE: Right . . . Well, as you know, this is an action film. There are a lot of dangerous stunts. Have you ever done any stunt work?

LARA: Oh, yes, I was in *Death Cops III*. I did all my own stunts. Do you remember that car chase – where they drove off the cliff? That was me!

MIKE: Really? Great!

LARA: And I've been in some westerns. I can ride really well and I know how to use a gun.

c) 🎧29 What do you think happens next? Do you think Lara gets the part? Listen to the end of the interview.

Past Simple or Present Perfect?

4 a) Read these sentences from Lara's interview. Which two sentences are in the Past Simple? Which two are in the Present Perfect?

1 I've done some commercials.
2 I did that ad for Tropical Cola last spring.
3 What part did you play?
4 Have you ever done any stunt work?

b) Now read the Language Box and fill in the gaps.

Present Perfect

We use the auxiliary verb *have* / *has* and the past participle.

Positive sentences

I / You / We / They	....	done some commercials.
He / She / It	....	

Negative sentences

I / You / We / They	....	had any problems.
He / She / It	....	

Yes / No questions	Short answers
.... you done any commercials?	Yes, I .... / No, I ....
.... he had any problems?	Yes, he .... / No, he ....

Look!

• When we speak we usually use contractions:
  I've done **NOT** ~~I have~~ done   It hasn't **NOT** ~~It has not~~

5 a) Read the interview in Exercise 3b) again and underline all the verbs in the Present Perfect. Put a box (☐) round the verbs in the Past Simple. Then fill in the Language Box with *Past Simple* or *Present Perfect*.

> ### Past Simple or Present Perfect?
>
> We use the .... to talk about past experiences in general:
> I've done some commercials.
> We use the .... to give more details about a past experience *(when? where? why? how?)*.
> I did that ad for Tropical Cola last spring.
> **Look!**
> • *ever / never* = at any time in your life
>   Have you **ever** done any stunt work?

b) Match the sentences about experience in A to the details in B.

Example: 1 = e)

A Experience
1 She's been in some pop videos.
2 She's worked in Europe and Asia.
3 She's directed quite a few blockbusters.
4 She's done some modelling jobs.
5 She's never ridden a horse.

B Details
a) Last year she was the highest paid director.
b) One bit her when she was a child.
c) She was on the front cover of *Vogue* last month.
d) She was in Tokyo two months ago.
e) She loved working with Madonna.

c) Fill in the gaps with the Present Perfect or Past Simple of the verbs in brackets.

Example: (jump)
> A: Have you ever jumped out of a plane?
> B: No, I haven't – but I jumped out of a flying bus in *Twister IV*.

1 (direct / be)
> A: .... she .... any comedies?
> B: No, she .... But she............... some very good thrillers and action films.
> A: What .... her last film?
> B: *Blue Fire*. It .... about a woman detective and her affair with a killer.

2 (work)
> A: .... they .... in Europe?
> B: No, they .... They............... mainly .... in South America and the USA.

3 (be / play / spend)
> A: .... you ever .... in a horror film?
> B: Yes, I ....
> A: What .... it like?
> B: Well, it .... really hard work. I .... the wife of a vampire and I .... five hours in make-up every morning.

Superlative Adjectives

6 a) ⊙⊙ 30 Listen to a man and a woman talking about films and fill in the gaps in these questions.
1 What's .... best film you've .... ?
2 What's .... worst film you've .... ?

b) ⊙⊙ 30 Listen again. What are their answers? Make notes.

c) In pairs. Ask and answer the questions in Exercise 6a).

d) *Best* and *worst* are Superlative Adjectives. Fill in the table with the correct forms of the adjectives. Then fill in the Language Box with *comparative* or *superlative*.

Adjective	Comparative	Superlative
Irregular		
good	better	....
bad	....	the worst
Regular	*-(e)r*	*-(e)st*
old	....	....
nice	....	....
sad	....	the saddest
funny	funnier	....
	more	*most*
popular	....	the most popular
interesting	more interesting	....
famous	....	....

> ### Comparative and Superlative Adjectives
>
> We use .... adjectives to compare two people or things and .... adjectives to compare three or more people or things.

4

Past experiences

7 a) Read the questionnaire. Fill in the gaps in the questions with the superlative form of the adjectives in brackets. Write one more question. Then fill in the questionnaire with information about your past experiences.

b) Go round the class and interview two students about their past experiences. Fill in the questionnaire about them.

Example: A: What's the worst thing you've ever bought?
B: My friend's car.
A: Why? What happened?
B: Well, it broke down two days after I bought it.

	You	Student A	Student B
1 What's the ......worst...... **(bad)** thing you've ever bought?			
2 What's the .... **(expensive)** place you've ever been to?			
3 What's the .... **(dangerous)** thing you've ever done?			
4 What's the .... **(frightening)** experience you've ever had?			
5 What's the .... **(valuable)** thing you've ever lost?			
6 What's the .... **(big)** mistake you've ever made?			
7 .... ?			

The Holly

starters
CAESAR SALAD £20.00
WILD MUSHROOM RISOTTO ... £21.00

main
STEAK TARTARE £39.00
FILLET STEAK £35.00
SEASONAL VEGETABLES x2 .. £20.00

desserts
HOME-MADE ICE CREAM £21.00
APPLE TART £21.00
FARMHOUSE CHEESES x2 .... £35.00
COFFEE x2 .... £13.00

wine
BOTTLE RED WINE £80.00
BOTTLE WHITE WINE £65.00
GLASSES DESSERT WINE x2 . £30.00

bar
CHAMPAGNE COCKTAILS x2 .. £50.00

SUB-TOTAL	£450.00
10% SERVICE CHARGE	£45.00
TOTAL	£495.00

Grammar reference
Present Perfect: page 104
Superlative Adjectives: page 107

Do you remember? Units 1–4

1 Money makes the world go round

a) In groups of four. How many "money" verbs can you think of? Make a list. What is the Past Simple of each verb?

Example: spend → spent

b) 🔟31 Listen to the conversation and fill in the gaps.

A: Can you .... me some .... ?

B: I'm .... I'm .... I .... a lot of .... last night – about £............ . I took my boss and his wife out to .... Why are you .... ?

A: Well, I .... some money from my brother and he wants me to .... him .... now.

c) In groups. Use the verbs from Exercise 1a) and write four more answers to the question *Why are you broke?*.

d) Go round the class and talk to as many students as possible. Have conversations like the one in Exercise 1b).

2 You used to buy me flowers

a) 🔟32 Look at the picture. Harry and Louise are married. They're having dinner in a restaurant. Listen. Are they happy?

b) 🔟32 Listen again. What do they say about each other? Use the words in the Word Box and make notes in the table.

| sweet ✓   complain   be   cook   buy   forget   talk   take |

Louise used to / didn't use to . . .	Harry used to / didn't use to . . .
used to be so sweet	

c) In pairs. You're a married couple but you're unhappy. Use the ideas from Exercise 2b) and have a conversation like Louise and Harry's.

3 Wanted!

We need stunt men and women URGENTLY

Have you done any stunt work?

Experienced actors and actresses wanted for a great new film

Phone today for an immediate interview

a) In pairs. Look at the advert and answer these questions.

1 What do stunt men and women do?

2 What kinds of films do you think use stunt men and women?

b) 🔟33 Listen to a TV interview with Karl Jordan. Tick (✓) the stunts he has done.

He's . . .

1 parachuted from a helicopter. ☐

2 fought with a shark. ☐

3 driven cars off cliffs. ☐

4 ridden a motorbike through a burning field. ☐

5 jumped from a plane without a parachute. ☐

c) Half the class are actors / actresses and half are directors. In groups of four. Actors / actresses look at page 132 and directors look at page 141.

Look at the Word lists for Units 1–4 on pages 113 – 116 and check that you know all the new words.

Puzzle 1 (Units 1–4): page 111

Reading for pleasure

① Interactivity

Your *Wavelength Pre-Intermediate* Coursebook has a Reader called *The wave and other stories* in the back. The first story is "Interactivity". Do the exercises on this page to help you understand and enjoy it.

1 Before you read the story, answer these questions.

1 Do you think technology has made communicating with other people easier or more difficult?
2 Do you have an answerphone?
3 Do you use e-mail? If you do, do you have e-mail friends that you've never met?

2 🔊 34 It's midnight on Monday 12th December. Read and listen to the first message on Alan Marshall's answerphone. Then answer the questions.

MONDAY 9:21
Alan? Alan, if you're at home, please answer the phone. Are you really not there? Well, I'd just like to say that I'm very angry with you – and your father is too. You know how much he loves our monthly family lunches. This is the fifth one you've missed. I hope you've got a really good reason this time. Oh, umm, this is your mother speaking.

1 What time did Alan's mother phone?
2 What did Alan miss?
3 How many of these has he missed?
4 Do you think that his mother finds it easy to leave messages on answerphones?

3 🔊 35 Read and listen to the second message. Then answer the questions.

MONDAY 10:02
Mr Marshall, this is Stefi Rosen, Mr Prince's assistant. I'm calling to confirm tomorrow's lunch with Mr Yamada of Rising Sun Computer Games. Mr Prince wants you to know that this meeting is **very important**. Please remember to bring the interactivity designs with you. He says that Mr Yamada is ready to pay for the world rights on your new game! The restaurant is The Four Stars in Gower Street and I've booked a table for quarter past one. Be there on time – please!

1 What time did Stefi Rosen phone?
2 Is this a meeting with friends or a business meeting?
3 Which country do you think Mr Yamada is from?
4 Who do you think Mr Prince is?

4 🔊 36 Read and listen to the third message. Then answer the questions.

MONDAY 11:23
My name is Karen Miller. I'm a producer at Interactive Computer Games, Australia. I saw your game "Kill the Enemy!" at the International Computer Games Fair. I think your work is great and I'd like to discuss buying the rights for my part of the world. Someone at the fair said that you're working on a new game which is even more interactive. How interactive can you get? Perhaps we can interact over lunch? I'm in London until Wednesday. My mobile number is 027747 6130800.

1 What time did Karen Miller phone?
2 Where is she from?
3 Why is she calling Alan?
4 What kind of meeting does she suggest?
5 What do you think Alan Marshall does for a living?

5 Now read the whole story. It starts on page 1 of *The wave and other stories*. Think about these questions while you read.

1 Who is Daisy?
2 Why was Pete's weekend so bad?
3 Who is Elizabeth?
4 Do you think the writer of the article in *The Sunday News* liked Alan's game?
5 Where did Daisy find the article she sent Alan?
6 What are the positive things about the game that this article talks about?
7 What are the negative things the article talks about?
8 Which country has banned the game?
9 What did the technician say is wrong with Pete's old computer?
10 What did Alan's mother phone about on Tuesday?
11 Who is Terry Watts and why did he phone Alan?
12 By the end of Tuesday 13th December, five people were angry with Alan. Who were they? Why were they angry?
13 Why do you think he tried to kill everyone in Finland?
14 What happened to Alan in the end?

5 Playing by the rules

Rules and regulations: *have to /
don't have to, can / can't*
Make and *let*
Conversations: *Really? Are you?*

Rules and regulations

1 In groups. Look at the signs and talk about these questions.

a SPEED LIMIT 55

b

c

d

1 Where do you see these signs?
2 What do you do when you see them?
3 Do you always obey them or do you sometimes break the rules?

2 **a)** In pairs. Look at pictures 1–3. Who are the people? Where are they?

b) 📢37 Listen and match the conversations (A–C) to the pictures (1–3). What are the people talking about? Is there a problem?

c) 📢37 Listen again. What did the people say? Fill in the gaps with words from the Word Box.

> can ✓   can't   have to /'hæftə/   don't have to

Example: You can work the hours you want.

1 You .... wear a suit and tie.
2 You .... come in here then.
3 You .... have a valid ticket.

3 Read the Language Box and fill in the gaps with the correct form of *have to*.

Obligation and permission

Obligation or no obligation?
Have to + infinitive = obligation.
Don't have to + infinitive = no obligation (you have a choice).

Positive

I / You / We / They	....	wear a suit.
He / She	....	

Negative

I / You / We / They	....	wear a suit.
He / She	....	

Yes / No questions
A: .... I .... wear a tie?
A: .... she .... have ID?

Short answers
B: Yes, you .... / No, you ....
B: Yes, she .... / No, she ....

Giving and refusing permission
• *Can* + infinitive = giving permission (it's OK):
  You can wear jeans in the office.
• *Can't* + infinitive = refusing permission (it isn't OK):
  You can't wear shorts in the office.

Pronunciation: *can, have to*

4 **a)** 🔊 38 Listen to the sentences in Exercise 2c). Underline the stressed words / syllables. How do they pronounce *can, can't, have to* and *don't have to*?

Example: You can /kən/ <u>work</u> the <u>hours</u> you <u>want</u>.

b) 🔊 38 Listen again and repeat.

Do you have to wear a tie?

5 **a)** In pairs. Look at the offices in pictures 3 and 4. Which is strict and which is relaxed? Which office would you like to work in? Why?

b) In pairs. Use *have to, don't have to, can* and *can't* and make as many sentences as you can about the two offices. Then work with another pair of students and compare your sentences.

Examples: Office in picture 3: You don't have to wear a suit and tie.
Office in picture 4: You can't make personal phone calls.

① Experience life on a farm

Do you love the fresh, clean air of the countryside?
Would you like to learn about country life?
Help to look after animals and pick fruit on a farm this summer.

Have a real country experience!

② Golden Voyages
luxury cruises

Do you like people – the excitement of the open sea – variety?
Do you want to see more of the world?
Active young people wanted to work aboard our modern cruise ships.

③ Teach your language

✓ Are you over eighteen?
✓ Do you like young people, sports and outdoor activities?

Be a counsellor in the USA this summer – teach your language and have a holiday in a small, friendly International Summer Camp.

Excellent modern facilities and accommodation.
Beautiful mountain location on Lake Shaska.

A great opportunity

6 a) In groups. Read the three adverts for summer jobs. Which one looks the most interesting? Why?

b) Ruth answered one of the adverts. Read her letter to a friend. Which advert did she answer? Is she enjoying the job?

Camp Shaska
Vermont
VT24901 USA

21st August

Dear Sophie,

1 How are you? I hope everything's OK and that you had a good time in Argentina. I can't wait to hear about it. I'm really depressed. It's horrible here. This is the worst job I've ever had. Why did I believe that stupid advert?

2 The work is really hard. There are five hundred noisy kids (and about a million mosquitoes!) and only twenty counsellors! I have to look after thirty kids all on my own for twenty-four hours a day! And the place is nothing like the picture I showed you. Modern facilities! What a joke! The "beautiful" lake is tiny – and really dirty!

3 Breakfast is at 6:30, so I have to get up at 5 a.m. and get the kids ready. It's a nightmare! The children have to be in bed by 9 p.m. and I don't let them make any noise after that. I don't think they like me very much. They think I'm really bossy, but I don't care. I need some peace and quiet!

2

4 The sports organiser used to be in the army and he loves giving orders. He shouts a lot and the kids are really frightened of him! He makes us do all the activities with the kids too. I've never been wind-surfing in my life, but he makes me go. Last week it took them an hour to get me back from the middle of the lake. I felt so stupid!

5 Fortunately we don't have to teach much – two lessons a week. And we have one day off a week (after we've given the kids their breakfast!). They let us use the camp van to drive into town. There's not much there, but at least we can do what we want. We can't drink or smoke back at the camp.

6 Anyway, I'll stop complaining now. I can't wait to leave this place. Please write when you can. I'm going crazy!

Love,

Ruth

c) In which paragraph does Ruth:

a) talk about her daily routine? ☐

b) talk about her free time? ☐

c) give an example of a bad experience and someone she doesn't like? ☐

d) describe the camp? ☐

d) Are these sentences true (T) or false (F)? Correct the false ones.

Example: Ruth loves her job. ☐F
It's the worst job she's ever had.

1 Ruth doesn't think the advert was truthful. ☐

2 She has to spend all day with the children when she's working. ☐

3 She thinks the facilities are good. ☐

4 She doesn't have to get up early every day. ☐

5 She works long hours. ☐

6 She's got a good relationship with the children. ☐

7 The sports organiser is popular. ☐

8 She works six days a week. ☐

e) Find the words or expressions in the letter that mean:

1 children (noun)

2 very small (adjective)

3 a very bad dream or a very bad experience (noun)

4 someone who tells people what to do all the time (adjective)

5 to speak in a very loud voice, often because you're angry (verb)

6 to say that you're angry or unhappy about something (verb)

Make and let

7 a) Read Ruth's letter again. Then fill in the Language Box with the correct forms of *make* and *let* (positive or negative).

Make and let

Make → have to
They .... us get up early. → We have to get up early.
He .... me go wind-surfing. → I have to go wind-surfing.

Don't make → don't have to
They .... us teach every day. → We don't have to teach every day.

Let → can
They .... us use the van. → We can use the van.

Don't let → can't
I .... them make any noise. → They can't make any noise.
They .... us drink or smoke. → We can't drink or smoke.

Look!
• With *he / she / it* we use *makes* and *lets*.
• We use object pronouns (*me, you, us, them, him, her, it*) after *make* and *let*.
• We do not use *to* after *make* or *let*:
  They let us smoke. **NOT** They let us ~~to~~ smoke.
---

b) In groups of four. You're going to play a guessing game about people that are very strict or very relaxed. Student A, look at page 131; Student B at page 134; Student C at page 137 and Student D at page 141.

What a nightmare!

8 a) In pairs. You're doing one of the jobs in Exercise 6a), but the advert wasn't truthful and you're having a very bad time. Talk about these questions.

1 How is the job different from the advert?
2 What's the place like?
3 What kind of things do you have to do?
4 What kind of things can't you do?
5 Do you have any problems with people?

b) In pairs. Write a letter to a friend like the one in Exercise 6b).

c) When you finish, read each other's letters. Who had the worst experience? Did anyone have a similar experience to you?

Grammar reference

Have to / don't have to, can / can't, make and *let*: page 108

33

Conversations *Really? Are You?*

Echo questions to show interest

1 **a)** Look at the photographs and read the conversations. Who are the people? Where are they?

b) In pairs. Can you fill in the gaps in the conversations?

1 WOMAN: Whereabouts in Italy are you from?
MAN: Pescara.
WOMAN: .... you? My brother lives there.
MAN: .... he? What's his name?

2 WOMAN: I didn't get the job.
MAN: .... you? Why not?
WOMAN: They gave it to someone in Accounts.
MAN: .... they? So, what are you going to do?

3 MAN: Well, I've booked my holiday. I'm going to Cuba.
WOMAN: .... you? I've been there.
MAN: .... you? Did you like it?

c) 🔊 39 Listen and check. Then read the Language Box.

Echo questions

In conversations we often ask short questions (echo questions) to show interest.
A: Whereabouts in Italy **are** you from?
B: Pescara.
A: **Are** you? My brother **lives** there.
B: **Does** he? What's his name?
A: I **didn't get** the job.
B: **Didn't** you? Why not?

Look!
• We also say *Really?* or *Oh?* to show interest.
A: My brother lives there.
B: **Really?** What's his name?

Pronunciation: intonation in echo questions

2 a) 🔊 39 Listen to the conversations again. Do the echo questions go up ↗ or down ↘ at the end?

b) In pairs. Practise the conversations.

Making connections

3 a) Fill in the gaps in the echo questions with the correct verb (positive or negative).

Example: 1 A: I'm not working for the BBC now.
B: Aren't you?

2 A: I've bought a motorbike.
B: .... you?
3 A: I was a bit of a rebel at school.
B: .... you?
4 A: Steve didn't marry Nancy, you know.
B: .... he?

b) 🔊 40 Listen and check.

c) We often add a sentence or question after the echo question. Add these sentences or questions after the echo questions in Exercise 3a).

Example: 1 = a)
A: I'm not working for the BBC now.
B: Aren't you? What are you doing?

a) What are you doing?
b) So was I.
c) Why not?
d) What kind have you bought?

d) 🔊 41 Listen and check.

e) Fill in the gaps in the echo questions and add a sentence or question from the Word Box.

> I knew he was clever. Is he a vegetarian?
> What was she like? What's she studying?

1 A: She was my teacher last year.
  B: .... she? ....
2 A: My girlfriend has gone to Paris to do a course.
  B: .... she? ....
3 A: My brother doesn't eat meat.
  B: .... he? ....
4 A: He speaks six languages.
  B: .... he? ....

f) Write five interesting sentences about yourself. Go round the class and talk to other students. Take it in turns to say one of your sentences and answer with an echo question and an extra sentence or question.

Example: A: I travelled round the world last year.
B: Did you? Who did you go with?

The echo game

4 a) In two teams A and B. Read these rules for the game.

1 Student 1 in Team A says a sentence.
2 Student 1 in Team B answers with an echo question and an extra sentence or question.
3 If the echo question and the extra sentence or question are all grammatically correct and if the connection is good and logical, Team B gets 2 points.
4 Student 2 in Team B says a sentence.
5 Student 2 in Team A answers with an echo question and an extra sentence or question. Your teacher gives the score.
6 The game continues until every student in both teams has said a sentence and answered a sentence.
7 The team with the most points wins.

Example:
STUDENT 1 (TEAM A): I went to a party at the weekend.
STUDENT 1 (TEAM B): Did you? So did I. / Was it good? / Where was it? / I love parties.
(2 points)
Did you? I love ~~swimming~~. (0 points)

b) In two teams. Team A, look at page 137 and Team B, at page 135.

Where on earth?

Describing places: *What's it like?*, *Where is it?*, *What's the weather like?*
The Future: Present Continuous, *be going to* + infinitive, *'ll (will)* + infinitive
Day to day English: *Can you tell me . . . ?*

What's it like?

1 In pairs. Look at these photographs of places. Use the nouns and adjectives in the Word Box and describe each place.

Nouns	Adjectives
mountains /ˈmaʊntɪnz/	mountainous
hills a lake countryside	green wild
moors /mʊəz/ trees	dramatic sandy
a beach /biːtʃ/ the sea	gentle hilly
the coast /kəʊst/	rocky white
vineyards /ˈvɪnjədz/	flat

Examples: There's a / some / a lot of . . .
The countryside is . . .
There are some / a lot of . . .
The cliffs are . . .

2 **a)** 🔊 42 Cheryl is from South Africa and Marcus is from the north of England but they both live in London now. Listen to them talking about where they're from. Which two of the photographs (1–4) are of South Africa? Which two are of the north of England?

b) 🔊 42 Listen again and make notes about Cheryl and Marcus's answers to these questions.

1 Where are you from?
2 What's the countryside like?
3 What's your favourite place? Why?
4 What are the people like?

①

②

c) Look at questions 2 and 4 in Exercise 2b) again. Then read the Language Box.

> ### What's he / she / it like?
>
> When we ask for a description of a person, a place or a thing, we say:
> What's he / she / it like?
> When we ask for a description of people, places or things, we say:
> What are they like?

Where is it?

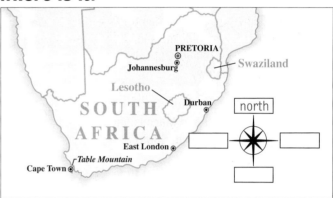

3 a) Look at the map and fill in the boxes on the compass with the words from the Word Box.

> north ✓   east   west   south

b) Look at the map again and fill in the gaps with the words from the Word Box.

> southern /ˈsʌðən/ ✓   in the south-west (x 2)
> on the coast (x 2)   south of   north of
> on the east coast   inland   near

Example: South Africa is in the <u>southern</u> hemisphere.

1 Durban is .... It's ....
 Swaziland.
2 Table Mountain is .... It's
 .... Cape Town.
3 Johannesburg is .... , but East
 London is ....
4 Pretoria is .... Johannesburg.
5 Cape Town is .... , ...

c) Think of a place. Where is it? What is it like? Prepare to describe it to other students. Make notes.

d) Go round the class. Talk to different students. Describe your place (but don't say the name) and guess which place your partners are describing.

What's the weather like?

4 **a)** Look at the photographs on pages 36 and 37 again. What do you think the weather is like in South Africa and the north of England? Use words from the Word Box to describe the weather.

> mild   changeable
> warm   freezing (cold)
> windy   boiling /ˈbɔɪlɪŋ/ (hot)
> rainy   cold   damp
> hot   humid /ˈhjuːmɪd/
> sunny   cloudy /ˈklaʊdi/
> wet   snowy

b) 🎧 43 Listen and check. What do Cheryl and Marcus say about the weather in South Africa and the north of England? When is the best time to go?

c) In groups. Talk about these questions.

1 What's the weather like today?
2 Do you like the weather in your country?
3 When is the best weather in your country?
4 What's your favourite place for weather?
5 What's the worst weather you've ever experienced?

Where are you going for your holiday?

5 Look at the pictures and read what Alan says. Then fill in the gaps in the Language Box with *be going to* + infinitive, *'ll (will)* + infinitive or *the Present Continuous*.

The Future

Possibilities
We use .... for ideas and possibilities, things we aren't sure about.
Intentions / plans
We use .... for our intentions and plans.
Arrangements
We use .... for things we have definitely arranged.

① I've got two weeks' holiday. What shall I do? Maybe I'll go to Iceland or perhaps I'll go to Alaska.

③ Hi, Sam. Guess what? I've booked my holiday. I'm flying to Alaska on Saturday.

② Hi, Mum. I've finally decided. I'm going to book a holiday to Alaska.

6 **a)** 🔊44 Listen to Julia talking to her friend, Wendy, about her holiday. Answer the questions.

1 Where is Julia going?
2 How long is her holiday?
3 Why is Wendy surprised?

b) Fill in the table below with these sentences (1–8) from Julia's conversation.

1 I'm going to Kerala.
2 I'm flying on Saturday.
3 Where are you staying?
4 I'm staying at a hotel on the beach.
5 Are you going to travel around?
6 Maybe I'll visit one other place.
7 I'm going to take it easy.
8 Perhaps I'll just sleep for a week!

Possibilities

....
....

Intentions / plans

....
....

Arrangements

....
....
....
....

7 In groups of four. You've all won holidays in a competition. Find out where. Student A, look at page 138; Student B at page 137; Student C at page 134 and Student D at page 140.

The shortest holiday I've ever had!

8 **a)** 🔊45 Listen. It's six months later. Julia is telling another friend, Ian, about her holiday in India. Put the pictures (a–d) in the correct order.

b) 🔊45 Listen again. Are these sentences true (T) or false (F)? Correct the false ones.

Example: She had a one-week holiday in India.   [F]
         She didn't have a one-week holiday in India.

1 She asked about a visa before she left. ☐
2 She started to worry on the plane. ☐
3 The pilot told her she could get her visa at the airport in Kerala. ☐
4 The officials at Kerala airport were all unfriendly. ☐
5 Julia cried at the airport in London. ☐
6 She spent one night in Kerala. ☐

c) In groups of four. Talk about these questions.
1 Have you ever had a bad or unusual holiday experience?
2 What happened? What did you do?
3 Did you learn anything from it?

> **Grammar reference**
> The Future: Present Continuous, *be going to* + infinitive and *'ll (will)* + infinitive: page 106

Day to day English Can you tell me . . . ?

Indirect questions

1 **a)** These people (1–4) want to know something. What are they asking? Match the questions (a–d) to the pictures.

a) Excuse me, do you know if there's a park near here?

b) Can you tell me if I need a visa for the USA?

c) Could you tell me where the post office is, please?

d) Excuse me, do you know what time the bank opens?

b) 〔oo〕46 Listen and check. Then listen again and repeat the questions. How do we say *Could you tell me . . . ? Do you know . . . ?* and *Can you tell me . . . ?*

c) 〔oo〕46 Listen again and fill in the gaps in the answers.

1 Yes, it's just .... , ... the pub.

2 Yes, it opens in about .... At ....

3 No, sorry, I .... I'm .... round here.

4 Yes, you ....

d) Read the Language Box. How are direct questions and indirect questions different?

Direct and indirect questions

Direct *Wh-* questions	Indirect *Wh-* questions
What time **does** the bank **open**?	Do you know what time the bank **opens**?
Where is the post office?	Could you tell me **where** the post office **is**?

Direct *Yes / No* questions	Indirect *Yes / No* questions
Is there a park near here?	Do you know **if there's** a park near here?
Do I need a visa?	Can you tell me **if I need** a visa?

e) Look again at the situations in Exercise 1a). Why do the people use indirect questions?

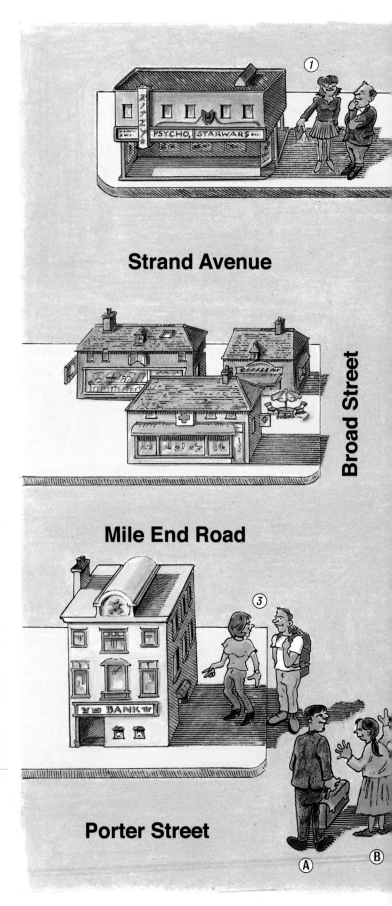

Strand Avenue

Broad Street

Mile End Road

Porter Street

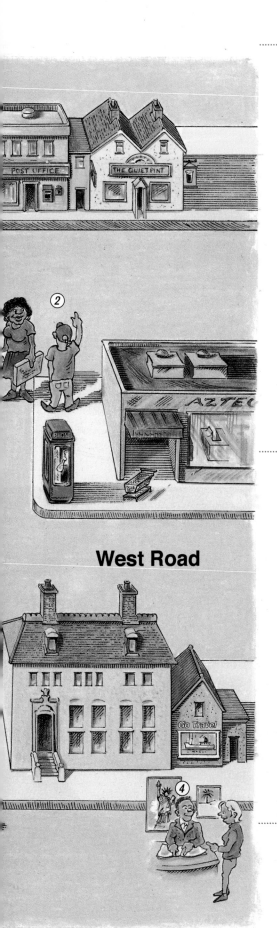

West Road

2 Fill in the table with direct or indirect questions with *Can / Could you tell me …?* or *Do you know …?*. Then, in pairs, compare your answers.

Example: Do the pubs close at 11:00 this evening?
Do you know if the pubs close at 11:00 this evening?

Direct questions	Indirect questions
1 Where's the nearest bank?	.... ?
2 .... ?	Could you tell me how often the ferry leaves?
3 Are these magazines free?	.... ?
4 .... ?	Do you know what time it is?
5 Is there a museum near here?	.... ?
6 .... ?	Can you tell me when the meeting starts?
7 When is the first train to Newport?	.... ?
8 .... ?	Can you tell me how much these bags are?
9 Does the coach stop here?	.... ?

Giving directions

3 **a)** In pairs. Adam (A) is in Porter Street. He's talking to a woman (B). Can you fill in the gaps in their conversation? Use the map and the words in the Word Box to help you.

> along ✓   the second turning   left   right (x 2)
> next to   corner (of) (x 2)   along   near   far

ADAM: Excuse me, can you tell me if there's a pub near here?
WOMAN: Yeah. Go .along. this street. Take .... on the .... It's on the .... , ... the post office.
ADAM: And sorry, do you know where the nearest phone is?
WOMAN: Er, let me think. Yeah. Just go .... this same street and er . . . there's a phone box on the .... , on the .... of West Road and Broad Street.
ADAM: West Road and . . . ?
WOMAN: Don't worry. Just remember – it's on the ....
ADAM: Right. Is it .... ?
WOMAN: No, it's quite .... A two-minute walk.
ADAM: Oh, thanks a lot!
WOMAN: No problem!

b) 🔟47 Listen and check.

4 In pairs. Look at the map again. One of you is A and one of you is B. Student A, look at page 132 and Student B, at page 140.

The cruel heart

First Conditional
Every-, some-, any-, no-
Skills: TV adverts and consumers

Joe Kelly

1 **a)** 🔊48 In pairs. Look at this picture from a Hollywood film about the life of Joe Kelly. Troy Tucker and his girlfriend, Estelle Kennedy, are at a party at Joe Kelly's mansion. Read and listen to their conversation and answer these questions.

1 What does Estelle think of Joe?
2 Does Troy know Joe well?
3 What does Troy think of Joe? Why?

SCENE 7

SCENE 1

ESTELLE: So . . . that's the famous Joe Kelly, America's most successful businessman. He's very handsome. Everyone wants to talk to him! He certainly has a lot of friends.

TROY: They aren't his friends. Joe Kelly has no real friends.

ESTELLE: What do you mean?

TROY: He has no heart . . . and he's ruthless. He'll do anything to get what he wants.

ESTELLE: Come on, darling. You're just jealous.

TROY: Look! I grew up with him. I know him. He can be very cruel. Sure he had a difficult childhood . . . but he's hurt a lot of really good people.

b) 🔊49 After Scene 1, the film goes back in time and tells Joe's story. Look at the pictures (a–f). Then Listen. What is the correct order of the scenes? Fill in the boxes.

c) Why did Troy Tucker say Joe Kelly "has no heart . . . and he's ruthless"?

SCENE ☐

SCENE ☐

SCENE ☐

SCENE ☐

SCENE ☐

d) Which scene(s) are these characters in? Find them in the pictures and fill in the table.

Character	Scene(s)
Joe Kelly	....
Nancy Banks	....
Joe's mother	....
Nancy's father	....
Joe's mother's boyfriend	....
Tania Vanderberg-Kelly	....
Troy Tucker	....

e) In pairs. Read sentences 1–12. Who's talking? Who are they talking to? Who are they talking about?

Example: 1 Joe's mother's boyfriend is talking to Joe's mother about Joe.

1 If that kid comes, I won't marry you.
2 They gave me a home when I had nothing.
3 You're so lucky. You've always had everything.
4 If she says "Yes", I'll be so happy.
5 Can you look after her for me when I'm at college?
6 If you help me, sir, you won't regret it.
7 Forget me. Find someone else.
8 If you ever need me, I'll be here.
9 If you do this, you'll destroy him.
10 If you don't help me, I'll fire you!
11 You don't care about anyone but yourself!
12 If you leave me, I'll kill myself!

f) 🎧 49 Listen again and check.

First Conditional

2 Read the Language Box. Then underline all the First Conditional sentences in Exercise 1e).

> ### First Conditional
>
> | Possible situation | | Possible result |
> |---|---|---|
> | If that kid comes, | → | I won't marry you. |
> | If she says "Yes", | → | I'll be so happy. |
> | If you do this, | → | you'll destroy him. |
>
> We use the Present Simple in the *if* part of the sentence.
> We use *'ll (will)* or *won't (will not)* + infinitive in the other part.

Pronunciation: sentence stress

3 **a)** 🎧 50 Listen to the sentences from Exercise 1e). Then underline the stressed words / syllables.

Example: If she <u>says</u> "<u>Yes</u>", I'll be <u>so</u> <u>happy</u>.

1 If you help me, sir, you won't regret it.
2 If you ever need me, I'll be here.
3 If you do this, you'll destroy him.
4 If you don't help me, I'll fire you!
5 If you leave me, I'll kill myself!

b) 🎧 50 Listen again and repeat.

Ruthless people

4 Fill in the gaps with the correct form of the verbs in brackets.

Example: If you <u>marry</u> (marry) my daughter, I'll <u>make</u> (make) you a partner.

1 If you ....(pay) me £10,000, I .... (not tell) your wife.
2 If you ....(not go) to the police, I ....(make) you a director.
3 If you ....(not lose) this match, you ....(not play) football again.
4 I................(destroy) him if he .... (not give) me the contract.
5 I ....(not tell) anyone about the fire if you ....(give) me the tapes.
6 You ....(not teach) again if my son ....(not pass) this exam.
7 I................(give) your daughter a job if you ....(advertise) my company.

5 Troy's girlfriend, Estelle Kennedy, is very ambitious. What is she thinking? Write her sentences.

Example: If I write a book about Joe Kelly, I'll make a lot of money. If I make . . .

If I . . . write a book about Joe Kelly → make a lot of money → become rich and famous → meet other rich and famous people → meet a rich man → get married → stop working → travel → meet other rich people → . . . ?

Every-, some-, any-, no-

6 **a)** Find all the words beginning with *every-*, *some-*, *any-*, and *no-* in Exercises 1a) and 1e). Then read the Language Box. Fill in the gaps with the words in brackets.

> ### Every-, some-, any-, no-
>
> **Positive sentences**
> *every-* (*everyone, everything, everywhere*)
> 1 He's got friends from .... (all the places) in the world.
> 2 .... (all the people) wants to talk to Joe.
> 3 He wants .... (all the things) he sees.
>
> *some-* (*someone, something, somewhere*)
> 1 He was born .... in Brazil. I'm not sure where.
> 2 I met .... from your company last week. I don't remember his name.
> 3 I saw .... strange in the sky. I think it was a UFO.
>
> **Negative sentences and questions**
> *any-* (*anyone, anything, anywhere*)
> 1 Did you meet .... interesting at Joe's party?
> 2 He was so rude. He didn't say .... nice all evening.
> 3 They didn't go .... exciting after the party.
>
> ***Look!***
> • Pronouns with *every-*, *some-*, *any-*, *no-* are singular:
>   What a great party! Everyone**'s** here. **NOT** Everyone ~~are~~ here.
> • Pronouns with *any* go with negative verbs:
>   I didn't have anything.
> • Pronouns with *no* go with positive verbs:
>   I had nothing. **NOT** I didn't have ~~nothing~~.
> • *-one* and *-body* are the same:
>   *someone = somebody*

b) Look at the picture and read what the spies say. Underline the correct word in brackets.

SPY 1: Does (<u>anyone</u> / someone)[1] know about this?

SPY 2: Only Mr Black. (Anyone / Someone)[2] told him. We think it was Raymond Jones.

SPY 1: Where's Raymond now?

SPY 2: I don't know. He went (everywhere / somewhere)[3] to make a phone call.

SPY 1: You idiot! Your job is to go (somewhere / everywhere)[4] with him! Now find him and don't let him go (anywhere / nowhere)[5] alone! He has to tell us (nothing / everything)[6] he knows.

SPY 2: I think he's fooling us. I don't think he knows (nothing / anything)[7].

SPY 1: You're an idiot! He knows (something / anything)[8]. I don't know what, but I'm going to make him tell me.

SPY 2: Be quiet! Did you hear that? (Someone / No-one)'s[9] in here.

SPY 1: I can't see (no-one / anyone)[10]. Oh look! It's a cat! Now relax. There's (someone / no-one)[11] in the office. It's empty. (Everyone / Someone)[12] left at 6 o'clock.

Reputations

7 a) Make two groups, politicians and Blackmailers. Politicians, your reputation is very important to you but you have some dark secrets. Blackmailers you know something about the politicians. What are you going to do with the information? Politicians, look at page 134 and blackmailers, look at page 132.

b) In pairs (a politician and a blackmailer). Have conversations. Politicians find out what the blackmailer knows, what they have and what they want. Then negotiate with them.

Example: BLACKMAILER: I know something about you. But if you give me £10,000 and promise to build a new supermarket in my town, I won't tell anyone.

POLITICIAN: I can't do that! I'll give you £100 if you tell me what you know.

Grammar reference
First Conditional: page 109

①

②

③

TV adverts and consumers

1 In groups. Talk about these questions.

1 Do you like any adverts on TV at the moment?
2 What do you like about them?
3 In your home, what do people do when the adverts are on the TV?

2 a) Look at the three TV adverts for *Savoury Delights*. Where are the people? What are they doing? How old are they?

b) 👀 51 Listen. Which of these adjectives and expressions are used in which advert? Fill in the boxes.

delicious [1]   tasty [ ]
low in calories [ ]   elegant [ ]
good for you [ ]   special [ ]

3 In groups. People in advertising use different styles of adverts for different types of people. Look at the information below. Who do you think each advert in Exercise 2a) is targeting? How do you know?

TARGET MARKET

Gender:
men, women, or both?

Age group:
children under thirteen? teenagers? young adults? the middle-aged? the old?

Family life:
single people? married couples? families? parents of young children?

Income:
people who earn large salaries? average salaries? small salaries?

Lifestyle:
school children? people with active, sporty lifestyles? people who are interested in their health? people with busy, stressful lifestyles? people who like glamour and luxury?

Designing a TV advert

4 **a)** Read the information on the right about a new drink called *Tropico*. Is it your kind of drink? Why? / Why not?

b) In small groups. You work for Vision Design, an advertising agency. You are going to write a short TV advert to sell *Tropico*. Look at the information again and decide:

1 which group of people you are going to design your advert for.
2 when you are going to advertise – during what kind of programmes.

Example: Our advert is going to be for teenage boys and we are going to advertise during sports programmes.

c) Design your advert. Use the TV adverts in Exercise 2a) and these questions to help you.

1 Who are the people in your advert? What is their relationship?
2 How old are they?
3 What type of people are they?
4 What are they wearing?
5 Where are they?
6 What are they doing?
7 What kind of music do you want?
8 Do you want to use any famous people? Who?

d) Write the script for your advert. Make sure everyone in your group has a part. Use some of the words and phrases in the Word Box and some of the adjectives from Exercise 2b).

> refreshing   non-fattening   cheap   smooth
> sophisticated /səˈfɪstɪkeɪtɪd/   fun   colourful
> sweet   it gives you energy   exotic

e) When you finish, practise your advert. Then act it out for the class. The class must say which target market your advert was for.

f) Which advert did you think was the cleverest? the funniest? the most original?

PRODUCT PROFILE

What's the product name?

Tropico

What is it?

Tropico is a new type of drink – and it's different. It's a fizzy drink but we only use real fresh fruit. There are no artificial additives.

What else is special about it?

- There are seven *Tropico* flavours: mango, papaya, banana, grape, pineapple, orange and strawberry.
- It has a lovely, sweet, fruity taste but it contains only natural fruit sugar. It's very low in calories so it's non-fattening.
- The packaging is attractive and recyclable so it's environmentally friendly.

Target markets

- Mothers of young children – it's the ideal healthy drink for children.
- People who are interested in their health and the environment.
- People who do a lot of entertaining – it's a great drink for barbecues or cocktail parties because it's delicious in cocktails.
- People who don't drink alcohol – it's delicious on its own and it has a sophisticated look.
- Older people who need a healthy diet.
- Young people who go clubbing or do a lot of sport.

Future dreams or nightmares?

Future predictions: *'ll (will)* and *might*
Adjectives and Adverbs of Manner
Do you remember? Units 5–8

How sure are you about the future?

1 a) In pairs. Read the questionnaire. Take it in turns to ask each other the questions and fill in your partner's answers.

b) Look at page 130 and work out your partner's score. Then read out the descriptions. Do you think they are right?

Are you an optimist or a pessimist?

1 How often do you gamble?
 a) Never. ☐
 b) A lot. ☐
 c) From time to time. ☐

2 If you work, do you think you'll get promotion / a pay rise in the next year? **OR** If you're a student or unemployed, do you think you'll find a job soon / when you start looking?
 a) Yes. ☐
 b) No. ☐
 c) I might. ☐

3 Are your first impressions of people usually positive?
 a) Sometimes positive and sometimes negative. ☐
 b) No. ☐
 c) Yes. ☐

4 Do you believe in true love?
 a) Yes. ☐
 b) No. ☐

5 Do you ever worry about the future?
 a) Sometimes. ☐
 b) Never. ☐
 c) Often. ☐

6 You have a good job but some friends have asked you to start a new business with them. Do you think:
 a) I'm going to try it! It sounds very interesting. ☐
 b) I'm sure we won't make any money. ☐
 c) I might try it. I'm a bit worried, but I'm excited too. ☐

7 There's a fire in the place where you work / study. Do you think:
 a) everyone will help each other? ☐
 b) no-one will help anyone? ☐
 c) one or two people might help but most people won't? ☐

8 How do you feel about next year?
 a) I'm sure it'll be better than last year. ☐
 b) I think it'll be worse than last year. ☐
 c) It might be better or it might be worse. ☐

Future predictions: *'ll (will)* and *might*

2 a) Underline the sentences with *'ll (will)* and *might* in the questionnaire in Exercise 1a). Which is more certain about the future: *'ll (will)* or *might*? Now read the Language Box.

b) Sandy is going to a job interview next week. Her friends said these things about her. How sure are they that she'll get the job? Write the sentences in the correct place in the table.

a) She might not get the job. ✓
b) I'm sure she'll get the job.
c) She probably won't get the job.
d) I'm sure she won't get the job.
e) She might get the job.
f) She'll probably get the job.

Definite *Yes*	1 ....
	2 ....
	3 ....
	4 a) She might not get the job. ....
	5 ....
Definite *No*	6 ....

c) In pairs. Read about these people. What do you think will happen? Make sentences from A and B and give your reasons.

1 You've invited Reg to your party at the weekend. He's a good friend and he likes your parties but he has to do some work at the weekend and he's not sure how long it will take.

> **Examples:** A: I'm sure he'll come because . . .
> B: He probably won't come because . . .

2 Sidney was a good student at university. He's a pleasant person and he works hard. He's just started his first job.
3 Joe is going for a job interview. He's got the qualifications and he's very intelligent, but he hasn't had a lot of experience.
4 Felix hardly ever comes to class and when he's here he doesn't do any work. He doesn't take anything seriously.
5 Freddie has a fast sports car and he drives really dangerously – like a maniac!
6 Stanley is an excellent runner and he's won a lot of races but he has had an injury so he hasn't had a lot of practice recently.

A	B
1 I'm sure he'll	a) come. ✓
2 He'll probably	b) pass the exam.
3 He might not	c) have an accident one day.
4 He might	d) do well.
5 He probably won't	e) get the job.
6 I'm sure he won't	f) win the race.

9 You're going to take a short flight in a small plane. Do you feel:

a) excited? ☐
b) excited, but also a bit nervous? ☐
c) terrified? ☐

10 If someone invites you to a party, do you:

a) make an excuse because you don't think it'll be any good? ☐
b) accept happily because you're sure you'll have a good time? ☐
c) accept and hope it'll be all right? ☐

What'll you do if . . . ?

3 a) In pairs. Jenny and her new boyfriend, Ken, are going to travel round Europe for two months on Ken's motorbike. It's their first holiday together. She's telling her friends, Mandy and Dan, about her plans. Mandy is an optimist, but Dan is a pessimist. What do you think they say about Jenny's trip? Talk about your ideas. Then make notes in the table.

	Mandy	Dan
1 weather	great	rain every day
2 their relationship		
3 people		
4 language	–	
5 the motorbike		
6 food		–

b) 🔈52 Listen. Do you hear any of your ideas? Tick (✓) them.

c) 🔈52 Listen again and write Mandy and Dan's opinions about Jenny's holiday.

d) 🔈52 Listen again and fill in the gaps. Use contractions.

1 .... you have an argument?

2 .... the bike breaks down?

3 .... the bike .... , ... it to a garage.

4 a) You're going to have conversations like the one in Exercise 3. First prepare your conversations. Make three groups. Group A, look at page 134; Group B, at page 138 and Group C, at page 137.

b) In groups of three (Students A, B and C), have three conversations.

CONVERSATION 1
Student A tells Student B (an optimist) and Student C (a pessimist) about his / her plans.

CONVERSATION 2
Student B tells Student C (an optimist) and Student A (a pessimist) about his / her plans.

CONVERSATION 3
Student C tells Student A (an optimist) and Student B (a pessimist) about his / her plans.

Adjectives and Adverbs of Manner

5 **a)** Read the Language Box and then find all the adjectives and Adverbs of Manner in the sentences in Exercise 2c).

Adjectives and Adverbs of Manner

Adjectives give information about nouns (people, things, places).
Adverbs of Manner give information about verbs (how we do things).
Most adverbs are adjectives + -ly:
He drives dangerously.
But there are some irregular adverbs:
He drives **well**.
Adverbs of Manner usually come after the main verb or after the verb + object:
She drives **fast**.
He drives his old car **slowly**.

Look!
• *Well* can also be an adjective:
A: How are you?
B: I'm very well thanks. (well = healthy, not ill)

b) Fill in the table with adverbs for these adjectives.

Adjectives	Adverbs	Adjectives	Adverbs
bad	badly	angry	angrily
calm		happy	
cold		sexy	
dangerous	dangerously		
efficient		careful	carefully
nervous		**Adjectives**	**Irregular adverbs**
passionate			
patient		fast	fast
pleasant		hard	hard
quick			
quiet		good	well
slow			
warm			

c) Put different adjectives and adverbs in these two sentences to make them more interesting.

1 The woman walked into the office.
2 The student did the grammar exercise.

Write as many different sentences as you can.

Examples: 1 The **nervous** woman walked **slowly** into the **busy** office.
2 The **young** student did the **long** grammar exercise **carefully**.

d) In pairs. Look at the picture and read this extract from a story. Make it more interesting by adding adjectives and adverbs where you see a number.

Example: The **young**(1) man . . .

The (1) man got off the plane and looked round the (2) airport. He walked (3) over to his (4) wife and kissed her (5). "How was the trip?" she asked. "Fine," he said. They got into their (6) car and their driver drove (7) through the city to the man's office. The driver gave the man his briefcase and he walked into the (8) building and took the lift to his office on the twentieth floor. "Hello, Mr Smith," his (9) secretary said. "Hello, Miss Jones. Can I see you in my office?" he said. He took a (10) package from his briefcase and said "Could you put this somewhere private?" "Of course," she said (11). At that moment his boss called him and told him to come up to his office. The lift was broken so he walked (12) up the stairs. A (13) woman was standing in his boss's (14) office. "Mr Sloane will be back soon," she said. Mr Smith walked out onto the terrace and looked down onto the (15) streets below. The woman walked over to him . . .

e) In groups. Read your stories to each other. Are your stories similar or very different?

Grammar reference
Future predictions: *'ll (will)* + infinitive and *might* + infinitive: page 106
First Conditional: page 109

Do you remember? Units 5–8

1 Do you have a choice?

a) Read the questionnaire. Write the endings for sentences 6–9.

Find someone who . . .

		Name
1	has to get up before seven o'clock.	....
2	doesn't have to get up early in the week.	....
3	has to use public transport.	....
4	can't wear jeans to school / work.	....
5	can use their father's car.	....
6	has to	....
7	doesn't have to	....
8	can't	....
9	can	....

b) Make questions for sentences (1–9).

Example: 1 Do you have to get up before seven o'clock?

c) Go round the class and ask your questions. Fill in the name column.

Example: 1 A: Carlos do you have to get up before seven o'clock?
B: Yes, I do because . . .

2 What are you going to do with the money?

a) Make four groups. You've all won the lottery but you are very different people. What are you going to do with the money? Group A, look at page 133; Group B at page 134; Group C at page 136 and Group D at page 141.

b) Make new groups of four with one student from each group (A–D). Take it in turns to tell the group your plans. The group has to guess what kind of person you are.

3 What do you think will happen?

a) Maxi Publishing (see page 10) is having its office party on Friday. Read about Maggie, Bill, Nina and Steve. Do they all like each other? Who do you think will go to the party at Maxi Publishing? Why?

Example: I'm sure Maggie will go. She loves parties, she's organising this one and she really likes Bill.

Maggie loves parties and she's organising this one. She's very excited because she really likes Bill. He doesn't know yet! Yesterday she had an argument with two of the temps, Nina and Steve, but today Nina smiled at her and Steve offered to do some photocopying for her.

Bill is going to the country this weekend and he doesn't know if he'll leave on Friday evening or Saturday. He likes Nina, but he doesn't know if she likes him. He wants to ask her out.

Nina loves parties and she thinks the new temp, Steve, is good-looking. She's tired because Maggie, her boss, made her work late again last night – she's still angry about it. Bill helped her with the work and she thinks he's very kind, but a bit boring.

Steve can't decide between going to the office party or having a drink with his friends. He wants a better job with Maxi Publishing and thinks Maggie can help him. She was angry with him yesterday, but this morning she was friendlier. He thinks Nina's a good laugh.

b) In pairs. What do you think will happen at the party if the things below happen? Make sentences.

Example: If Bill goes to the party, he'll try and talk to Nina.

1 If Bill doesn't go to the party, . . .
2 If Bill asks Nina out, . . .
3 If Maggie sees Bill with Nina, . . .
4 If Steve talks to Nina, . . .

Look at the Word lists for Units 5–8 on pages 116 – 118 and check that you know all the new words.

Puzzle 2 (Units 5–8): page 111

Reading for pleasure

② The Stranger

1 This is a story about a town where people turn against a young man because he is different. Before you read the story, look at this list. How many of these things might make you think badly of a stranger? Can you add to the list?

1 A man with an earring and very long hair.
2 A girl with a tattoo and no hair.
3 Someone who wears strange clothes and no shoes.

2 🆗 53 Read and listen to the first part of the story. Then answer the questions.

> Children always see unusual things long before anyone else. It was little Sam Donnelley, the hotel owner's son, who said to me, "Look, there's a man at the top of the Ford Building!"
>
> I looked up at the top of our town's tallest building – all of seven floors – and I saw the man. He was on the parapet, with his legs over the edge. From where I was, he didn't look worried. He just sat there, looking up at the sky. Waiting, perhaps, for the first evening star.
>
> Soon there was a small crowd of people looking up.
>
> "Someone should call the Fire Department," said Millie Banks, the hairdresser.
>
> "But who is it? Can you see?" asked old Mrs Harper who owns the bookstore.
>
> "It's the Stranger," said Sam, who has the best eyesight of all of us.
>
> "The Stranger". That's what we called him, because he was a new, unknown person in our small town. And also because, by our small town's standards, he was strange.

1 Where was the young man?
2 What time of day was it?
3 Do you think the Stranger might jump?
4 Who identified him?

3 Now read the whole story. It starts on page 7 of *The wave and other stories*. Think about these questions while you read.

1 Who is telling the story?
2 Why does he have a lot of free time?
3 What did Randall Dodge do for a living before he retired?
4 Did the Stranger take a room in a hotel?
5 How did he spend his days?
6 What kind of relationship did Doc Dodge have with the Stranger?
7 What was Mary-Lou Carpenter like?
8 Where did she go when she disappeared?
9 How did people's attitude to the Stranger change after Mary-Lou disappeared?
10 How did the Stranger react?
11 Why couldn't anyone go up to the top of the Ford Building to talk to him?
12 Did the people in the square change their attitude to the Stranger? How did they feel?
13 What did the people shout to the Stranger?
14 Who, in the end, was the Stranger?
15 Were there any clues in the story that pointed to his true identity?

⑨ *My place*

Talking about rooms
Present Perfect: *for* or *since*
Conversations: *Could I speak to . . . ?*

Talking about rooms

1 a) Look at the photographs (a–c). Which is a bedroom, which is a kitchen and which is a living room? Do you like any of the rooms? Why / Why not?

b) In pairs. Take it in turns to ask and answer these questions.

1 Do you live in a house or a flat?
2 Where do you spend the most time? Why?
3 Where do you listen to music?
4 Where do you work / do your homework?
5 Where do you relax?

2 a) 🔊 54 Listen to Kate, Liz and Nick talking about where they live. Do they live in houses or flats? Which photographs are they talking about? Fill in part 1 of the table.

	1	2	3
Kate	Photograph ☐	She's lived there since	simple
Liz	Photograph ☐	She's lived there for	
Nick	Photograph ☐	He's lived there for	

b) 🔊 54 Listen again and fill in part 2 of the table.

c) Look at the adjectives in the Word Box. Which adjectives did you hear? Fill in part 3 of the table.

> simple ✓   large   bright /braɪt/   cosy /ˈkəʊzi/
> welcoming   relaxing   light   tidy
> comfortable /ˈkʌmftəbəl/   untidy   warm
> colourful   traditional /trəˈdɪʃənəl/   dark

d) 🔊 54 Listen and check.

54

3 Look at the words in the Word Box. Find the things in the photographs in Exercise 1a). Write the words on the word map.

Example: duvet = 29 sofa = 13 dishwasher = 9

duvet /ˈduːveɪ/ ✓ sofa /ˈsəʊfə/ ✓ dishwasher ✓
carpet chair chest of drawers /tʃest əv ˈdrɔːz/
TV coffee table cooker cupboard /ˈkʌbəd/
curtains /ˈkɜːtnz/ cushion /ˈkʊʃən/ bed
fridge lamp mirror microwave /ˈmaɪkrəweɪv/
picture freezer pillow /ˈpɪləʊ/ plant pot
rug sheet sink blanket shelves table
stereo vase toaster wardrobe

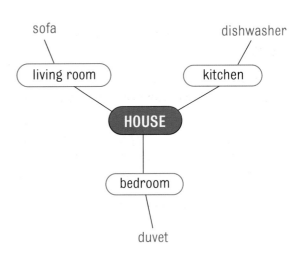

This is nice. How long have you had it?

4 a) 🔘 55 Listen to Kate, Liz and Nick. Who says these sentences? What are they talking about? Match the photographs (a–c) to the sentences (1–3).

1 I've had it for about seven years.
2 We've had it since we got married.
3 I've had it for ages.

b) Read the sentences in Exercise 4a) again. Fill in the gaps in the Language Box with *for* or *since*.

Present Perfect: for or since?

We can use the Present Perfect for a period of time that began in the past and continues to now:

We've had this chair **for** six months.

PAST ←——————————————→ NOW
(January)   (June)

We've had this chair **since** January.

We use .... with a period of time:
I've had this .... five years / a week.
We use .... with the start of the period (a point in time):
She's lived there .... 1999 / she left college.

---

c) Which expressions in the Word Box go with *for* and which go with *since*? Make two lists.

---

twelve weeks   last year   this morning   a year
the day before yesterday   Friday   three o'clock
six days   he left school   a couple of months
a week   they got married   an hour

---

d) Fill in the gaps with the Present Perfect of the verbs in brackets and *for* or *since*. Use contractions if you can.

1 He...............(live) here .... he got divorced.
2 A: How long .... they ....(know) him?
   B: Only .... yesterday.
3 A: What's Sarah doing these days?
   B: I don't know. I ....(not see) her .... about three months.
4 She................ (have) this picture .... years. Her grandmother gave it to her.
5 A: Sorry for the delay. We're very busy today. How long .... you .... (be) here?
   B: We................ (be) here .... 2 o'clock!

Pronunciation: weak forms

5 a) 🔘 56 Listen. Underline the stressed words / syllables.

1 How long has he had it?
2 How long have you lived here?
3 I haven't seen her for nine years.
4 A: How long have they known her?
   B: Since they were at school.
5 A: How long has she been here?
   B: For ages.
6 I've loved him since I was a little girl.

b) 🔘 56 Listen again and answer the questions.

1 How do we pronounce *have, has, for, was, were*?
2 Can you hear the "h" sound in *have* and *has*?

c) 🔘 56 Listen again and repeat.

My favourite things

6 a) Use these questions and make notes about your favourite things.

1 Why is it important to you?
2 How long have you had it?
3 Who gave it to you?

b) Go round the class and ask and answer questions about your favourite things.

c) Write a paragraph about your favourite thing.

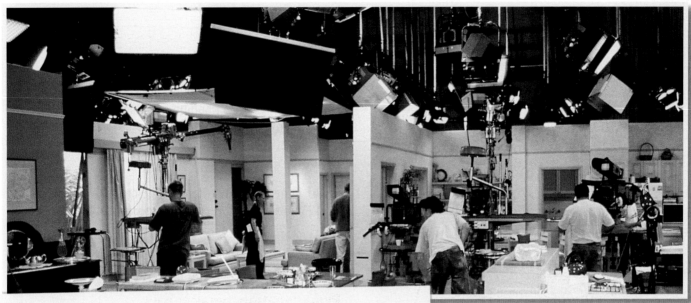

Different lives – different dreams

This is a modern psychological drama about the very different lifestyles, ambitions and dreams of the members of one family. All of the action takes place in the different living rooms of the main characters.

Cordelia and Henry O'Connell

Cordelia and Henry are in their late fifties. Cordelia is from a very rich family but she and Henry don't have a lot of money any more. They have an old house in the country and they've lived there for many years. They used to be hippies and they still have a free and easy lifestyle. They've travelled a lot and love India and Latin America. Their house is full of things they've bought on their travels.

Bob: (Cordelia and Henry's son)

Bob is in his late twenties and is an ambitious young businessman. He has worked in a bank in London since he left university and he's now very successful. He always has beautiful, rich girlfriends. He has a large luxury flat in the city centre. His flat is a financial investment and so are the things in it.

Carol: (Cordelia and Henry's daughter)

Carol is a fashion designer and her husband, Justin, is an architect. They're both in their early thirties. They have a modern house in the city. They're always looking for new ideas and hate anything traditional. They want to be different from other people. Their friends are designers and artists and they often buy their work. They don't have children and they don't want them – children are too untidy!

Ophelia: (Cordelia's sister)

Ophelia is in her late fifties, but thinks she's still twenty. She has been married seven times. She's single at the moment, but she's looking for husband number eight. She loves romance and glamorous parties. She has spent a lot of time on the French Riviera. She writes romantic novels and makes a lot of money.

Designing rooms

7 **a)** You work in television. You design sets. You're going to design the set for a new TV drama *Different lives – different dreams*. Read about the main characters. Do you think their homes are similar?

b) In pairs. Design one of the four living rooms. Talk about these things and then write your ideas.

1 What kinds of things do you think are in the living room (furniture, flowers, books, CDs, pictures, magazines, things from holidays, etc.)?

2 What does the room look like? Is it modern or traditional? Is it tidy or untidy? What colours are there?

c) In groups of four. Read your descriptions to each other but don't say whose room it is. Can the other pair guess?

Example: It's a very modern room with big windows. The walls are white and there's a . . .

Grammar reference
Present Perfect: page 104

Conversations Could I speak to . . . ?

On the phone

1 a) 🔊57 Patsy has bought a new flat and it needs decorating. She's phoning an interior design company. Listen and answer the questions.

1 Which interior design company is Patsy phoning?
2 What's the problem?

b) In pairs. Look at Recording script 57 on page 126 and practise reading the conversation.

c) 🔊58 Patsy tries again and gets through to Mann Interior Design this time. She talks to the receptionist. Listen and fill in the message pad.

mann interior **design**

Message for: Jason Lombard
Caller's name: ....
Company: ....
Phone number: ....
Message: ....
....
....
....
....
....

d) 🔊58 Listen again. Underline the words you hear.

Example: <u>Can</u> / Could I speak to Jason Lombard, please?

1 One moment / Just a minute.
2 Who's calling / Who's speaking, please?
3 It's / This is Patsy Wright.
4 Hold on / Hold the line, please.
5 Can I take / Can I leave a message?
6 Can you / Could you ask him to phone me?
7 May I take your / What's your number?
8 Right. I'll give him / I'll pass on the message.

Pronunciation: stress and intonation

2 a) ⊙⊙59 Listen to these sentences from the conversation in Exercise 1c). Underline the stressed words / syllables. Which word / syllable in each sentence has the most stress?

1 Can I speak to Jason Lombard, please?
2 One moment.
3 Hold the line, please.
4 I'm afraid he's in a meeting.
5 Can I take a message?
6 May I take your number?

b) ⊙⊙59 The caller and the receptionist both sound polite. Listen again and repeat the sentences.

3 In pairs. Student A, look at page 138 and Student B look at page 136.

Can you repeat that?

4 a) ⊙⊙60 Patsy is trying to have a phone conversation with her friend, Bob, but she's having problems with her mobile phone. The line keeps breaking up and she can't hear him very well. Listen and write the questions Patsy asks to get the information she missed.

1 .... see?
2 .... go?
3 .... ask for?
4 .... call?

b) ⊙⊙60 Listen again. Underline the word Patsy stresses most in each question.

c) ⊙⊙61 Listen and repeat the questions. Then read the Language Box.

> ### *Can you repeat that?*
>
> When we ask someone to repeat information we stress the question word and our intonation goes up:
>
> A: I saw ★ ★ ★ last week. ➚
> B: Sorry? ➚ **Who** did you see?

5 In pairs. Student A, look at page 138 and Student B at page 133.

Wavelength page

10 He loves me,
he loves me not . . .

Love stories
Past Continuous or Past Simple?
Skills: Jealousy and revenge

Love stories

1 In pairs. Are you a secret romantic? What is your idea of a romantic evening for two? Which of these ideas do you think is the most romantic?

1 Walking along a beach in a hot country. The sea is calm and there's a full moon.
2 A candle-lit dinner in an expensive restaurant. There's violin music playing in the background.
3 Sitting by an open fire in a comfortable old cottage in the country with your favourite music and good food and drink.

2 a) In pairs. Look at picture a) in this love story. What do you think happened next? Put the other pictures (b–j) in order.

b) Match these sentences (1–9) to the pictures (b–j).

1 They **split up**.
2 He **fancied** her.
3 They **fell in love**.
4 They **had rows** /raʊz/ all the time.
5 He **asked** her **out**.
6 They **went out**.
7 They **went off** each other.
8 They discovered that they **had a lot in common**.
9 He **chatted** her **up**.

3 a) Do you remember Jenny, her boyfriend, Ken and Mandy (see page 50)? What do you think happened to them? Read Jenny's story, on the right and answer the questions.

1 How many men does Jenny talk about?
2 Where did she meet two of them?

b) Fill in the gaps with the words and expressions in green from Exercise 2b). Use the correct form of the verbs and change the pronouns.

c) 👀 62 Listen and check.

Why did you do it?

4 a) In groups. You're going to hear Jenny's friend, Mandy, talking to Roger, her psychotherapist. Before you listen, why do you think people:

- get engaged?   • have an affair?
- get married?   • separate?
- get pregnant?   • get divorced?

b) 👀 63 Now listen to Mandy. Make notes about her reasons.

When Ken and I split up, I was really miserable. I didn't go out for two weeks! I was sitting at home alone one evening when my crazy friend, Mandy, rang and invited me to a party at John's. What was I doing at the time? Nothing – so I decided to go.

When we got to the party everyone was dancing and Mandy immediately disappeared, so I got a drink and sat down on my own in a corner. I was sitting there when a man came over and started to ...chat me up...(1). His name was Greg.

At first I didn't ....(2) him at all. He wasn't my type. But after about an hour I realised he wasn't bad, just a bit nervous. I decided to give him a chance and when he ....(3) I said "Yes".

The first time we ....(4) we had a really nice time and we discovered that we ....(5). That was the beginning of our relationship. We saw each other all the time after that. Why did I ....(6) with him? I don't know . . . it just happened . . . and we were really happy at first.

It was really romantic. Then things began to change and we started to ....(7) each other. I suppose we just got bored.

Then things really got worse! We ....(8) about everything . . . money . . . the car . . . TV programmes. And he didn't like my cooking. After a few months we ....(9). I felt bad about it at first and I was really depressed. Then one evening I was watching TV when Mandy rang. She made me go to another party.

That was when I met Paul. Mandy and I were talking in the kitchen when I saw him. He was talking to some people. He was laughing – it was a wonderful laugh. Anyway I went over and asked him to dance and he said "Yes".

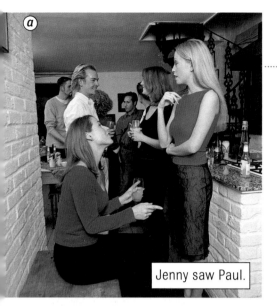

Jenny saw Paul.

Jenny asked Paul to dance and he said "Yes".

Mandy and Jenny were talking in the kitchen.

Past Continuous or Past Simple?

5 a) Look at the photographs (a–c). Put them in the correct order.

b) Look at the time line in the Language Box. Then read Jenny's story in Exercise 3a) again and underline all the examples of the Past Continuous. Then fill in the gaps in the Language Box.

Past Continuous

• We form the Past Continuous with *was / were* + verb + *-ing*

(Past Continuous)
Paul **was talking**

PAST ⟵————————————————————————| NOW

when Jenny saw him.
(Past Simple)

Questions	Positive answers	Negative answers
.... he laughing?	Yes, he	No, he ....
.... you talking?	Yes, we	No, we ....
What .... you drinking?	I .... water.	I .... beer.

---

c) Read these sentences about Jenny's story. Correct the mistakes.

Example: Jenny was having dinner with friends at home when Mandy phoned her about John's party.
She wasn't having dinner with friends. She was sitting at home alone.

1 The people at John's party were talking in the kitchen when Jenny and Mandy arrived.
2 Jenny was talking to a man when Greg came over.
3 When Mandy rang the second time Jenny was washing her hair.
4 When Jenny first saw Paul he was dancing.

d) Fill in the gaps with the Past Continuous or Past Simple of the verbs in brackets.

1 **A:** I ....(sit) in a café when I ....(see) my future husband. It ....(be) love at first sight.
 B: .... he ....(see) you?
 A: No, he ....(do). He ....(talk) to a young woman.

2 **A:** What .... you ....(do) when I ....(phone) you? Why .... you ....(not answer) the phone?
 B: Sorry, Patrick and I ....(have) another row.

3 **A:** What .... you ....(do) when you ....(meet) your first wife?
 B: Believe it or not, I ....(study) English.

e) 🔊 64 Listen and check. How do we say *was* and *were*?

Shades of anger

6 **a)** 🔘65 Listen to two conversations and answer the questions.

1 Where are the people?
2 What are they angry about?
3 In which conversation are the people angrier?

b) 🔘65 Listen again. Which expressions do the people use in conversations 1 and 2? Fill in the boxes.

1 It really irritates me when she does that. `1`
2 She makes me so angry. `2`
3 It drives me crazy when she does that. `☐`
4 She gets on my nerves too. `4`

7 **a)** In groups. Look at the pie chart from a newspaper survey. What do you think couples row *(row)* about? Fill in the gaps with words from the Word Box.

housework	children	work
money	personal habits	friends

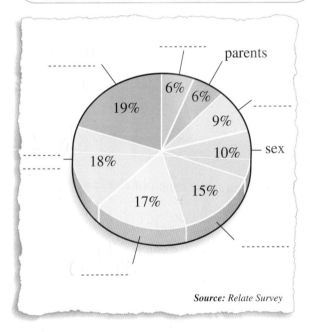

Source: Relate Survey

b) Look at page 133 and check your ideas.

c) What do people you know do that drives you crazy? Use the expressions in Exercise 6b) and write sentences about family, friends, colleagues, etc.

Examples: My sister really gets on my nerves sometimes – especially when she borrows my things and doesn't ask me.

My boyfriend always talks about his job. It drives me crazy!

Chat show interviews

TERRY *Stinger*

8 **a)** 🔘66 Listen to the introduction to a television show where people talk about their lives and the audience joins in. The show's host is Terry Stinger. What's the subject of tonight's show?

b) You're going to be chat show hosts (like Terry Stinger) or "couples from hell". The chat show hosts are going to interview the couples. The most miserable couple wins a free instant divorce and two holidays (to different places!). In two groups. Chat show hosts, look at page 133 and couples look at page 139.

c) Chat show hosts each find a couple. Take it in turns to interview your couples for the audience (the class). The class then decides which couple is the most miserable.

> *Grammar reference*
> Past Continuous: page 105

Who's Shakespeare?

1 a) What do you know about William Shakespeare? Do the questionnaire and find out.

b) In pairs. Compare your answers. Then look at page 141 and check.

1 Shakespeare was:
a) English b) American c) German
2 He wrote:
a) *War and Peace* b) *Macbeth* c) *Gone With The Wind*
3 Which pronunciation of Shakespeare is correct?
a) /ʃaɪkspɪə/ b) /ʃɑːkəspɪrə/ c) /ʃeɪkspɪə/
4 How does this line from *Hamlet* end?
"To be, or not to be – that is the ...."
a) problem b) answer c) question

Jealousy and revenge

2 a) In pairs. Look at the pictures. What is happening?

①

②

③

④

b) Read the letter (A) from William Shakespeare to his friend, Francis, and the newspaper article (B). Match one of the pictures (1–4) to each story. Who took revenge on their partner (lover / wife / husband) in each story and why?

c) Read the letter and newspaper article again. Now answer these questions about each story.

1 Who are the three main characters in the story?
2 Which of the main characters lied? What about?
3 What did Othello and Jenny do to take revenge on their partners? Were they sorry about what they did afterwards?

Ⓐ

Dear Francis,

1 Sorry I haven't written to you for so long, but I've been busy on a new play. It's a love story and a tragedy.

The main character, Othello, is a general in the Venetian army. He's black. Othello loves Desdemona and she loves him. They run away
5 together and get married. Her father is very, very angry.

Iago, a soldier in the Venetian army, is angry because Othello has promoted another soldier (Cassio) and not him. He pretends to be Othello's friend, but really he hates him and wants to destroy him. He tells Othello that Desdemona is having an affair with Cassio.
10 At first Othello doesn't believe Iago, but in the end Iago convinces him. Then Othello goes crazy with jealousy and kills Desdemona. Later, Othello finds out that Iago was lying – Desdemona really loved him. When he realises his terrible mistake, he kills himself.
14 So, basically that's the story. What do you think?

Your good friend,

William

Wavelength page

d) Look at the letter (A) and the newspaper article (B) again. Who or what do these words refer to?

Example: it (A, line 2) = Shakespeare's new play.

A Shakespeare's letter	B Newspaper article
1 he (line 3)	6 she (line 2)
2 she (line 4)	7 he (line 4)
3 they (line 4)	8 her (line 4)
4 him (line 7)	9 they (line 18)
5 he (line 7)	10 it (line 23)

e) Find these words and expressions in the letter and the newspaper article. Then match them to their meanings.

Example: 1 = e)

A Shakespeare's letter

1 tragedy	a) to damage someone or something completely (verb)
2 promote	b) when you are angry or unhappy because someone you like or love is showing interest in another person (noun)
3 destroy	c) to make someone believe that something is true, even if it's not (verb)
4 convince	d) to give someone a better or more important job (verb)
5 jealousy	e) a serious play that has a very sad ending (noun)

B Newspaper article

6 get your own back	f) something that you don't tell other people because you don't want them to know (noun)
7 cheating	g) to take revenge on someone (expression)
8 secret	h) to make someone leave a place (phrasal verb)
9 helping	i) behaving dishonestly, not telling the truth (adjective)
10 throw someone out	j) the amount of food that someone gives you or that you take (noun)

Lover's Dog Food Revenge

1 A blonde woman told millions of TV viewers yesterday how she served her unfaithful boyfriend dog food pie. It happened after he told her
5 about his affair with another woman. Jenny Bloor, twenty-six, has kept her secret for six years. But she decided to tell all on the TV show *The Time, The Place*.
10 The TV audience laughed as she told them how she got her own back on her cheating live-in lover, David Spencer, twenty-seven.
Jenny went to visit him in hospital
15 after he had a serious car crash but there was another woman (not his nurse) by his bedside. The woman was his lover and they were having a secret affair.

20 When David came home from hospital Jenny baked him a pie which she made from a tin of dog food. He enjoyed it so much he asked for more.
25 "He really liked it and had a second helping," said Jenny on the show. Later that day she threw him out of the house.
"I've never told him what was in the
30 pie," Jenny said. "But now he'll know and I hope he's sick! I haven't seen him since then and I hope I never will."

(from the *Daily Express*)

Revenge is sweet!

3 a) In small groups, at least one for each scene. You're going to write one scene from a play about *Lover's Dog Food Revenge*. Read about the four scenes and choose your scene.

SCENE 1: Jenny Bloor with her live-in boyfriend, David Spencer, in a restaurant before she finds out about his affair.

SCENE 2: David with his secret lover in a park before Jenny finds out about his affair.

SCENE 3: David and his secret lover in his hospital room. Jenny comes in and sees them. Jenny and David have a big row.

SCENE 4: Jenny and David in their kitchen. Jenny makes dog food pie and serves it to David. Then she throws David out.

b) Before you write your scene, answer these questions:

1 Who in your group will play which character? Everyone in the group must have a part. Add more characters if you like (a waiter, a person in the park, a doctor, a neighbour etc.).
2 What are the characters doing? (going for a walk? dancing? having a row?)
3 How does each character feel? (happy? sad? angry? fed up? worried?)
4 What are the characters talking about?

c) Write your scene and practise it.

d) Join up with three other groups who have written different scenes. Act out the four scenes in the correct order for the class.

If . . .

> **Second Conditional:** *If I had . . .*
> **Inventions and gadgets**
> **Day to day English:** *I think you should . . .*

In the beginning there was nothing

1 In pairs. Look at the mixed up words (a–d). They are all inventions. Put the letters in the correct order and match them to the pictures (1–4). Which of the inventions is the most important and useful to you? Why?

Example: a) = 4 (space shuttle)

a) EASCP LETTUSH   b) LWEHE   c) IISNELEVOT   d) EWVACRIMO

2 a) Look at the pictures (a–d) on the right. Albert Einstone is a caveman. He's also a genius and he has a lot of great ideas for inventions. Match the sentences (1–4) to the pictures (a–d).

Example: 1 = b)

1 If the pictures moved, this would be fun.
2 If this stone had wheels, it wouldn't be difficult to move.
3 If we cooked this food, it would taste nice.
4 If we had a space shuttle, I could take you to the moon!

b) 🎧 67 Listen and check. Then listen again and repeat.

c) Look at the pictures again. Answer the questions with *Yes* or *No*.

1 a) Do they cook their food?
  b) Does it taste nice?
2 a) Do the pictures move on their rock?
  b) Does Albert think "watching" the rock is fun?
3 a) Do they have a space shuttle?
  b) Can Albert take them to the moon?
4 a) Does the stone have wheels?
  b) Is it difficult to move?

d) Now read the Language Box and tick (✓) the correct answer.

Second Conditional

We use the Second Conditional to talk about unreal / impossible situations:

If we had a space shuttle, I could take you to the moon!
BUT We don't have a space shuttle and I can't take you to the moon.

If this stone had wheels, it wouldn't be difficult to move.
BUT It doesn't have wheels and it is difficult to move.

Is Albert talking about:
the present / future? ☐
the past? ☐

If	I / you / we / they / he / she / it	Past Simple	I / you / we / they / he / she / it	would could wouldn't couldn't	infinitive

Both parts of the sentence can have a positive (+) or negative (–) verb.
If I **didn't have** a television, I'd **be** really bored.
The *if* part can come first or second in the sentence.
I'd be really bored **if** I didn't have a television.

Look!
• We often use the contraction *'d* (would) when we speak.
  She would → she'd

3 **a)** In pairs. Albert has more ideas to make their lives easier. Match the beginning of sentences (1–5) in A to the end of sentences (a–e) in B. Then finish sentences 6–10 with your own ideas.

Example: 1 = b)

A
1 If we had a car,
2 If we had umbrellas,
3 If we had a washing machine,
4 If we didn't eat meat,
5 If we had pens,

B
a) we wouldn't have to go hunting.
b) we could get to places faster.
c) it would be easier to write.
d) we wouldn't get wet.
e) we wouldn't have to wash our clothes in the river.

6 If we had soap, . . .
7 If we had phones, . . .
8 If we had electricity, . . .
9 If we had money, . . .
10 If we had supermarkets, . . .

b) Write a Second Conditional sentence for each situation (+ = positive, – = negative).

Example: He doesn't help her so she gets angry with him. If . . . `+ –`
If he helped her, she wouldn't get angry with him.

1 I don't have a car, so I have to walk to work. If . . . `+ –`
2 Joe has to look after his little brother, so he can't go out. If . . . `– +`
3 I don't have enough money, so I can't buy that jacket. If . . . `+ +`
4 Mrs Jones has nine children, three dogs and two cats, so she's very busy. If . . . `– –`

If I didn't have my . . .

4 **a)** Match the words in the Word Box to the photographs (a–g). Do you have any of the things in the photographs? Which ones do you have?

> mobile phone   laptop   hairdryer   Swiss army knife
> travel iron   umbrella   dishwasher

b) 🎧 68 Listen to three people talking about things that are really important to them. Which three things in the photographs do you think they are talking about? Why do they like them? Fill in the table.

What are they talking about?	Why do they like it / them?
1	....
2	....
3	....

c) 🎧 68 Listen again. Which things are these sentences about? What or who do the words in green refer to?

a) I just pop **them** in … turn **it** on … and that's it!
b) **It's** like my best friend!
c) I know **they** irritate some people.
d) I keep in touch with **them** this way.

d) What is the most useful thing you have? Why?

e) Go round the class and talk to other students. Make notes about what they say.

Example: I don't know what I'd do if I didn't have my travel iron. I really
need it because . . .

Pet hates

5 **a)** In pairs. Think of one modern invention or gadget that really irritates you. You now have the chance to get rid of it forever! Think of how the world would be a better place if we didn't have this thing. Prepare a short speech to convince the class to get rid of it.

Example: The world would be a better place if we didn't have cars. If
we didn't have them, we wouldn't have to worry about the
traffic. The air would be cleaner. There wouldn't be any car
accidents. We could cycle everywhere. Everyone would be
fitter and healthier.

b) Make groups of four with people from different pairs. Each student makes their speech. The group chooses the best speech and gets rid of that thing.

If things were different . . .

6 a) In pairs. Look at the pictures. What are the people thinking? Can you fill in the gaps?

1 If I were the .... , I wouldn't have to work.

2 If she weren't so .... , we'd do more business.

3 If they were more .... , they wouldn't lose things all the time.

b) Read the Language Box and then fill in the gaps in sentences 1–5 with *were* or *weren't*.

Second Conditional: be

With the verb *be*, we usually use *were / weren't* with all subjects. (*If I were . . . If you weren't . . . If he were . . .*):

If	I / you / we / they / he / she / it	were (positive) / weren't (negative)	I / you / we / they / he / she / it	would could wouldn't couldn't	+ infinitive

1 If Joe's job .... so stressful, he'd be happier.

2 If they .... over eighteen, they could get into that nightclub.

3 If he .... late every day, the boss wouldn't shout at him.

4 If she .... nicer, people would like her more.

5 If I .... the boss, I'd fire him!

7 a) Choose six of these sentences and make them true for you.

Example: If I weren't married, I'd leave my job and travel round the world.

 1 If I weren't . . .

 2 I'd be happier if I were . . .

 3 My life would be easier if I had . . .

 4 My life would be better if I didn't have to . . .

 5 I wouldn't be happy if I had to . . .

 6 It would be great if I knew how to . . .

 7 It would be nice if I lived near . . .

 8 I'd be really unhappy if I didn't have . . .

 9 I'd be fed up if I . . .

10 Life would be more fun if I were a . . .

b) In groups. Compare your sentences. Take it in turns to ask and answer questions about them.

Example: A: It would be nice if I lived near a lake.

 B: Really, why?

 A: Well . . .

Grammar reference
Second Conditional: page 109

A problem at work

1 a) 🔊 69 Sam has worked in the Marketing Department of his company for four years, but he has a problem at work. He's talking to some friends about it. Listen. Why is he fed up?

a) Because he didn't get a pay rise.

b) Because his boss doesn't socialise with the staff.

c) Because he didn't get promoted.

d) Because his boss doesn't let people have any time off.

b) 🔊 69 Listen to the conversation again. Tick (✓) the advice that his friends give him.

1 a) Have you thought about stopping her?	☐
b) Have you thought about talking to her?	☐
2 a) Why don't you ask her about it then?	☐
b) Why don't you ask her out then?	☐
3 a) I think you should explain.	☐
b) I think you should complain.	☐
4 a) I don't think you should bother her.	☐
b) I don't think you should go above her.	☐
5 a) If I were you, I'd look for another boss.	☐
b) If I were you, I'd look for another job.	☐

c) 🔊 69 Listen again. Does Sam accept or reject his friends' advice? Read the Language Box below.

Advice

Giving advice

Have you thought about	talking to her?
Why don't you	talk to her?
I think you should I don't think you should If I were you, I'd If I were you, I wouldn't	talk to her.

Accepting advice

That's a good idea.

Hmm, maybe you're right.

Rejecting advice

Yes, but . . .

Well, . . .

Wavelength page

Pronunciation: sentence stress

2 a) 🔊 70 Listen and underline the stressed words / syllables.

Example: I don't <u>think</u> you should <u>talk</u> to her.

1 Why don't you talk to her?
2 I think you should talk to her.
3 If I were you, I'd talk to her.
4 If I were you, I wouldn't talk to her.
5 Have you thought about talking to her?

b) 🔊 70 Listen again and repeat.

If I were Sam, . . .

3 In groups. What would you do if you were Sam?

Example: A: If I were Sam, I'd talk to the boss.
B: I think he should leave.

Help me, please!

4 a) In pairs. You're unhappy because you have one of these problems. Work together, choose one of the problems and talk about the details. Make notes.

1 My boyfriend / girlfriend / wife / husband can't stand my best friend.
2 I think my wife / husband is having an affair.
3 I'm having terrible problems with my son / daughter at the moment.
4 No-one likes me.
5 Someone at work / school is jealous of me and it's making my life very difficult.
6 My husband's / wife's habits are driving me crazy.

b) Make groups of four, with people from four different pairs. Take it in turns to describe your problem. The others give you advice.

Example: What do you think I should do? My wife . . .

Love me, love my car

Cars and stars
Reported Commands: *tell / ask* +
someone + *to* + infinitive
Do you remember? Units 9–12

Cars and stars

1 In groups. Talk about these questions.

1 Have you got a car?
2 How important are cars in your life? Why?

2 In groups. Which of the adjectives in the Word Box can describe people, which can describe cars, which can describe both? Fill in the table.

> lively /ˈlaɪvli/ ✓ curious /ˈkjʊərɪəs/ spontaneous efficient /ɪˈfɪʃənt/
> nervous /ˈnɜːvəs/   comfortable   proud   independent
> cautious /ˈkɔːʃəs/ popular /ˈpɒpjʊlə/ creative reliable /rɪˈlaɪəbəl/
> optimistic   passionate /ˈpæʃənət/   irritating   moody   safe

People	Cars	Both
lively		

3 a) Look at the signs of the zodiac. Which astrological sign are you? When is your birthday?

b) Read part of a magazine article about astrology and cars. Which sign (a–l) do you think describes you?

c) In groups. Tell each other which description you think is yours and why. Then look at page 139 and find out which description goes with which sign of the zodiac. Did you choose the right description? Do you agree with the description of you? Can you find any descriptions that fit people you know?

d) In groups. What car would you buy, if money were no problem? Why?

Aquarius
(21st January – 20th Febuary)

Pisces
(21st Febuary – 21st March)

Aries
(22nd March – 21st April)

Taurus
(22nd April – 22nd May)

Gemini
(23rd May – 22nd June)

Cancer
(23rd June – 23rd July)

Leo
(24th July – 23rd August)

Virgo
(24th August – 23rd September)

Libra
(24th September – 22nd October)

Scorpio
(23rd October – 22nd November)

Sagittarius
(23rd November – 22nd December)

Capricorn
(23rd December – 20th January)

It's in the Stars

a You want a different car for every day of the week, from a 2CV to a Rolls Royce – it depends on your mood. (Some people say you're moody!)

b You like a car with style and elegance – with somewhere to put your caviar and champagne! It also has to be reliable and comfortable.

c You're very lively. You want to live life in the fast lane. Your ideal car is a Porsche or a Lamborghini. You make passengers nervous – your friends and family probably prefer to take the bus.

d You're proud and independent, but you'd love to have a chauffeur. You drive a luxury car (in your dreams, at least!). You worry about whether the bar is full – and where to put the music system.

e You love privacy and mystery. Your car has tinted windows – so you can see out but no-one can see in. In other areas of your life you're passionate and you love drama but surprisingly, you drive cautiously.

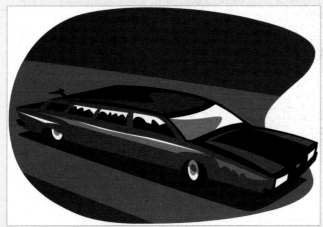

f You don't want a car – you want a cupboard on wheels. Somewhere to put your cassettes, sandwiches, maps and a world atlas – you're terrified of getting lost. You're curious too – you'd like a car with a periscope so you can see what the other drivers are doing.

g You're a creative person. You think the practical things in life are boring. You use the mirrors to look at yourself – not to see possible dangers on the road. You choose your car because of the colour. You're not the most popular driver on the road!

h You're a spontaneous person so you never plan things. Your fantasy car is a two-seater sports car with an ejector seat for irritating passengers.

i You're optimistic and full of big ideas. You love speed and excitement. If you're rich, you probably have a car with a jet engine. How many cars have you crashed? Slow down!

j You need a safe car like a Volvo. You're usually quiet and calm, but in a car you shout at everyone who irritates you. Your language can get so strong that it's better (and safer!) if no-one can hear you.

k Your ideal car is probably a BMW or a Mercedes. If you don't own one of these cars, it's probably because you think you can't afford it – but go on, live a little! You want your car to be reliable – but you also like a bit of status!

l You're a very independent person. You don't like rules and regulations. You think red lights, stop signs and No Entry signs are for other drivers, not you. You love to be different – and you never wear a seat belt!

The driving lesson

4 a) In groups. Talk about these questions.

1 Can you drive?
2 Who taught you to drive?
3 Did you pass your driving test the first time?

b) In pairs. Look at the pictures (a–f) of Mrs White's driving lesson. They're in the wrong order. What do you think happened?

c) 🔘71 Listen to Mrs White's driving lesson with her driving instructor, Ron Johnson. Put the pictures (a–f) in the correct order.

d) 🔘71 Listen again. Who says these things: Ron Johnson, Mrs White, the cyclist or the owner of the Mercedes?

Example: Can you slow down?
= Ron Johnson

1 Please don't shout.
2 Get off the road!
3 Don't worry about the cyclist.
4 Could you turn left, please?
5 Get out of the car.
6 Please don't hit him.

e) 🔘72 The policeman asked Mrs White what happened. Listen and fill in the gaps. Which two details did Mrs White change in her story?

1 He told me to .... – right in the middle of the road.
2 I asked .... shout.
3 He told .... get off the road.
4 Mr Johnson told .... worry about the cyclist.
5 He asked .... right.
6 The man told Mr Johnson .... of the car.
7 I asked .... Mr Johnson.

f) Read the Language Box on the right. Then put sentences 1–5 from the conversation into Reported Commands.

Example: RON: Could you show me your licence, please?

He asked her to show him her licence.

1 RON: Start the car.
2 RON: Could you turn the windscreen wipers off?
3 RON: Check your mirrors and then pull out.
4 RON: Slow down!
5 RON: Don't stop in the middle of the road.

My car

5 **a)** Look at the photograph and read the words of the first part of a famous 1950s rock and roll song. Don't fill in the gaps. Do you think the singer's car is important to him because:

1 he has a very busy job and he needs his car?
2 he can drive around with his girlfriend and have fun?
3 he's teaching his daughter to drive?

b) 🔊 73 Listen to the first part of the song. Was your guess in Exercise 5a) right?

c) Read these lists of words. Which word in each list has a different vowel sound?

Example: 1 **automobile**: wheel, feel, steal, smile
smile /smaɪl/ has a different vowel sound. The others are all /iː/.

1 **automobile**: wheel, feel, steal, smile
2 **mile**: style, wild, dial, meal
3 **go**: too, radio, slow, road
4 **sincere**: wear, ear, beer, here

d) 🔊 73 Fill in the gaps in the song with words from Exercise 5c). Then listen again and check.

e) Find words in the song that mean:

1 next to (preposition)
2 driving around just for fun (verb)
3 spoke very, very quietly (verb)
4 hugging and kissing the one you love (verb)

f) 🔊 74 Now look at Recording script 74, page 127 and listen to the whole song.

Reported Commands

• We use *ask / tell* + someone + *to* + infinitive.

Direct Commands	Reported Commands
"Could you turn left, please?"	→ He **asked her to** turn left.
"Get out of the car."	→ He **told him to** get out of the car.
"Don't worry about the cyclist."	→ He **told her not to** worry about the cyclist.
"Please don't shout."	→ She **asked him not to** shout.

SUBJECT PRONOUN		OBJECT PRONOUN	
I / You / He She / We / They	asked told	me / you / him her/ us / them	to turn left. not to shout.

Look!
• *Tell* is stronger than *ask*.

No Particular Place To Go

Ridin'* along in my automobile
My baby beside me at the .... [1] .
I stole a kiss at the turn of a mile,
My curiosity runnin' .... [2]
Cruisin' and playin' the .... [3] ,
With no particular place to go.

Ridin' along in my automobile
I'm anxious to tell her the way I .... [4] ,
So I told her softly and sincere,
And she leaned and whispered in my .... [5]
Cuddlin' more and drivin' .... [6] ,
With no particular place to go.

* ridin' = riding, runnin' = running, cruisin' = cruising etc.

Grammar reference
Reported Commands: page 109

Do you remember? Units 9–12

1 How long have they lived there?

a) In groups. Read the information about four neighbours, George, Peter, Rick and Mike. Who lives in which house? How long has each person lived there?

1 Rick has been George's next-door neighbour since he moved to Brighton.
2 George has lived in his house four years longer than Peter.
3 Rick's house isn't red and he doesn't have a garage.
4 Rick moved into the house next to the yellow one four years ago.
5 The man in the black house has never lived in London.
6 Peter has lived here since he left his job in London two years ago.
7 Mike moved here two years before Peter.

b) How long have George, Peter, Rick and Mike lived in their houses? Make sentences with *for* and *since*.

2 Where were you?

a) In pairs. Where were you and what were you doing at midnight on 31st December 1999?

b) In pairs. A man went to a party on New Year's Eve 1999. What do you think happened? Use the words in the Word Box.

> garden   glasses   girlfriend
> best friend   swimming pool   kiss
> push   scream   bar   drunk

c) 🎧 75 Listen to the man's story. Were you right? Was it a happy night for him? Why / Why not?

d) 🎧 76 A woman went to the same party. Listen. Was it a happy night for her? Why / Why not? What mistake did the man in Exercise 2c) make?

e) 🎧 75 and 76 Listen again. Are these sentences true (T) or false (F)? Correct the false ones.

Example: The man went into the garden to look for his friend, Brad. ☐F☐
He went into the garden to look for his girlfriend.

1 He wasn't wearing glasses. ☐
2 A couple were sitting by the pool. ☐
3 The man by the pool wasn't kissing the woman. ☐
4 The woman laughed when the man pushed them into the pool. ☐
5 Johnny asked the woman to marry him and she agreed. ☐

f) In pairs. Complete this story about New Year's Eve 1999. You don't have to tell the truth!

On New Year's Eve 1999 the strangest thing happened to me. I went to a party .... (where?). I was with .... (who?). We were .... (what were you doing?), when suddenly this .... (who?) came up to me and .... (what did he / she do?). We were both .... (how did you feel?) and then .... (what happened next?) . . .

g) Make new pairs. Tell each other your stories.

3 If I were a . . .

a) Finish these sentences for yourself. Write each sentence on a different piece of paper.

1 If I were a film director. . .
2 If I were a writer. . .
3 If I had three wishes I'd wish for. . .
4 If I didn't have to work / study. . .

b) In groups. Put your papers together. Take it in turns to pick up a piece of paper and read out the sentence. Guess who wrote it.

> Look at the Word lists for Units 9–12 on pages 118 – 120 and check that you know all the new words.

Puzzle 3 (Units 9–12) page 112

Wavelength page

Reading for pleasure

③ The wave

1 Before you read the story, look at the title and the picture. What do you think the title means?

1 A person who is waiting for you at the end of a journey.
2 A surprise meeting with someone you haven't seen for a long time.
3 A signal you make with your hand or arm.

2 🎧 77 Read and listen to the first part of the story. Then answer the questions.

> "Ladies and gentlemen, this is Frances Grant, your captain, speaking. We're beginning our descent to John F Kennedy Airport. Local time is 9:15. The temperature is 25° Celsius, 77° Fahrenheit . . ."
>
> Kim is almost home. She makes a few more notes. Then she shuts down her laptop. There are nearly fifty orders in a file on her little computer: large orders from big stores and designer shops in Seoul, Tokyo and Hong Kong. The buyers there loved the casual clothes that her company makes. This has been her most successful trip this year. She's feeling very pleased with herself.

1 Where does the story begin?
2 Which city is Kim's home?
3 Where has she been?
4 Why did she go there?
5 Why is she feeling so happy?

3 🎧 78 Read and listen to the second part of the story. Then answer the questions.

> In Arrivals, Kim calls her office on her cell phone. "Monica? It's Kim. I'm at JFK."
>
> "Welcome back, Miss Leeson!" says Kim's secretary. "How was your flight?"
>
> "Fine. I didn't sleep much, but I'm OK."
>
> "You must be very tired. You don't have to come into the office today. There's nothing urgent. Everything can wait until tomorrow."
>
> "I'm not really tired. But if there isn't anything urgent, I think I'll take the day off."
>
> "That's a great idea. Put your feet up. You've earned it!"
>
> "Thanks, Monica," she says. "I'll see you tomorrow."

1 Does Kim make her phone call before or after the plane lands?
2 Who does she speak to?
3 What does Kim decide to do?

4 Now read the whole story. It starts on page 13 of *The wave and other stories*. Think about these questions while you read.

1 Is Kim expecting someone to meet her?
2 Who does she wave to when she's leaving Arrivals?
3 What is he holding?
4 How does he react when she introduces herself?
5 Why does he suggest showing her the city?
6 Where does he decide to take her?
7 What two surprising things does Kim find they have in common?
8 Why does Kim ask Dan a lot of questions?
9 What particular place can Kim see from the top of the Empire State Building?
10 Why does Dan take Kim to lunch in an Italian restaurant?
11 What is Kim's first real lie?
12 Who does she see in the restaurant?
13 What does Kim do then?
14 What do Kim and Dan do after lunch?
15 Why do you think Kim decides to tell Dan the truth?
16 How does Dan react?

13 What a holiday!

Countable and uncountable nouns
Be going to + infinitive for predictions and plans
Present Perfect + *yet*
Day to day English: *There's a problem . . .*

Countable and uncountable nouns

1 a) Guests at Club Torso (a holiday resort) said these sentences to the receptionist. Some of the words in green are wrong. Correct them.

Examples: The people in the next room ̶i̶s̶ very noisy. are
There isn't any whisky in my mini-bar. ✓

1 How many people were on the coach trip yesterday? ....
2 The airline has lost my luggages. ....
3 We'd like to see some of the sights. Can you give us an advice? ....
4 There's some problem with the air conditioning in my room. ....
5 Do you have any informations on the sports and activities? ....
6 **A:** I'm just going to buy some magazines for the flight. ....
7 **B:** Well hurry up. We don't have many time. ....
8 There was a lot of children in the bar last night. ....
9 **A:** Can I change some Italian money here? ....
10 **B:** Certainly. How much money would you like to change? ....

b) ⊙⊙ 79 Listen and check. Then read the Language Box.

(How) much / (How) many and a lot (of) / lots (of)

Questions and negative sentences
We use *much* and *How much…?* with uncountable nouns.
A: How much luggage have you got?
B: Not much.
(I haven't got much luggage.)
We use *many* and *How many…?* with plural countable nouns.
A: How many children are in the swimming pool?
B: Not many.
(There aren't many children in the pool.)

Positive sentences
We can use *a lot (of)* or *lots (of)* with plural countable nouns and uncountable nouns.
There's a lot of / lots of luggage in reception.
There are a lot of / lots of children in the pool.
A: How much money have you got?
B: A lot. / Lots.

13

Club Torso: sports and activities

2 **a)** In pairs. Look at Club Torso's noticeboard. Match the activities (1–8) to the pictures (a–h).

1 painting	5 Latin American dancing
2 water skiing	6 jet skiing
3 aerobics	7 paragliding
4 wind-surfing	8 horse-riding

b) In pairs. Look at the students in your class and talk about these questions.

1 Which students in the class do you think have done the activities on the noticeboard?
2 Which activities do you think they would like to do?

c) Go round the class. Ask questions to find out if your guesses in Exercise 2b) were correct.

Examples: Have you ever been wind-surfing?
Have you ever done any painting?
Would you like to go horse-riding?

Look out! He's going to . . . !

3 **a)** In pairs. Look at the picture on the left. Ann and Maggie are on the beach at Club Torso. Who are they looking at? What are the people in the sea doing and why are they in danger?

b) 🔊 80 Listen to part of Ann and Maggie's conversation and fill in the gaps.

MAGGIE: He's .... crash into that boat!
ANN: Look at that huge .... behind them!
MAGGIE: They're .... fall into the water!

c) Look at Maggie's sentences and the picture again and answer these questions. Then read the Language Box.

1 What two predictions does Maggie make?
2 Why does she make them?

Be going to + infinitive

We use *be going to* + infinitive to make future predictions when we can see the evidence now:

Evidence now	**Prediction**
Look at that huge wave behind them. →	They're going to fall into the water.

Look!
We can also use *be going to* + infinitive for future intentions.

4 a) In pairs. Look at these people (1–4) at Club Torso. They're also having problems. What's happening? What do you think is going to happen? Use the verbs in the Word Box and make predictions.

> attack /əˈtæk/   drop   crash into   fall off

b) 🎧 81 Listen and check.

5 a) In pairs. Look at the predictions below. Choose three predictions and write a possible situation (the evidence now) for each one.

Situation	Prediction
1 Two children are fighting on the diving board of a swimming pool.	They're going to fall into it!
2	They're going to get wet!
3	They're going to fall off!
4	They're going to crash into it!
5	They're going to drop it!

b) In groups of four (Pair A and Pair B). Pair A describes one of their situations and Pair B makes a prediction from Exercise 5a). Pair B then describes one of their situations and Pair A makes a prediction.

Have you done that yet?

6 a) 🎧 82 Ann is talking to Ray and Simon about the activities at Club Torso. What activities do they say they've done? What haven't they done, but are planning to do? One person has had an accident. What was he / she doing when they had the accident? Make notes in the table.

	Has done	Hasn't done yet / is going to do	Accident
Ray			
Ann			
Simon			

b) 🎧 82 Listen again and fill in the gaps.

RAY: .... you .... wind-surfing .... ?

ANN: No, ... But I'm .... tomorrow.

SIMON: I .... jet skiing yesterday. I was having a great time when I suddenly .... this rock. I .... it and .... my ....

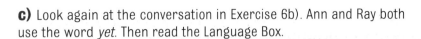

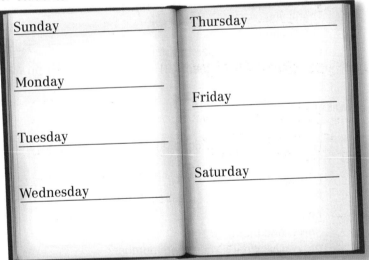

c) Look again at the conversation in Exercise 6b). Ann and Ray both use the word *yet*. Then read the Language Box.

> ### Present Perfect + yet
>
> We use *yet* in questions and negative sentences:
> Have you been wind-surfing yet? (Club Torso offers wind-surfing. I think you've probably done it or are going to do it.)
>
> Look at the difference between B's and c's answers:
> A: Have you done any of the activities?
> B: No, I haven't.
> c: No, not yet. (I haven't done any of the activities on this holiday up to now but it is my plan / intention to do some.)

7 **a)** In groups of four. You're all on a week's holiday (Sunday to Saturday) at Club Torso. Today is Thursday. You've done different activities every day and you've had one accident this week. Student A, look at page 131; Student B at page 139; Student C at page 140 and Student D at page 132.

b) Fill in every day of your diaries with activities you've done (and your accident!) and activities you're going to do. Don't show your diaries to other students.

Sunday	Thursday
Monday	Friday
Tuesday	
	Saturday
Wednesday	

c) In your groups. Have conversations about your week. Talk about what you've done, describe your accidents and talk about what you're going to do.

Example: A: Have you been water skiing yet?
B: Yes, I have. I went yesterday – but I had an accident.
A: Oh? What happened?
B: Well, I was . . .

> **Grammar reference**
>
> Present Perfect: page 104
> Future predictions: *be going to* + infinitive: page 106

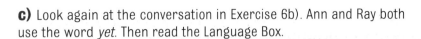

Making complaints

1 In groups. Talk about these questions.

1 Have you ever complained in a shop, hotel or restaurant? What about? What happened?
2 When was the last time you wanted to complain, but didn't? Why not?

2 a) 🔘 83 Guests in three different hotels are telling hotel receptionists about problems with their rooms. What are the problems? Are the receptionists polite and helpful? Listen and fill in the table.

	Problem	Is the receptionist polite?
Conversation 1	....	....
Conversation 2	....	....
Conversation 3	....	....

b) Put these two conversations from Exercise 2a) in the correct order. Fill in the boxes. Who says each line? Fill in the gaps with G (guest) and R (receptionist).

CONVERSATION 1

..R.. ☐1 Reception. How can I help you?
...... ☐ Yes, that's right. Thank you.
...... ☐ Thank you.
...... ☐ That's room 401.
...... ☐ Oh, I'm sorry. We'll see to it straightaway.
...... ☐ Oh, hello, er, I'm in Room 401 – I'm afraid there's no water in the mini-bar.

CONVERSATION 2

...... ☐ Room 215.
...... ☐ I'm sorry, but the air conditioning in our room doesn't work.
...... ☐ Thanks very much.
...... ☐ Excuse me.
...... ☐ Right, I'm very sorry. I'll get someone to look at it as soon as possible.
...... ☐ Sorry, one moment. Yes?
...... ☐ Oh, really? What's your room number?

c) 🔘 83 Listen to Conversations 1 and 2 again and check. Then in pairs, practise the conversations.

3 a) In pairs. Look at the hotel room in the picture. What are the problems? Match A and B to make sentences about the problems.

Example: 1 = b)

A	B
1 There's no beer	a) any toilet paper.
2 The blind	b) in the mini-bar.
3 There aren't	c) are very noisy.
4 There isn't	d) any towels.
5 The people in the room above	e) doesn't work.
6 The television	f) is broken.

Wavelength page

b) In pairs. Take it in turns to be a guest and a receptionist. Have two phone conversations.
Guest You have a problem in your room. Choose a problem from Exercise 3a). Then make a complaint. Begin: *I'm afraid / I'm sorry . . .*
Receptionist Deal with the complaint.

There's no need to be rude!

4   **a)** Look at these sentences from Conversation 3 in Exercise 2a). Fill in the boxes with G (guest), R (receptionist) and M (manager).

1 ☐G☐ . . . you were going to see to it straightaway but it's been an hour!
2 ☐ Well . . . I'm afraid there's nothing I can do at the moment.
3 ☐ Can I speak to the manager, please?
4 ☐ Look. We're very busy. We'll see to it as soon as possible, OK?
5 ☐ I'd like to speak to the manager.
6 ☐ Is there a problem?
7 ☐ Yes, the light in my bathroom doesn't work.
8 ☐ Oh, I am sorry, sir. I'll get someone to look at it straightaway.

b) 🔊 84 Listen and check. Then answer these questions.

1 Was the receptionist polite and helpful? What did he sound like?
2 How did the guest feel? What did he sound like?
3 What was the manager like?

c) 🔊 84 Listen again and mark the stressed words / syllable in the sentences in Exercise 4a). Then in pairs. Practise the conversation.

5   **a)** In groups of three. One of you is an unhelpful receptionist, one of you is a guest with a complaint and one of you is the manager. Plan a conversation. Decide if the guest is successful or unsuccessful in the end.

b) Act out your conversations for the class. Answer these questions about each conversation.

1 What is the guest's complaint?
2 Is the guest successful in the end?

Wavelength page

Crime doesn't pay!

Criminals and crimes
Countable and uncountable nouns
Describing people
Prepositions of place and movement
The Passive: Past Simple, Present Perfect
   and Present Simple
Skills: *Guilty or not guilty?*

Criminals and crimes

Countable and uncountable nouns

1 a) In pairs. Look at the picture of Sheila Dixon and answer the questions.

1 Where is she?   3 Who do you think the man is?
2 What's she doing? 4 Why is he watching her?

b) Sheila is a shoplifter. She steals things from shops. What has she stolen? Look at the picture on page 130 for one minute.

c) Make a list of the things you remember.

Example: Sheila's stolen an apple, some . . .

d) In pairs. Compare your lists, who remembered more things? Look at page 130 again and check.

2 A shoplifter is a type of thief. There are four other types of thief in the Word Box. Which verbs can you use with which types of thief? Fill in the gaps with words from the Word Box.

Types of thief	Verbs
bank robbers burglars /'bɜːgləz/	steal (x 4) rob (x 2)
muggers /'mʌgəz/ pickpockets	break into

1 .... usually "work" in crowded, busy places. They .... things from people when they're not looking.
2 .... often "work" at night or when people are away on holiday. They .... houses, shops and offices and .... things.
3 .... usually "work" in quiet streets or places where there aren't any witnesses. They .... people and .... anything valuable that the person has on them. They are sometimes violent.
4 .... often carry guns. They .... banks. Sometimes they .... a lot of money.

14

Can you give us a bit more information?

3 **a)** In pairs. Look at these scenes. What do you think is going to happen?

b) Fill in the table with descriptions of the four criminals.

	He's	He has / 's got	He's wearing	He's holding / carrying
A	tall in his thirties	short, blonde hair a moustache	a white T-shirt black trousers a black jacket	He's holding a brick.
B				
C				
D				

c) 🔊 85 Listen to four witnesses (the people who saw the crimes). Match their descriptions to the pictures.

Example: 1 = B

d) 🔊 85 Listen to the witnesses again. Use the prepositions in the Word Box and fill in the gaps.

> out of ✓   across   at
> in front of   into   next to   past
> towards /təˈwɔːdz/   opposite

1 Well, I was looking <u>out of</u> this window when I saw the burglar. He was climbing .... the Smiths' house.

2 Well, I was on the Underground and the pickpocket was standing .... a tall man in a suit.

3 Yes, I first saw him when I was walking .... the street. The car park is .... the bank, you see. He was walking .... the chemist's – going .... the bank.

4 I saw him when I was standing .... the bus stop. He was just standing .... the jeweller's.

① **Burglar Gets Five Years**

② **Mugger Gets Five Years**

③ **Mugger Says Sorry To Victim**

"I've been framed – I'm innocent."

Reginald Kramer has been found guilty of mugging seventy-year-old Mabel Thompson. Mrs Thompson was mugged six weeks ago in the High Street. A witness, Josie Robinson, saw the mugging and gave evidence to the police.

Kramer was arrested the day after the mugging and questioned by police, but he was released on bail the following day. He then jumped bail and left the country. He and his girlfriend were picked up by Spanish police at Málaga airport two weeks ago. His girlfriend was released after questioning, but Kramer was brought back to England.

Kramer pleaded not guilty. But he was sentenced yesterday to five years in prison. He has been sent to Brixton prison.

The Passive

4 a) Read the newspaper article about a mugging outside a café. Which is the best headline (1–3) for this article?

b) In pairs. Reginald Kramer says he's innocent! What really happened? Student A, look at page 139 and Student B at page 135.

5 The verbs in green in the article in Exercise 4a) are in the Passive. Read the Language Box and fill in the gaps with the correct form of *be*. Then read the article again. Why are there so many passive verbs?

The Passive

We use the correct tense of *be* + the past participle:

Past Simple Passive

	be	PAST PARTICIPLE
Kramer	....	questioned.
He and his girlfriend	....	picked up.

Present Perfect Passive

	be	PAST PARTICIPLE
Kramer	....	found guilty.
He and his girlfriend	....	questioned.

Present Simple Passive

	be	PAST PARTICIPLE
That shop	....	broken into regularly.
440 people	....	sent to prison in the UK every day.

We use the Passive when:

1 what happens is more important than who does the action.
2 we don't know who does the action.

When we want to use the Passive and say who does the action we use *by*:

Kramer was questioned by the police.

Pronunciation: weak forms

6 🎧 86 Listen to the sentences in the Language Box. How do we pronounce *is / are, was / were* and *has / have been?* Listen again and repeat.

The long arm of the law

7 Fill in the gaps with the Passive (Past Simple, Present Perfect, Present Simple) of the verbs in brackets.

Example: Why <u>were</u> you <u>arrested</u> in 1999? (arrest)

1 Excuse me, officer. I.........................(rob) and my passport
.........................(steal).
2 132,100 people ....(send) to prison in the UK each year.
3 We ....(question) by the police yesterday, but they let us go.
4 Lord and Lady Bracknell ....(murder) ten years ago, but
their murderer ....(find) yet.
5 A year ago he ....(sentence) to ten years in prison because
he broke into a jeweller's shop and stole jewellery worth £1,000,000.

8 a) In pairs. Charlie Dixon, Sheila the shoplifter's son, used to be a bank robber. Five years ago he robbed a bank and this is what happened to him. Put the sentences in the correct order.

a) He was found guilty. ☐
b) He was sent to prison. ☐
c) He was sent to court and tried. ☐
d) He was charged with robbery. ☐
e) He was questioned. ☐
f) He was arrested. ☐1
g) He was sentenced to five years. ☐
h) He was taken to the police station. ☐

b) 🔘🔘 87 Listen to Charlie's story and check your answers. He's just been released from prison. What's he going to do now?

Excuse me, officer . . .

9 a) In pairs. Look at the picture. What has happened to these people? Student A, look at page 140 and Student B at page 136.

b) You were interviewed by a newspaper reporter after the police caught the criminal who stole your car or burgled your house. Write a short newspaper article like the one in Exercise 4a) about what happened. Write the headline for your article.

Examples: Brave woman fights off burglar!
Man fights car thief!

> *Grammar reference*
> The Passive: Present Simple, Past
> Simple and Present Perfect: page 110

Skills *Listening, speaking, reading, writing*

Wavelength page

Guilty or not guilty?

1 **a)** [oo] 88 Look at the photograph and read the beginning of the magazine article on the right. Then listen to these sounds from the night of the murder. Make notes about what you think happened.

b) In pairs. Compare your notes. Do you think Dr Payne murdered his wife?

c) Read the rest of the article. Is it similar to your ideas about what happened on the night of the murder?

d) Read the article again and answer the questions. Then, in pairs, compare your answers.

1 What was the first thing Dr Payne did when he got home?
2 Why didn't he worry when his wife didn't answer?
3 Why did he make himself a stiff drink?
4 Why didn't he phone the police immediately?
5 Have you changed your mind about Dr Payne? Who do you think murdered his wife?

e) Read the article again. Who or what do these words refer to?

1 him (line 8)	4 it (line 14)	7 them (line 35)
2 he (line 11)	5 she (line 17)	8 it (line 35)
3 it (line 12)	6 her (line 28)	9 he (line 40)

f) Match the questions in A to their answers in B.

A	B
1 Why did Dr Payne stay late at the hospital?	a) To tell them about Ellen's death.
2 Why did he go upstairs?	b) To do an emergency operation.
3 Why did he go into the bedroom?	c) To have a bath.
4 Why did he phone the police?	d) To close the window.

Writing stories

Past Continuous

2 Read the Language Box. Then underline the Past Continuous verbs in the story.

Past Continuous

When we tell stories we use the Past Continuous to describe scenes, add information and add interest to the story:
The wind **was blowing** hard and it **was raining** heavily.

"The night that changed my life . . ."

Top doctor, Geoffrey Payne, talks for the first time about the night his wife was murdered. Dr Payne, was found guilty of his wife's murder and is now serving a life sentence. He wrote to this magazine from his prison cell about what happened on the night of 13 October 1999.

1 "I had to stay late at the hospital that night to do an emergency operation. I finally left at about 11 p.m.

I drove home slowly because the weather
5 was terrible – the wind was blowing and it was raining heavily. I was turning into our road when a man suddenly ran in front of my car. I almost hit him but I stopped just in time. I was terrified and
10 the man looked terrified too. I got out of the car but he ran away before I could ask if he was all right. It was very strange.

Linkers and time expressions

3 **a)** Read the article again. Find the linkers and time expressions from the Word Box and underline them.

> because   so   and   but   suddenly   finally   after   before

b) Fill in the gaps with the correct linkers and time expressions.

1 **because / so**
  a) I didn't know what to do .... I phoned the police.
  b) I phoned the police .... I didn't know what to do.

2 **and / but**
  a) I phoned my neighbours .... they came straightaway.
  b) I phoned my neighbours .... they weren't in.

3 **suddenly / finally**
  a) I was taking a short cut through the park. It was very late on a dark night. .... a cat jumped out of a tree right on my head! I was terrified!
  b) We waited for ages. .... the train arrived.

4 **after / before**
  a) The ambulance arrived an hour .... the accident.
  b) She robbed nine banks .... she was arrested.

c) Read the Language Box. Then fill in the gaps in sentences 1–5 with *when* or *during*.

When I got home the lights were on but it
15 was very quiet. I called to my wife but there was no answer. Then I remembered that she was out at a concert.

I was still very upset about what happened on the road, so I made myself a
20 stiff drink. Then I went upstairs to have a bath. I saw that the window in the bedroom was open. This was strange because my wife always locked the doors and windows before she went out. She
25 was afraid of burglars. When I went to close it, I found Ellen. She was lying on the floor. There was blood everywhere. I rushed over and felt for her pulse but she was dead. I sat on the floor beside her
30 body in a state of total shock.

The next thing I knew, the sky was getting light. I can't remember a thing about that night. In the morning I phoned the police. They arrived about half an
35 hour after I phoned them, but it seemed like hours. During that time I tried desperately to remember anything I could about the night before. I couldn't stop thinking about the man in the road.
40 What was he doing at that time of night in our quiet neighbourhood? Why did he look so terrified? Why did he run away?"

When *and during*

We use *when* with verbs:
When I went to close it, I found Ellen.

We use *during* with nouns:
During that time I tried desperately to remember anything I could about the night before.

---

1 I was waiting for the bus when two men came up to me.
2 He left .... the film to make a phone call.
3 The police didn't discover anything .... the investigation.
4 .... the police arrived, I showed them the gun.
5 Everyone stopped talking .... she came into the room.

4 In pairs. You discovered a crime. You were the only witness. Write a story like Dr Payne's. Use these questions to help you.

1 What was the crime?
2 Where and when did it happen?
3 How did you discover the crime?
4 What did you do when you discovered the crime?
5 Did you see anybody else at the scene of the crime?
6 Who do you think committed the crime?

Wavelength page

15 What are you talking about?

> *One* and *ones*
> Defining Relative Clauses: *who, which, that*
> *Look, look like, be like*
> Conversations: *What do you call . . . ?*

Which one?

1 In pairs. Talk about these questions.

1 Do you like shopping for clothes?
2 Who do you like going shopping with?
3 When did you last go to a party?
4 What did you wear? Did you wear anything new?

2 **a)** Look at the pictures. Where is Kim? What's she doing? What do you think she's talking about?

b) 🔵 89 Listen to her conversations and check.

c) 🔵 89 There's a mistake in each of these sentences. Listen to the conversations again. Find the mistakes and correct them.

Example: The one which didn't ~~rip~~. The one which didn't fit.

1 Do you mean the one that was next to the window?
2 If I get the white one, I'll need a different pair of shoes.
3 The ones that have really nice heels.
4 Do you mean the one that's dancing with Edward?
5 She's the one who's having an affair with the nice Marketing Manager.

Kim

d) What or who do the words *one* / *ones* refer to in the sentences in Exercise 2c)?

Example: The one which didn't fit.
one = dress

e) Read the Language Box and fill in the gaps.

> ### One and ones
>
> We can use .... to replace singular countable nouns and .... to replace plural countable nouns:
>
> **Singular**
> A: Which woman?
> B: The tall one.
>
> **Plural**
> A: Which shoes?
> B: The black ones.

f) Write the second sentence in each pair (1–6) again. Use *one* or *ones*.

Example: I like the blue dress.
I don't like the purple dress.
I don't like the purple **one**.

1 A: What job would you like to do?
  B: A job that pays a big salary.
2 They didn't stay in expensive hotels. They stayed in cheap hotels.
3 A: Which pub did you go to?
  B: The pub near the cinema.
4 A: Where's my CD?
  B: Which CD?
5 A: Who's that woman?
  B: The woman with the red hair?
6 I've lost my sunglasses. My pink sunglasses.

g) 🔊 90 Listen and check.

Who, which, that

3 **a)** Read the sentences in Exercise 2c) again. Then read the Language Box.

> ### Defining Relative Clauses
>
> We use Defining Relative Clauses to identify which person or thing we are talking about:
>
> **People** (*who / that*)
> She's the one **who's** having an affair with the new marketing manager.
> Do you mean the one **that's** talking to Edward?
>
> **Things** (*which / that*)
> Roger likes the one **which** didn't fit.
> Kim likes the ones **that** have really high heels.
>
> ### Look!
> • In conversation we often use *that*, especially for things.

b) Replace *that* in each of these sentences with *who* or *which*.

Example: He's the guy that sold me my car.
He's the guy who sold me my car.

1 Where's the magazine that was on the sofa?
2 Are they the boys that shouted at you?
3 This is Sarah. She's the girl that shares a flat with my sister.
4 I want the one that has the chocolate on top.
5 Are you the person that wanted to see me?

4 Look at the picture of the room at the end of the party. Where are the people? What are they doing? Where do you think the other people and the cats are? What are they doing? Student A, look at page 135 and Student B look at page 137.

And this is a photo of . . .

5 🔊 91 Listen to Edward's conversation with Clare at the party. He's telling her about his family. Find these people in the "photographs" and then fill in the boxes with the correct letters.

1 his ex-wife ☐
2 his daughter, Camilla ☐
3 his daughter, Priscilla ☐
4 his son, Robert ☐

Look or look like?

6 a) 🎧91 Listen again to what Clare says about Edward's family and fill in the gaps. Who's she talking about each time?

1 She .... a fashion model.
2 She .... glamorous and sophisticated.
3 She .... very sweet.
4 They .... angels.
5 He .... very sensitive and intelligent.

b) Answer the questions. Then fill in the Language Box with *look* and *look like*.

1 Clare says "She looks very sweet" about Camilla. Has she met Camilla?
Yes ☐ No ☐
2 Does she know if Camilla is sweet?
Yes ☐ No ☐
3 Clare says "She looks like a fashion model"about Edward's ex-wife. Has she met Edward's ex-wife?
Yes ☐ No ☐
4 Does she know what his ex-wife's job is?
Yes ☐ No ☐

> **Look and look like a / an . . .**
>
> We use .... + noun and .... + adjective when we make guesses about people from what we can see.

c) Look at the jobs in the Word Box. Look back at the picture of the party on pages 90 and 91. Make sentences about the people (a–f).

> boxer ✓ dancer artist
> journalist /ˈdʒɜːnəlɪst/
> pop singer accountant

Example: a) He looks like a boxer.

Uses of *like*

7 a) Match the questions with *like* in A to their answers in B.
Example: 1 = b)

A
1 Does he like going shopping?
2 What's her brother like?
3 Do you look like your sister?
4 Would you like a drink?
5 He looks like a spy. You know, mysterious.

B
a) Really? Do you think so? That's funny. He's a dentist, actually.
b) Not much. He always complains.
c) Nice and very funny.
d) No, thanks. I'm OK.
e) Not really. She's taller, with very blonde hair.

b) 🎧92 Listen and check.

Now tell me all about your family

8 a) Draw a "photograph" like this one of four people in your family.

b) In pairs. Show your "photographs" to each other. Talk about your families and ask and answer questions to find out as much as you can.

Example: Who's this?
What's he / she like?
Does he / she look like you / your father?
Is he / she like you / your mother?
Does he / she like . . . ?
Is he / she the one who . . . ?

Wavelength page

What's the word?

1 In pairs. Talk about what you do when:

1 you're having a conversation in your own language and you can't remember the word.
2 you're trying to say something in English and can't remember or don't know the word.

2 Look at the picture. Where's the man? What's he doing? What do you think he wants to buy?

3 a) 🔊 93 Look at the photograph of Roberto, talking to an English friend, Jill, about his boss. Listen. Does he like his boss? Why / Why not?

b) 🔊 93 Listen again and fill in the gaps.

ROBERTO: I don't like her. She's, um, I .... the .... She's not ....

JILL: .... she's rude?

ROBERTO: No, no, it's .... – .... rude exactly. She speaks to me .... I know she .... she's .... than me, ... than .... her family has a lot of ....

JILL: Oh, is she .... ?

ROBERTO: Oh, yeah, ... very ....

c) In pairs. Practise Jill and Roberto's conversation. How did Roberto make his meaning clear?

4 a) In pairs. Look at the words in the Word Box. Check their meanings. Then decide on the best way from Exercises 2 and 3 (miming or "talking round" the word) to make them clear to another person.

> stupid   boring   friendly   moody
> optimistic   suntan lotion /ˈləʊʃən/
> ashtray   mobile phone   shampoo

b) Make new pairs. Use the ways you talked about in Exercise 4a) to try to make the meaning of the words in the Word Box clear. Take it in turns to guess each other's words.

Example: A: I really don't like her. She never wants to go out. She only talks about work.
B: Do you mean she's boring?

5 a) 🔊94 Look at the picture and listen to Helga and Mike's conversation. Why does Mike look hot? What are they eating?

b) 🔊94 Listen again and fill in the gaps. What are the two words that Helga doesn't know?.

1 Can you pass that .... ? The .... that you .... to open the bottle.
2 I put in the .... that makes it hot.

c) Read the Language Box and fill in the gaps with *stuff* or *thing / things*.

> ### Stuff and thing / things
>
> When we don't know, or can't think of a word, we can use .... to replace countable nouns and .... to replace uncountable nouns.

d) Match the words in B to the questions in A. In pairs. Check your answers.

Example: 1 = f)

A *What do you call. . . ?*

1 the stuff that stops you burning and makes you brown?
2 the things you wear to see under water?
3 the thing you put flowers in?
4 the stuff that keeps mosquitoes away?
5 the thing with dates that you put on the wall?
6 the stuff you put on your hair to make it soft?
7 the thing you use to keep you dry when it's raining?
8 the things you use to cut paper?

B

a) a calendar
b) scissors
c) goggles
d) conditioner
e) an umbrella
f) suntan lotion
g) insect repellent
h) a vase

Have you got any . . . ?

6 a) In pairs. You're on holiday in a very hot English-speaking country. You've forgotten to bring some things and you've gone to the chemist's to buy them. Decide on four things that you need. Then decide on the best way to make those things clear to the chemist.

b) Make new pairs. Take it in turns to be the chemist and the customer. Customers try to make the chemist understand so you can buy the things you need.

Example: Have you got any of the stuff that . . . ?

The strangest thing happened to me . . .

Reported Speech: statements and questions
So and *such*
Do you remember? Units 13–16

Strangers on a train

1 **a)** Imagine you're on a train journey. Think of two people you'd like to sit next to. Why? What would you like to talk to them about? Who wouldn't you like to sit next to? Why?

b) In groups. Talk about your answers.

2 **a)** 🔊95 Look at the photographs on page 97. Listen to the conversation between two colleagues, Laura and Charles, about Charles's business trip to Paris. Answer the questions.

1 Why didn't Charles enjoy the journey from London to Paris?
2 Who did Charles meet on the train to London?
3 How does Laura know the man Charles met?

b) 🔊95 Listen again. Why does Laura say "What a coincidence"?

"I'm in advertising."

"I said I was in advertising."

Reported Speech

3 a) Match the things Charles said on the train to the things he said later to Laura in the office.

Example: 1 = f)

On the train	In the office
1 "I'm in advertising."	a) He said he worked in publishing.
2 "Where do you work?"	b) He asked me if you still lived in North London.
3 "Do you know Laura Brett?"	c) He said he was going to a conference.
4 "I work in publishing."	d) He asked me where I worked.
5 "I'm going to a conference."	e) He asked me if I knew you.
6 "Does Laura still live in North London?"	f) I said I was in advertising.

b) Read the Language Box and fill in the gaps with the past forms of the verbs in green.

Reported Statements

Verbs in Reported Speech often go into the past:

Direct Speech	Reported Speech
"I'm in marketing."	He said (that) he was in marketing.
"I work in London."	She said (that) she .... in London.
"We're flying to Munich."	They said (that) they .... to Munich.
"I love your book."	I told him (that) I .... his book.
"I don't like my job."	He told me (that) he .... his job.
"We can come on Friday."	They said (that) they .... on Friday.
"She's going to Paris."	You said (that) she .... to Paris.

Look!
- We can use *that* /ðæt/ or not in Reported Speech.
- We don't use quotes (" ") in Reported Speech.

c) Fill in the table with the correct pronouns.

Pronouns

SUBJECT	OBJECT		SUBJECT	OBJECT
....	me		....	him
you	....		she	....
....	us		....	it
they	....			

d) Do we use object pronouns after *say*? Do we use them after *tell*? Fill in the gaps in these Reported Statements with the correct form of *say* or *tell*.

Example: I said I loved working in advertising.

1 He .... he often thought about you.
2 I .... him we were good friends.
3 He didn't .... her where he lived.
4 You didn't .... why you liked your job.

4 a) Read the Language Box. Then answer the questions. When we report a question:
1 what happens to the question mark (?)?
2 what happens to the auxiliary verbs *do* and *does*?

Reported Questions

Wh- questions
We don't use the auxiliary *do / does* and the word order changes:

Direct Questions	Reported Questions
"Where does she live?" →	He asked me where she lived.
"What's she saying?" →	He asked me what she was saying.

Yes / No questions
We use *if*:

Direct Questions	Reported Questions
"Do you like Paris?" →	They asked us if we liked Paris.
"Are you in the media?" →	I asked if she was in the media.

Look!
• We don't use question marks (?) or quotes (" ") in Reported Questions.

b) Put these questions into Reported Speech. Change the Subject Pronouns if necessary.

Example: Are they staying in a hotel?
He asked me if they were staying in a hotel.

1 What languages do you speak?
He asked me what ....
2 Where are you from?
He asked me ....
3 Do you work a lot?
I asked him ....
4 Can you speak Spanish?
He asked her ....
5 When are they coming back?
I asked him ....

So, what did you say to each other?

5 a) You had a conversation with a stranger on a train. You're going to write about your experience. In pairs. Think about these questions:

1 Was this a good or bad experience?
2 How did you feel? (bored? happy? frightened?)
3 Who was the stranger?
4 Where were you going? (the same place? different places?). Why?
5 Why did you start talking?
6 How did the conversation end?

b) Write your conversations. Use these questions and sentences. Then write your conversation in Reported Speech.

1 I live in . . .
2 I work for . . .
3 I am . . .
4 Why are you . . . ?
5 I like / hate . . .
6 Where are you . . . ?
7 What are you . . . ?
8 Do you know . . . ?

Strange but true . . .

6 a) The magazine article on the right is about coincidences that two people have had in their lives. Read the people's stories. Who did Carol and Maria meet or speak to?

b) Read the stories again and answer these questions.

1 Were Carol and Maria following their usual routines or was something different?
2 Was there something familiar that helped them to recognise the other person? What was it?
3 Why were they surprised?

c) In pairs. Compare your answers. Which coincidence do you think is the most surprising? Why?

So and such

7 a) Read the Language Box and fill in the gaps with *such, such a / an* or *so*.

Such, such a / an and so

When we describe people or things, we often use *such, such a / an* and *so* to make our meaning stronger:

It was **so** funny.
He had **such** *a* familiar face.
She's had **such** strange experiences.
He does **such** important work.

We use ....*so*.... with adjectives, ...*such*... with uncountable nouns and plural countable nouns, and .... with singular countable nouns.
such a

b) Read the stories again and underline the examples of *such, such a / an* and *so* where they are used to make meaning stronger.

It's a small world!

Strange things really do happen to people like you and me. Here are two coincidences that ordinary people have had.

A

When the London Underground goes on strike my journey to work can be a nightmare. I remember a strike a few summers ago – the station near my house was closed and I had to use another station and take a different train. This added about an hour to my journey, so I wasn't very happy. There was chaos at the station. People were late and they were panicking! By the time I got on the train, I was feeling fed up and sorry for myself. Then I saw this man. There was something about him – he had such a familiar face. It took me a few minutes to realise that it was someone I knew – he was Ian, a friend from my school days in Scotland. He recognised me too and we started talking about school and the people we both used to know. I was even more surprised when the train came into my station and he started to get off too! I asked him where he was going and he said he was going to work. He told me he worked in Fitzroy Street. You see, I work in Fitzroy Street, too. It was such an amazing coincidence. It's a small world!

(Carol McDonald, London)

B

I was sitting at home one evening watching television when the phone rang and a voice asked, in Italian, "Is that the book shop in via del Corso?". I'm Italian and I spoke to her in Italian and told her it was a London number. I don't know why, but I had this strange feeling. Her voice was so familiar. Anyway I just said, "Cristina, is that you?" She sounded really surprised and then she said, "Maria, is that you?" We couldn't believe it. We were friends in Italy and we used to work together – I moved to London five years ago and we lost touch. She didn't have my new phone number because I've moved several times since I first came to England. It was so strange. She dialled the number of a book shop in Italy and for some reason my phone rang in London!

(Maria Valli, London)

Pronunciation: *so* and *such*

8 👓 96 Listen and repeat four sentences from the stories in the magazine article. Make sure you stress *so* and *such* to make the meaning stronger.

9 Fill in the gaps with *such, such a / an* or *so*.

Example: Some people have such interesting lives.

1 I was ...*so*..... surprised when she told me that we both lived in the same town.

2 She had *such a* strange look on her face when I told her that I knew Martin Howard.

3 We were ...*so*...... shocked when we discovered that we were going out with the same man.

4 We had *such an sorprendevT* .... amazing time when we got together again.

5 They've lived in ...*such*.... beautiful places.

What a coincidence!

10 a) In groups. Have you ever had a coincidence? Has someone you know had a coincidence? Tell each other your stories. Listen carefully so you don't forget important details.

b) Make new groups. Take it in turns to tell each other about the coincidences from your first group. Has anybody had a similar coincidence?

Grammar reference

Reported Statements and Questions: page 109

Wavelength page

1 Defining Relative Clauses

a) In pairs. Ann has just come back from her holiday at Club Torso. She's showing her photographs to her sister, Judith. What do the people look like? What are they wearing?

b) 🔊97 Listen to Ann and Judith talking about one of the photographs. Who are the people? Fill in the boxes.

Alex ☐ Damian ☐ Debbie ☐ Martin ☐ Sheila ☐

c) 🔊97 What did Ann say about the people in the photograph? Listen again and fill in the gaps.

Alex is .... me when I went wind-surfing.

Debbie is .... love with Martin.

Martin is .... us breakfast in bed.

Damian and Sheila are the .... the ....

d) In pairs. Write sentences about four students. Then read them out. The other students must guess who you're talking about.

Example: A: He's the one who came to class late.
B: You're talking about Carlo.

Would you like to be on the *Terry Stinger Show?* Have you ever been abducted by aliens? Have you ever been mistaken for a Hollywood film star? Have you ever been attacked by a shark? If you have, call 07181 443 0559

2 The Passive

a) In pairs. The *Terry Stinger Show* is looking for people to interview. They want people who have had incredible experiences. Choose one of the questions in the advert and invent a story. Think about these questions.

1 What happened?
2 Where were you when it happened?
3 What were you doing?
4 How did you feel?
5 Were there any witnesses?

b) Go round the class and talk to three people. Find out about each other's experiences. Use the questions in Exercise 2a) to help you.

3 Reported Speech

a) In pairs. Talk about these questions.

1 Would you like to live abroad?
2 What would you miss about your country?

b) Yesterday, Carlo and Helen were talking about London and Italy. Read some of Helen's questions and Carlo's answers and put them into Reported Speech.

Direct Speech	Reported Speech
1 Where are you from?	I asked him where he was from.
2 I'm from Salerno.	
3 What do you think about London?	
4 I don't like the food.	
5 Do you miss Italy?	

c) 🔊98 Listen and check. What did Carlo say he missed about Italy?

Look at the Word lists for Units 13–16 on pages 120 – 121 and check that you know all the new words.

Puzzle 4 (Units 13–16): page 112

Reading for pleasure

④ Watch it!

1 This play takes place in an exclusive health club called The Temple. Before you read it, look at this list of facilities. Which would you expect to find at an exclusive health club? Can you add to the list?

1 squash courts
2 luxurious changing rooms
3 a sauna
4 a fast-food restaurant
5 a shop which sells designer sports clothes

2 🔊99 Read and listen to the first part of the play which describes the stage. Then answer the questions.

The stage is in two parts.

One half is the big, comfortable office of Lisa Shaw, the owner and manager of The Temple Health Club – the most expensive and most exclusive gym in town. Behind her desk are video monitors which show the different parts of the building: the Olympic-sized swimming pool; the squash courts; the modern dance studio; the gym full of body-building equipment; the changing rooms; the restaurant; the snack bar; the sauna; the massage rooms.

The other half of the stage is the luxurious men's changing room. The wall on the left has a lot of large lockers where clients put their clothes and valuables. The wall on the right has ten showers. The wall in the centre is one huge mirror. There is a bench in front of it.

The play opens with the lights on only in Lisa's office. Lisa is sitting at her desk. Her chair is turned towards the monitors. She has her back to the audience. She is checking every part of her empire. Now and then she presses a zoom button and we see close-ups of the swimmers, the dancers, the handsome men, the attractive women.

1 Who is the manager and owner of The Temple?
2 Why do you think there are monitors in her office?
3 What facilities does the Temple have?
4 Where do clients keep their things when they are using the club's facilities?
5 What is Lisa doing when the play begins?

3 Now read the whole play. It starts on page 20 of *The wave and other stories*. Think about these questions while you read.

1 How do we know that Lisa wants people to spend money at The Temple?
2 What does Lisa do which shows that she wants to be attractive?
3 What are the three young men doing when the scene changes from Lisa's office to the other half of the stage?
4 How do we know that Matt has money problems?
5 What does Mark offer to do?
6 Why do you think Lucas is worried about his weight?
7 How is Jonathan different from the other men?
8 Matt, Lucas and Mark are interested in one of Jonathan's things. What?
9 Lisa is talking on the phone when Jonathan goes into her office. What do you think she is talking about? Who is she talking to?
10 What do we learn from Jonathan and Lisa's conversation?
11 What happens between the time the lights go off in Lisa's office and the time they come on when the three men go back into the changing room?
12 Which of the three men's watches are stolen?
13 How does Jonathan know who is guilty?

Grammar reference

The Present

Present Simple (Unit 1)

Positive

SUBJECT	VERB
I / You / We / They	work.
He / She / It	works.

Negative

SUBJECT	DO	VERB
I / You / We / They	don't (do not)	work.
He / She / It	doesn't (does not)	

Wh- questions

	DO	SUBJECT	VERB
Where	do	I / you / we / they	work?
	does	he / she / it	

Yes / No questions

DO	SUBJECT	VERB
Do	I / you / we / they	work?
Does	he / she / it	

Positive short answers

	SUBJECT	DO
Yes,	I / you / we / they	do.
	he / she / it	does.

Negative short answers

	SUBJECT	DO
No,	I / you / we / they	don't (do not).
	he / she / it	doesn't (does not).

Form

Spelling and pronunciation: he, she, it
- With *he, she, it*, add *-s* to positive verbs: He buys a newspaper every day. **NOT** He ~~buy~~ a newspaper every day.

BUT
- Add *-es* to verbs ending in *-o, -ch, -s, -sh* and *-x*: do → does, teach → teaches, kiss → kisses, wish → wishes, mix → mixes. We pronounce these endings /ɪz/.
- Change *-y* to *-i* and add *-es* to verbs ending in a consonant + *-y*: study → studies, marry → marries, try → tries. We pronounce these endings /z/.
- *Have* changes to *has*.

Use

General habits, routines, permanent situations
- For habits, routines and permanent situations, often with frequency adverbs *(always, usually, often, sometimes, hardly ever, never).*
  She works for a large company in London.
  I **always** eat breakfast.
  I **usually** eat breakfast.
  I **often** eat breakfast.
  I **sometimes** eat breakfast.
  I **hardly ever** eat breakfast.
  I **never** eat breakfast.

Present Continuous (Unit 1)

Positive

SUBJECT	BE	VERB + -ING
I	'm (am)	
You / We / They	're (are)	studying.
He / She / It	's (is)	

Negative

SUBJECT	BE	VERB + -ING
I	'm not (am not)	
You / We / They	aren't (are not)	studying.
He / She / It	isn't (is not)	

Wh- questions

	BE	SUBJECT	VERB + -ING
	am	I	
What	are	you / we / they	studying?
	is	he / she / it	

Yes / No questions

BE	SUBJECT	VERB + -ING
Am	I	
Are	you / we / they	studying?
Is	he / she / it	

Positive short answers

	SUBJECT	BE
	I	am.
Yes,	you / we / they	are.
	he / she / it	is.

Negative short answers

	SUBJECT	BE
	I	'm (am) not.
No,	you / we / they	aren't (are not).
	he / she / it	isn't (is not).

Form

Spelling: -ing
- Add *-ing* to most verbs: work → working.

BUT
- Short verbs (all one-syllable and some two-syllable verbs) ending in a vowel + a consonant, double the consonant: get → getting, run → running.
- Verbs ending in *-e* take off the *-e:* live → living, joke → joking.
- *Be* is irregular: be → being.

Contractions
- *Is* and *are* have two possible negative contractions:
  She isn't. **OR** She's not.
  They aren't. **OR** They're not.

Use

Activity happening now
- For things that are happening now:
  That man is stealing the old woman's bag! Phone the police!

Activity happening around now
- For temporary things that are happening around now, for a limited period of time:
  I'm working in the evenings at the moment to make some extra money for my holiday.

Present Simple or Present Continuous?
- Zoltan's a doctor and **he lives** in Budapest (his permanent home), but **he's studying** English in London at the moment (this is temporary – for a limited period of time).

The Past

Past Simple (Units 2 and 3)

Positive

SUBJECT	VERB	
I / You / We / They / He / She / It	rented	a flat.

Negative

SUBJECT	DO	VERB	
I / You / We / They / He / She / It	didn't	buy	a flat.

Wh- questions

	DO	SUBJECT	VERB
When	did	I / you / we / they / he / she / it	arrive?

Yes / No questions

DO	SUBJECT	VERB	
Did	I / you / we / they / he / she / it	rent	a flat?

Positive short answers

	SUBJECT	DO
Yes,	I / you / we / they / he / she / it	did.

Negative short answers

	SUBJECT	DO
No,	I / you / we / they / he / she / it	didn't.

Form

Regular verbs: spelling
- Add -ed to verbs ending in a consonant: ask → asked, play → played.
- Add -d to verbs ending in -e: like → liked.
- With verbs ending in a consonant + -y, change -y to -i and add -ed: try → tried, marry → married.
- Double the consonant in short verbs (one syllable) ending in one vowel + one consonant: stop → stopped.

Irregular verbs
- See the Irregular verb list on page 143 for positive Past Simple forms. In questions and negatives, irregular verbs follow the same rules as regular verbs.
- Remember be is different:
  I lived in California when I **was** a child.
  They lived in Chicago when they **were** children.
  A: **Were** they rich then? B: Yes, they **were**.
  A: **Was** she a good student? B: No, she **wasn't**.

Use

For single events that happened in the past
- She met him last year.

For past states
- I was afraid of the dark when I was a child.

For things that happened regularly in the past (past habits)
- I walked to school every day when I was a child.

With time expressions
- at + times: at eight o'clock, at lunch, at the weekend, at Christmas.
- on + days and dates: on Sunday, on 23rd June.
- in + parts of the day, months, seasons, years: in the afternoon, in May, in (the) spring, in 1492.
- last with no preposition: last week, last month, last year NOT in last week.
- ago to measure time back from now: two weeks ago = two weeks back from now.
- yesterday morning / afternoon / evening BUT last night.

Used to / didn't use to + infinitive (Unit 2)

Positive

SUBJECT	USED TO	VERB	
I / You / We / They / He / She / It	used to	like	Mary.

Negative

SUBJECT	DO	USE TO	VERB	
I / You / We / They / He / She / It	didn't	use to	like	Mary.

Wh- questions

	DO	SUBJECT	USE TO	VERB
Where	did	I / you / we / they / he / she / it	use to	live?

Yes / No questions

DO	SUBJECT	USE TO	VERB	
Did	I / you / we / they / he / she / it	use to	live in France?

Positive short answers

	SUBJECT	DO
Yes,	I / you / we / they / he / she / it	did.

Negative short answers

	SUBJECT	DO
No,	I / you / we / they / he / she / it	didn't.

Use

Past habits that are finished
- For things that happened regularly in the past but don't happen any more: I used to smoke. (But I don't smoke now.)

Past states that are now finished
- For things which were true in the past but which are not true now: She used to be shy. (But she isn't any more.)

Look!
- Don't confuse used to /juːstə/ and didn't use to + infinitive with the regular verb use /juːz/.
- There is no present form of used to. To talk about present habits and states we usually use the Present Simple.

Past Simple NOT used to / didn't use to + infinitive
- For single events, things which happened only once:
  He left New York five years ago.
  NOT He used to leave New York five years ago.
- For how many times things happened in the past:
  I visited Paris seven times when I lived in France.
  NOT I used to visit Paris seven times when I lived in France.

Present Perfect (Units 4, 9 and 13)

Positive

SUBJECT	*HAVE*	PAST PARTICIPLE	
I / You / We / They	've (have)	worked	in TV.
He / She / It	's (has)	made	a film.

Negative

SUBJECT	*HAVE*	PAST PARTICIPLE	
I / You / We / They	haven't (have not)	worked	in TV.
He / She / It	hasn't (has not)	made	a film.

Wh- questions

	HAVE	SUBJECT	PAST PARTICIPLE
What	have	I / you / we / they	done?
	has	he / she / it	

Yes / No questions

HAVE	SUBJECT	PAST PARTICIPLE	
Have	I / you / we / they	worked	in TV?
Has	he / she / it	made	any films?

Positive short answers

	SUBJECT	*HAVE*
Yes,	I / you / we / they	have.
	he / she / it	has.

Negative short answers

	SUBJECT	*HAVE*
No,	I / you / we / they	haven't (have not).
	he / she / it	hasn't (has not).

Look! The past participles of all regular verbs are the same as the Past Simple and end in *-ed* (see page 103). For the past participles of irregular verbs, see page 143.

Use

Unit 4

General past experience
- For past experiences (finished actions or events in the past), but we don't say when these things happened:
  I've travelled a lot in Europe but I've never visited Asia.
  Have you seen the film *Casablanca?*

With *ever* and *never*
- With *ever* (= in your whole life) and *never* (= not in your whole life):
  A: Have you ever met a famous person?
  B: No, I've never met a famous person.

Been* or *gone?
- Look at the difference between *been* and *gone:*
  She's been to Africa. (She has visited Africa at some time in the past but she's here now, not in Africa.)

here now ⇄ Africa

  She's gone to Africa. (She's in Africa now.)

here → Africa now

  Been can be the past participle of *be* and *go:*
  She's **been** in a western. (= past participle of *be*)
  She's **been** to Africa. (= past participle of *go*)

Present Perfect or Past Simple?
- If we say **when** things happened, we use the Past Simple. Look at the difference:
  I've been to Berlin. (= Present Perfect. It's the experience, not **when** it happened which is important.)
  I went to Berlin last summer. (= Past Simple. The time is important.)
- We often begin a conversation with a Present Perfect question or sentence to talk generally about a past experience. Then we go on to use the Past Simple to give more information about the experience (*when, where, who, how, why,* etc.):
  A: Have you ever been to Poland? (= Present Perfect)
  B: Yes, I have. (= Present Perfect)
  A: When did you go? (= Past Simple)
  B: I went two years ago. (= Past Simple)

Unit 9

A period of time that began in the past and continues to now
- For habits and states that began in the past and have continued to the present we use the Present Perfect **NOT** the Present Simple.

With *for* and *since*
- Look at the difference between *for* and *since*. We use *for* with a period of time. We use *since* with the start of the period (a point in time):

		PERIODS OF TIME
I've had this briefcase	for	a few days.
		six months.
		ten years.
		ages.
		POINTS OF TIME
	since	yesterday.
		last month.
		I left university.
		1999.

Unit 13

With *yet* in negative sentences and questions
- With *yet* (= up to now) in negative sentences and questions for actions we are expecting to happen:
  I haven't been to the village yet. (I'm planning / expecting to go).
  Have you been wind-surfing yet? (I think you've tried it because the hotel offers wind-surfing. I'm checking.)
- There are two possible negative answers to questions with *yet:*
  A: Have you been to the village yet?
  B: No, I haven't. **OR** No, not yet.

Past Continuous (Unit 10)

Positive

SUBJECT	BE	VERB + -ING	
I / He / She / It	was	watching	TV.
You / We / They	were		

Negative

SUBJECT	BE	VERB + -ING	
I / He / She / It	wasn't (was not)	watching	TV.
You / We / They	weren't (were not)		

Wh- questions

	BE	SUBJECT	VERB + -ING
What	was	I / he / she / it	doing?
	were	you / we / they	

Yes / No questions

BE	SUBJECT	VERB + -ING	
Was	I / he / she / it	watching	TV?
Were	you / we / they		

Positive short answers

	SUBJECT	BE
Yes,	I / he / she / it	was.
	you / we / they	were.

Negative short answers

	SUBJECT	BE
No,	I / he / she / it	wasn't (was not)
	you / we / they	weren't (were not).

Form

Spelling: -ing
• See page 102.

Use

Activities that happened at or around a time in the past
• To talk about what was going on at or around a time in the past. We don't know and aren't interested in when the action started or finished: I was living in São Paulo.

Present Continuous or Past Continuous?

It's 10:30 on Tuesday morning. Pedro **is sitting** in his English class.

Yesterday morning at 10:30 Pedro **was sitting** in his English class too.

Past Continuous or Past Simple?
• We use the Past Continuous to talk about what was going on (the background activity) when something happened (a single action in the Past Simple):

Pedro **was sitting** in class when his mobile phone **rang**.

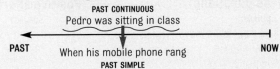

PAST CONTINUOUS
Pedro was sitting in class

PAST ← When his mobile phone rang → NOW
PAST SIMPLE

• We can use *when* to link the two parts of the sentence. We can change the order of the two parts:
When Pedro's phone **rang** he **was sitting** in class.
• We use the Past Simple when one single action follows another:

When his mobile phone **rang** he **left** the room.

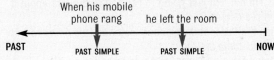

When his mobile phone rang / he left the room

PAST ← PAST SIMPLE / PAST SIMPLE → NOW

• When we tell stories we use the Past Simple to talk about the events (the things which happen) in the story. We use the Past Continuous to describe what was going on in the background when the events happened and to give more information:
I **walked** (Past Simple) down to the beach. The sun **was setting** (Past Continuous). Some people **were sitting** (Past Continuous) at the bar. They **were talking** and **laughing** (Past Continuous). A fisherman **was working** (Past Continuous) on his boat. I **went** (Past Simple) to the bar and **ordered** (Past Simple) a drink.

The Future

See page 102 for form.

Present Continuous (Unit 6)

Be going to + infinitive (Units 6 and 13)

Positive

SUBJECT	BE		VERB
I	'm (am)		
You / We / They	're (are)	going to	work.
He / She / It	's (is)		

Negative

SUBJECT	BE		VERB
I	'm not (am not)		
You / We / They	aren't (are not)	going to	work.
He / She / It	isn't (is not)		

Wh- questions

	BE	SUBJECT		VERB
	am	I		
What	are	you / we / they	going to	do?
	's (is)	he / she / it		

Yes / No questions

BE	SUBJECT		VERB
Am	I		
Are	you / we / they	going to	work?
Is	he / she / it		

Positive short answers

	SUBJECT	BE
	I	am.
Yes,	you / we / they	are.
	he / she / it	is.

Negative short answers

	SUBJECT	BE
	I	'm not.
No,	you / we / they	aren't.
	he / she / it	isn't.

'll (will) + infinitive (Units 6 and 8) and might + infinitive (Unit 8)

Positive

SUBJECT		VERB	
I / You / We / They /	'll (will)	help	her.
He / She / It	might		

Negative

SUBJECT		VERB	
I / You / We / They /	won't (will not)	help	him.
He / She / It	might not		

Wh- questions

		SUBJECT	VERB
What	will	I / you / we / they /	do?
	might	he / she / it	

Yes / No questions

	SUBJECT	VERB
Will	I / you / we / they /	leave?
Might	he / she / it	

Positive short answers

	SUBJECT	
Yes,	I / you / we / they /	will.
	he / she / it	might.

Negative short answers

	SUBJECT	
No,	I / you / we / they /	won't.
	he / she / it	might not.

The Future: Present Continuous, be going to + infinitive and 'll (will) + infinitive (Unit 6)

Use

Present Continuous
- We use the Present Continuous for definite future arrangements:
  I'm flying on Saturday. (I've booked my flight.)

be going to + infinitive
- We use be going to + infinitive for future intentions and plans:
  A: Are you going to travel around when you're on holiday?
  B: No, I'm not. I'm just going to relax. (I've thought about it and I've decided.)
- We use the Present Continuous instead of be going to with the verbs come and go:
  I'm going for a walk. NOT I'm going to go for a walk.

'll (will) + infinitive
- We use maybe / perhaps + 'll (will) + infinitive for things we're not sure about, for ideas and possibilities:
  A: Are you going to travel around when you're on holiday?
  B: Well, maybe I'll go to the mountains. (I'm not sure.)

Future predictions: 'll (will) + infinitive and might + infinitive (Unit 8)

Use

- We use 'll (will) / might + infinitive to make predictions when we know something about a person or a situation:
  He'll pass the English exam. (He works hard, does all the homework and he has a good level of English.)
  He might pass the English exam. (He has a fifty per cent chance of passing.)
  He might not pass the English exam. (He doesn't do any work, but he's clever.)
  He won't pass the English exam. (He doesn't work in class, he never does the homework and his English isn't good.)
- We also use expressions like I'm sure, probably, with 'll (will) + infinitive to show how sure we feel about the situation.

Future predictions: be going to + infinitive (Unit 13)

Use

- We use be going to + infinitive to make predictions because of evidence we can see, hear or feel now:
  It's going to rain. (There are big dark clouds in the sky.)

Comparing

Comparative Adjectives (Unit 2)

Form

Than

- We use *than* in comparisons when there is an object. Look at the pictures of Alan's house and Rick's house:
  Rick's house is bigger **than** Alan's house.

Regular Adjectives

- Short adjectives (all one-syllable and some two-syllable adjectives), add *-er*: old → older
- Short (one syllable) adjectives ending in a vowel + consonant, double the consonant and add *-er*: sad → sadder
- Short adjectives ending in *-e*, add *-r*: nice → nicer
- Short adjectives ending in *-y*, change the *-y* to *-i* and add *-er*: sunny → sunnier
- Longer adjectives (two or more syllables), use *more* or *less*: interesting → more interesting, interesting → less interesting

Irregular Adjectives

- good → better, bad → worse

not as + adjective + as

- We can use comparative adjectives or *not as* + adjective + *as* to compare things. We can say:
  Alan's house wasn't as expensive as Rick's house.
  It means the same as:
  Rick's house was more expensive than Alan's (house).
  Alan's house was cheaper than Rick's (house).
  Alan's house was less expensive than Rick's (house).

Use

- We use Comparative Adjectives to compare two people or things or two groups of people or things.

Alan's house - £50,000

Rick's house - £200,000

Superlative Adjectives (Unit 4)

Form

The

- We use *the* with Superlative Adjectives. Look at the picture of Mike's house and compare it with the other two houses:
  Mike's house is the biggest and the most expensive.

Regular Adjectives

- Short adjectives (all one-syllable and some two-syllable adjectives), add *-est*: old → the oldest
- Short (one syllable) adjectives ending in a vowel + consonant, double the consonant and add *-est*: sad → saddest
- Short adjectives ending in *-e*, add *-st*: nice → the nicest
- Short adjectives ending in *-y*, change the *-y* to *-i* and add *-est*: sunny → the sunniest
- Longer adjectives (two or more syllables), use *the most* or *the least*: interesting → the most interesting, interesting → the least interesting

Irregular Adjectives

- good → the best, bad → the worst

Use

- We use Superlative Adjectives to compare three or more people or things.

Mike's house £2,000,000

Obligation and permission

Have to / don't have to, can / can't,
make and *let* (Unit 5) and *must / mustn't*

Have to

Positive

SUBJECT		VERB	
I / You / We / They	have to	wear	a suit.
He / She / It	has to		

Negative

SUBJECT	DO		VERB	
I / You / We / They	don't	have to	wear	a suit.
He / She / It	doesn't			

Wh- questions

	DO	SUBJECT		VERB
What	do	I / you / we / they	have to	wear?
	does	he / she / it		

Yes / No questions

DO	SUBJECT		VERB	
Do	I / you / we / they	have to	wear	a suit?
Does	he / she / it			

Positive short answers

	SUBJECT	DO
Yes,	I / you / we / they	do.
	he / she / it	does.

Negative short answers

	SUBJECT	DO
No,	I / you / we / they	don't.
	he / she / it	doesn't.

Form

Can / can't and *must / mustn't*

- *Can / can't* and *must / mustn't* are modal verbs.
- Modal verbs use the infinitive without *to:*
  She can wear jeans. **NOT** She can ~~to~~ wear jeans.
  He must wear a suit and tie. **NOT** He must ~~to~~ wear a suit and tie.
- Modal verbs never change. They are the same for all subjects *(I / you / we / they / he / she / it).*
- Modal verbs never have the auxiliary *do / does / did* in questions, negatives or short answers:
  A: Must she go?
  B: Yes, she must. Her boss can't go.

Make and *let*

- We use the infinitive without *to* after *make* and *let* but, unlike modals, these verbs change:
  Our teacher doesn't make us do any homework.
  NOT Our teacher doesn't ~~to~~ make us do any homework.

  His parents make him tidy his room.
  NOT His parents make him ~~to~~ tidy his room.

  The boss lets me leave early.
  NOT The boss lets me ~~to~~ leave early.

  The managers don't let the workers leave early.
  NOT The managers don't let the workers ~~to~~ leave early.

Use

Obligation

- We use *have to* when the obligation comes from outside (a law, a rule, or an agreement when some other person has given orders):
  We have to do military service in my country. (It's the law.)
  I have to stop smoking. (My doctor ordered me to.)
- We can use *must* to give an order or strong advice to someone. The obligation comes from the person who is speaking:
  DOCTOR (to patient): You must stop smoking.
  FRIEND (to friend): I must leave now. I've got an appointment in half an hour.

No obligation (there is a choice)

- We use *don't / doesn't have to* when there is no obligation:
  You don't have to be at the office by 9 a.m. (It's OK to arrive later. You can choose when you arrive.)

Negative obligation (there is no choice)

- We use *can't* when a rule, law or person says "No!":
  You can't buy alcohol until you're eighteen years old.
- We can use *mustn't* when we order (or strongly advise) someone not to do something:
  MOTHER (to child): You mustn't hit your little sister.
  FRIEND (to friend): You mustn't work so hard. You'll have a heart attack.

Permission

- We use *can* when the rules or laws say it's OK or when we give someone permission to do something:
  MANAGER (to worker): You can leave early today.

Conditional sentences: *If . . .*

First Conditional (Units 7 and 8)

Form

- We use the Present Simple in the *if* part of the sentence and *'ll (will)* / *won't* + infinitive in the other part:
  If they work hard, they'll be successful.
  If she doesn't work hard, she won't be successful.
  What'll (will) you do if you don't like your new job?
- Both parts of the sentence can be positive or negative and the *if* part can come first or last in the sentence.

Use

- We use the First Conditional for possible future situations and possible future results:
  If you take the job, you'll be successful. (It's possible you'll take the job and it's possible that you won't regret your decision.)
  I'll phone his mobile number if he doesn't arrive soon. (It's possible he won't arrive soon and it's possible that I'll phone his mobile number.)

Second Conditional (Unit 11)

Form

- We use the Past Simple in the *if* part of the sentence and *would* / *could* + infinitive in the other part. We often use the contraction *'d (would)*:
  If we had more money, we'd (would) buy a new car.
  If she didn't work, she could come to the party.
- With the verb *be* we usually use *were* / *weren't* with all subjects, but we do sometimes use *was* / *wasn't* with *he* / *she* / *it* in conversation.
- Both parts of the sentence can be positive or negative and the *if* part can come first or last in the sentence.

Use

- We use the Second Conditional for unreal / impossible situations in the present or near future:
  If she were nicer, she'd have more friends. (But she isn't nice and she doesn't have many friends.)

Reported Speech

Reported Commands (Unit 12)

Form

Tell + *someone* + *to* + infinitive

- We use the Past Simple of *tell* + *someone* + *to* + infinitive.

DIRECT SPEECH	REPORTED SPEECH
"Turn right at the next corner"	He told me to turn right at the next corner.
"Don't tell anyone."	She told me not to tell anyone.

Ask + *someone* + *to* + infinitive

- We use the Past Simple of *ask* + *someone* + *to* + infinitive.

DIRECT SPEECH	REPORTED SPEECH
"Would you turn the music down, please?"	I asked them to turn the music down.
"Please don't go."	She asked him not to go.

- We use object pronouns in Reported Commands:
  He asked them (object pronoun) to be quiet.
- *Tell* is stronger than *ask*.
- We report orders with *tell* + *someone* + *to* + infinitive.
- We report requests with *ask* + *someone* + *to* + infinitive.
- We often change other words when we use Reported Speech:
  here → there, this → that, etc.

DIRECT SPEECH	REPORTED SPEECH
"Please don't park your car here."	She asked him not to park his car there.
"Take this to the manager."	He told me to take that to the manager.

Reported Statements (Unit 16)

Form

- We use *say* and *tell* in Reported Statements.
- The verb usually moves one step back into the past:
  Present Simple → Past Simple
  Present Continuous → Past Continuous

DIRECT SPEECH	REPORTED SPEECH
"I'm a doctor."	He said (that) he was a doctor.
"I'm staying with friends."	He told me (that) he was staying with friends.

- With *tell* we need an indirect object:
  "I work in the city." → She told **him** that she worked in the city.

Use

- We often leave out *that* in conversation:
  He said he was staying with friends.

Reported Questions (Unit 16)

- We use *ask* in Reported Questions.
- The verb usually moves one step back into the past:
  Present Simple → Past Simple
  Present Continuous → Past Continuous
- The word order of Reported Questions is the same as for statements. We don't use the auxiliary *do* / *does*.
- In *Yes* / *No* questions we use *if*.

DIRECT SPEECH	REPORTED SPEECH
"Why are you here?"	He asked us why we were there.
"What are they doing?"	She asked me what they were doing.
"Do you like New York?"	He asked me if I liked New York.

The Passive

Present Simple, Past Simple and Present Perfect (Unit 14)

Active

SUBJECT		OBJECT
They	make	these watches in Switzerland.
They	made	this skirt in Portugal.
The police	questioned	them.
Someone	has stolen	my wallet.

Passive

OBJECT	
These watches	are made in Switzerland.
This skirt	was made in Portugal.
They	were questioned by the police.
My wallet	has been stolen.

Form

- We use the correct tense of the verb *be* and the past participle:
  I'm stopped by the police regularly. (Present Simple)
  They were stopped yesterday. (Past Simple)
  They've been stopped. (Present Perfect)
  He wasn't stopped. (Past Simple)
  When were you stopped? (Past Simple)
  Why has he been stopped? (Present Perfect)
  A: Are you often stopped?
  B: Yes, I am. / No, I'm not. (Present Simple)
  A: Have you ever been stopped?
  B: Yes, I have. / No, I haven't. (Present Perfect)

Use

- When the object or the action is more important than the subject (the person or thing that does the action).
- When we don't know the subject.
- We use the Passive more in written English than in conversation.
- When we use the Passive and want to say who did the action, we use *by*.

Modal verbs

Form

- Modal verbs never change. They don't have an *-s* for *he / she / it* in the present.
  He should leave his job. **NOT** He shoulds leave his job.
- They don't have the auxiliary *do / did* in negatives, questions or short answers.
  Can you drive? **NOT** Do you can drive?
- We never use *to* after modal verbs:
  I can drive. **NOT** I can to drive.

Positive	Negative
can	can't (cannot)
could	couldn't (could not)
might	mightn't (might not)
must	mustn't (must not)
shall	shan't (shall not)
should	shouldn't (should not)
will	won't (will not)
would	wouldn't (would not)

Use

- **Requests**
  Could you repeat that, please?
  Can you post these letters for me?
  Would you phone the office for me?
- **Offers**
  Can I help you?
  I'll get you a sandwich.
  Shall I answer the phone for you?
- **Asking for and giving permission**
  Can I use your phone?
  You can borrow that CD.
- **Talking about ability**
  Can you play a musical instrument?
  He can't speak Spanish.
- **Rules and regulations, giving orders and instructions**
  You can't come in here.
  You must stop smoking.
  Can we wear shorts in the office?
- **Giving and asking for advice**
  (I think) you should talk to the boss about it.
  You shouldn't complain. **OR** I don't think you should complain.
  Should I leave him?
  What do you think I should do?
- **Talking about the future**
  Maybe I'll stay in and watch a video this evening.
  She might phone later.
  They'll probably get married.

Grammar and vocabulary puzzles

Puzzle 1 (Units 1–4)

ACROSS

2 Philip and Rose aren't married any more. They got .... last year. (8)
6 She lives in a neighbourhood on the edge of the city. It's very .... (8)
8 That story isn't true. It's .... (7)
10 Can I borrow that dictionary or .... you using it? (3)
12 Anna and Silvio .... born in Rio de Janeiro. (4)
13 It's not for me – it's for .... (3)
14 I .... lose my money at the casino. I lost it at the hotel. (3, 3)
16 When I got my new computer I did a course in information .... (10)
17 Have you .... been to Latin America? (4)

DOWN

1 When Kenny was a teenager, he .... to like rock music, but now he loves classical music. (4)
2 A: Charlotte went to Cambridge University.
   B: Really? So .... I. (3)
3 Jill is a .... She doesn't eat meat or fish. (10)
4 James .... ever goes out. He's always too tired. (6)
5 The money they pay you every month for doing your job is your .... (6)
7 It was my dad's fiftieth .... yesterday. We had a big party for him. (8)
9 I'm very hungry. I .... something to eat now. (4)
11 She's been to France but she .... been to Italy. (contraction) (5)
15 Jane is .... oldest child in the family. (3)

Puzzle 2 (Units 5–8)

ACROSS

3 A: I come from Poland. B: Oh, ... in Poland?
   A: Kraków – it's a beautiful old city. (11)
7 When you ask someone to a party, you .... them. (6)
8 Perhaps the Smiths .... move to the country. They don't like city life and they hate London. (4)
11 I can't see you before the meeting but I can see you .... it. (5)
13 The boss never wastes time. She's very .... (9)
17 She worked very hard and she got a .... at the end of last year. Her new job is very important and she earns a lot of money. (9)
20 It's .... or nothing. (3)
21 No, I don't want a return ticket. I want a .... (6)
22 Margaret Thatcher was the first woman .... Minister of Britain. (5)
23 I love Saturdays because I don't .... get up early and go to work. (4, 2)
24 What .... you do yesterday evening? (3)
25 I'd like you to meet my daughter, Amy, and my .... , John. (3)

DOWN

1 Those trousers don't .... you. They're too big. (3)
2 The contraction of *it is* is .... (3)
4 Geoff and Celia were married for more than fifty years. They had a really good .... (12)
5 What do you want to .... when you grow up? A lawyer or a doctor? (2)
6 The past participle of *see* is .... (4)
9 A: Does your boss .... you smoke in the office?
   B: No, he doesn't. We have to go outside. (3)
10 .... you help me with this work, I'll take you out for a drink later. (2)
12 Everyone hated Joe. He had a really bad .... (10)
14 This food is disgusting. I'm going to .... to the waiter. (8)
15 I hate this job. Why .... they make us wear these awful uniforms? (2)
16 His new film is a big .... It made $5 million in its first week. (7)
18 I think my interview went well this morning but I .... not get the job because they're interviewing more people tomorrow. (5)
19 One of the ten things on the end of your feet. (3)
21 On holiday, we're going to .... at a new hotel. (4)

Puzzle 3 (Units 9–12)

ACROSS

1 I'd like to .... a teacher, but it's hard work! (2)

3 I don't know what's wrong with the phone. I get .... every time. (3, 5, 6)

7 The bank is in the centre of town, ... the cinema. (4)

8 A: What's Elizabeth's new house like?
   B: Well, it isn't modern. In fact, it's very .... (11)

10 Sophie .... a game when her computer crashed! (3, 7)

15 I've known James .... years. We used to go to school together. (3)

17 I've always wanted to have a lot of money, but I don't know what I'd do if I .... the lottery. (3)

20 When my daughter was learning to drive, her .... was very strict. But he taught her well. (7, 10)

21 If I .... rich, I'd travel round the world. (4)

DOWN

2 Have you .... been to the USA? (4)

3 Please .... on the light. It's getting dark in here. (4)

4 Who .... you .... to on the phone when I came in? (4, 8)

5 I'm going to the shop. Can I .... you anything? (3)

6 There's a .... in the car outside. I think he's waiting for you. (3)

9 Could you put these plates in the .... over there? (8)

10 Where .... you stay if you went on holiday in the south of France. (5)

11 The contraction for I .... is I'm. (2)

12 The opposite of old is .... (3)

13 After their wedding Gloria and Wayne went to Barbados for their .... (9)

14 The mobile phone was the most irritating .... of the late twentieth century. (9)

16 He .... her to turn right, but she turned left! (4)

18 They've lived in that house .... they got married seven years ago. (5)

19 We use a .... to tell the time. (5)

Puzzle 4 (Units 13–16)

ACROSS

5 The noun from *mysterious* is .... (7)

7 They always go .... for their holidays. They never stay in England. (6)

9 The infinitive of *is / are* is .... (2)

10 The burglar was arrested .... the police. (2)

11 In Britain, you phone 999 if there's an .... The operator will put you through to the police, the fire service or the ambulance service. (9)

13 *Worse* is the comparative of .... (3)

14 My mother told me .... go out last night. She shouted, "Don't go out!" but I didn't listen! (3, 2)

15 In England you don't have to carry .... with you all the time. (1, 1)

17 You really need a car with .... in the summer. It's so hot! (3, 12)

18 An informal way of saying "father". (3)

DOWN

1 If you want to know your exam results, look on the .... (11)

2 The ten-year-old son of the millionaire, James Smith, ... last night. The police are looking for the murderer. (3, 8)

3 A burglar .... their house during the night and stole some valuables. (5, 4)

4 Another word for *taxi*. (3)

5 A .... attacked Mrs Jones in the street. He hit her on the head and stole her handbag. (6)

6 I know it's a difficult job, but if you really .... hard I'm sure you can do it. (3)

8 We usually begin letters with .... (4)

10 There's a Reader called "The wave and other stories" at the .... of *Wavelength Pre-Intermediate*. (4)

12 Look at that water skier – she's .... crash into that rock! (5, 2)

16 I met Jane's new boyfriend last night. I really liked him, he was .... interesting! (2)

Word lists

A list of useful words from each unit (n = noun, v = verb, adj = adjective, adv = adverb, det = determiner, prep = preposition, pron = pronoun)

Unit 1 Finding out about people

abroad (adv) /ə'brɔːd/
accounts (n) /ə'kaʊnts/
action point (n) /'ækʃən pɔɪnt/
active (adj) /'æktɪv/
advanced (adj) /əd'vɑːnst/
advertisement / advert / ad (n)
  /əd'vɜːtɪsmənt, 'ædvɜːt, æd/
aikido (n) /aɪ'kiːdəʊ/
all right (adj) /ɔːl 'raɪt/
anyone (pron) /'eniwʌn/
anyway (adv) /'eniweɪ/
appointment (n) /ə'pɔɪntmənt/
article (n) /'ɑːtɪkəl/
Asia (n) /'eɪʃə, 'eɪʒə/
boring (adj) /'bɔːrɪŋ/
business (n) /'bɪznɪs/
busy (adj) /'bɪzi/
call (v) /kɔːl/
cancel (v) /'kænsəl/
chance (n) /tʃɑːns/
choose (v) /tʃuːz/
coffee break (n) /'kɒfi breɪk/
company (n) /'kʌmpəni/
compare (v) /kəm'peə/
computer (n) /kəm'pjuːtə/
confident (adj) /'kɒnfɪdənt/
confirm (v) /kən'fɜːm/
connect [with] (v) /kə'nekt wɪð, wɪθ/
copy (n) /'kɒpi/
course (n) /kɔːs/
crazy (adj) /'kreɪzi/
current affairs (n) /ˌkʌrənt ə'feəz/
database (n) /'deɪtəˌbeɪs/
daughter (n) /'dɔːtə/
defend (v) /dɪ'fend/
delay (v) /dɪ'leɪ/
department (n) /dɪ'pɑːtmənt/
design (n) /dɪ'zaɪn/
diploma (n) /dɪ'pləʊmə/
discuss (v) /dɪ'skʌs/
dream (n) /driːm/
e-mail (n) /'iː meɪl/
engineer (n) /ˌendʒɪ'nɪə/
event (n) /ɪ'vent/
everything (pron) /'evriθɪŋ/
exam (n) /ɪg'zæm/
excuse (v) /ɪk'skjuːz/
exercise (n) /'eksəsaɪz/
experience (adj) /ɪk'spɪəriəns/
famous (adj) /'feɪməs/

fashion (n) /'fæʃən/
favourite (adj) /'feɪvərɪt/
fill in (v) /fɪl 'ɪn/
film (n) /fɪlm/
find out /faɪnd 'aʊt/
fit (adj) /fɪt/
foreign (adj) /'fɒrən/
form (n) /fɔːm/
free (adj) /friː/
friendly (adj) /'frendli/
get up (v) /get 'ʌp/
group (n) /gruːp/
guitar (n) /gɪ'tɑː/
gym (n) /dʒɪm/
habit (n) /'hæbɪt/
ham (n) /hæm/
happen (v) /'hæpən/
hard (adv) /hɑːd/
hardly ever (adv) /ˌhɑːdli 'evə/
headline (n) /'hedlaɪn/
hungry (adj) /'hʌŋgri/
husband (n) /'hʌzbənd/
important (adj) /ɪm'pɔːtənt/
industry (n) /'ɪndəstri/
informal (adj) /ɪn'fɔːməl/
information technology (n) /ɪnfə'meɪʃən
  tekˌnɒlədʒi/
intensive (adj) /ɪn'tensɪv/
interesting (adj) /'ɪntrəstɪŋ/
interior design (n) /ɪnˌtɪəriə dɪ'zaɪn/
introductory (adj) /ˌɪntrə'dʌktəri/
leave (v) /liːv/
lifestyle (n) /'laɪfstaɪl/
long (adj) /lɒŋ/
look for (v) /'lʊk fə, fɔː/
lunchtime (n) /'lʌntʃ taɪm/
manage (v) /'mænɪdʒ/
married (adj) /'mærɪd/
maths (n) /mæθs/
meeting (n) /'miːtɪŋ/
mind (n) /maɪnd/
music (n) /'mjuːzɪk/
musician (n) /mjuːˈzɪʃən/
need (v) /niːd/
[at] night (n) /'naɪt /
nightclub (n) /'naɪtklʌb/
novel (n) /'nɒvəl/
once (adv) /wʌns/
order (v) /'ɔːdə/
part-time (adj) /'pɑːt taɪm/
patient (adj) /'peɪʃənt/
people /'piːpəl/

permanent (adj) /'pɜːmənənt/
person (n) /'pɜːsən/
photocopier (n) /'fəʊtəʊˌkɒpiə/
photograph (n) /'fəʊtəgrɑːf/
photography (n) /fə'tɒgrəfi/
piano (n) /pi'ænəʊ/
plant (n and v) /plɑːnt/
polite (adj) /pə'laɪt/
post (v) /pəʊst/
professional (adj) /prə'feʃənəl/
project (n) /'prɒdʒekt/
publishing (n) /'pʌblɪʃɪŋ/
questionnaire (n) /ˌkwestʃə'neə/
quite (adv) /kwaɪt/
really (adv) /'rɪəli/
refuse (v) /rɪ'fjuːz/
safe (adj) /seɪf/
sandwich (n) /'sænwɪdʒ/
sell (v) /sel/
send (v) /send/
short (adj) /ʃɔːt/
skill (n) /skɪl/
something (pron) /'sʌmθɪŋ/
sometime (adv) /'sʌmtaɪm/
son (n) /sʌn/
stress (n) /stres/
stressed (adj) /strest/
study (n) /'stʌdi/
subject (n) /'sʌbdʒɪkt/
sure (adv) /ʃɔː/
system (n) /'sɪstəm/
team (n) /tiːm/
temp (n) /temp/
temporary (adv) /'tempərəri, -pəri/
the Internet (n) /ði 'ɪntənet/
tired (adj) /taɪəd/
travel (v) /'trævəl/
trip (n) /trɪp/
true (adj) /truː/
try (v) /traɪ/
TV script (n) /ˌtiː 'viː skrɪpt/
university (n) /ˌjuːnɪ'vɜːsəti/
urgent (adj) /'ɜːdʒənt/
use (v) /juːz/
useful (adj) /'juːsfəl/
usually (adv) /'juːʒuəli, 'juːʒəli/
video (n) /'vɪdiəʊ/
violin (n) /ˌvaɪə'lɪn/
violinist (n) /ˌvaɪə'lɪnɪst/
voice (n) /vɔɪs/
waiter (n) /'weɪtə/
well (adv) /wel/

wife (n) /waɪf/
word processing (n) / ˈwɜːd ˌprəʊsesɪŋ/
world (n) /wɜːld/
worry (v) / ˈwʌri/
writer (n) / ˈraɪtə/
yeah (adv) /jeə/
year (n) /jɪə/
yourself (pron) /jəˈself/

Unit 2 Money matters

absolutely (adv) / ˈæbsəluːtli, ˌæbsəˈluːtli/
adult (n) / ˈædʌlt, əˈdʌlt/
adventurous (adj) /ədˈventʃərəs/
afford (v) /əˈfɔːd/
ago (adj) /əˈgəʊ/
agree (v) /əˈgriː/
apartment (n) /əˈpɑːtmənt/
attractive (adj) /əˈtræktɪv/
awful (adj) / ˈɔːfəl/
bald (adj) /bɔːld/
bank (n) /bæŋk/
borrow (v) / ˈbɒrəʊ/
broke (adj) /brəʊk/
building (n) / ˈbɪldɪŋ/
businessman (n) / ˈbɪznɪsmən/
camp (n) /kæmp/
careful (adj) / ˈkeəfəl/
casino (n) /kəˈsiːnəʊ/
change (v) /tʃeɪndʒ/
clothes (n.pl) /kləʊðz, kləʊz/
college (n) / ˈkɒlɪdʒ/
completely (adv) /kəmˈpliːtli/
conversation (n) /ˌkɒnvəˈseɪʃən/
cost (v) /kɒst/
couple (n) / ˈkʌpəl/
decide (v) /dɪˈsaɪd/
die (v) /daɪ/
disagree (v) /ˌdɪsəˈgriː/
disappear (v) /ˌdɪsəˈpɪə/
disgusting (adj) /dɪsˈgʌstɪŋ/
dress (n) /dres/
earn (v) /ɜːn/
expensive (adj) /ɪkˈspensɪv/
experimental (adj) /ɪkˌsperɪˈmentl/
eyesight (n) / ˈaɪsaɪt/
fat (adj) /fæt/
flat (n) /flæt/
flight (n) /flaɪt/
gamble (v) / ˈgæmbəl/
game (n) /geɪm/
generous (adj) / ˈdʒenərəs/
glamorous (adj) / ˈglæmərəs/
grow (n) /grəʊ/
hair (n) /heə/
happiness (n) / ˈhæpinɪs/
hate (v) /heɪt/

helpful (adj) / ˈhelpfəl/
inherit (v) /ɪnˈherɪt/
invest (v) /ɪnˈvest/
joke (v) /dʒəʊk/
kid (n) /kɪd/
lend (v) /lend/
life (n) /laɪf/
look like (v) / ˈlʊk laɪk/
lose (v) /luːz/
lovely (adj) / ˈlʌvli/
lucky (adj) / ˈlʌki/
luxury (adj) / ˈlʌkʃəri/
maybe (adv) / ˈmeɪbi/
meat (n) /miːt/
miserable (adj) / ˈmɪzərəbəl/
modern (adj) / ˈmɒdn/
moustache (n) /məˈstɑːʃ/
museum (n) /mjuːˈziːəm/
neither (adv) / ˈnaɪðə/
noise (n) /nɔɪz/
on [his] own (adj) /ˌɒn ɪz ˈəʊn/
opinion (n) /əˈpɪnjən/
owe (v) /əʊ/
pay (v) /peɪ/
perhaps (adv) /pəˈhæps/
poor (adj) /pɔː/
popular (adj) / ˈpɒpjʊlə/
promise (v) / ˈprɒmɪs/
pub (n) /pʌb/
quiet (adj) / ˈkwaɪət/
rain (n) /reɪn/
refund (v) /rɪˈfʌnd/
rent (v) /rent/
report (n) /rɪˈpɔːt/
rich (adj) /rɪtʃ/
rude (adj) /ruːd/
salary (n) / ˈsæləri/
same (adj) /seɪm/
save (v) /seɪv/
saying (n) / ˈseɪɪŋ/
service (n) / ˈsɜːvɪs/
shop (v) /ʃɒp/
short (adj) /ʃɔːt/
silly (adj) / ˈsɪli/
simple (adj) / ˈsɪmpəl/
smoking (n) / ˈsməʊkɪŋ/
so (adv) /səʊ/
sound (v) /saʊnd/
spend (v) /spend/
staff (n) /stɑːf/
stick (n) /stɪk/
store (n) /stɔː/
stressful (adj) / ˈstresfəl/
stuck (adj) /stʌk/
stupid (adj) / ˈstjuːpɪd/
thin (adj) /θɪn/

ticket (n) / ˈtɪkɪt/
tiny (adj) / ˈtaɪni/
tip (v) /tɪp/
too (adv) /tuː/
traffic (n) / ˈtræfɪk/
translate (v) /trænsˈleɪt/
type (n) /taɪp/
uncle (n) / ˈʌŋkəl/
unfortunately (adv) /ʌnˈfɔːtʃənətli/
unhappy (adj) /ʌnˈhæpi/
used to (v) / ˈjuːst tə/
vegetarian (n) /ˌvedʒeˈteərian/
waitress (n) / ˈweɪtrɪs/
waste (v) /weɪst/
wealthy (adj) / ˈwelθi/
weather (n) / ˈweðə/
win (v) /wɪn/
young (adj) /jʌŋ/

Unit 3 It's your life!

actor (n) / ˈæktə/
actually (adv) / ˈæktʃuəli, -tʃəli/
address book (n) /əˈdres bʊk/
afternoon (n) /ˌɑːftəˈnuːn/
alphabet (n) / ˈælfəbet/
ambitious (adj) /æmˈbɪʃəs/
armchair (n) / ˈɑːmtʃeə/
author (n) / ˈɔːθə/
baby (n) / ˈbeɪbi/
back (n) /bæk/
bank manager (n) / ˈbæŋk ˌmænɪdʒə/
bat (n) /bæt/
beach (n) /biːtʃ/
become (v) /bɪˈkʌm/
bedroom (n) / ˈbedruːm, -rʊm/
best-seller (n) /ˌbest ˈselə/
bike (n) /baɪk/
biography (n) /baɪˈɒgrəfi/
birthday (n) / ˈbɜːθdeɪ/
blood (n) /blʌd/
boat (n) /bəʊt/
body (n) / ˈbɒdi/
book cover (n) / ˈbʊk kʌvə/
bring up (v) /ˌbrɪŋ ˈʌp/
brush (v) /brʌʃ/
cassette recorder (n) /kəˈset rɪˌkɔːdə/
change (v and n) /tʃeɪndʒ/
chapter (n) / ˈtʃæptə/
childhood (n) / ˈtʃaɪldhʊd/
clever (adj) / ˈklevə/
commune (n) /kəˈmjuːn/
countable (adj) / ˈkaʊntəbəl/
crime (n) /kraɪm/
cut (v) /kʌt/
dangerous (adj) / ˈdeɪndʒərəs/
dead (adj) /ded/

detective (n) /dɪˈtektɪv/
dictionary (n) /ˈdɪkʃənəri/
director (n) /dɪˈrektə, daɪ-/
divorced (adj) /dɪˈvɔːst/
doll (n) /dɒl/
early (adj) /ˈɜːli/
economics (n) /ˌekəˈnɒmɪks, ˌiː-/
exciting (adj) /ɪkˈsaɪtɪŋ/
fall off (v) /ˌfɔːl ˈɒf/
family (n) /ˈfæməli/
fashionable (adj) /ˈfæʃənəbəl/
fiction (n) /ˈfɪkʃən/
floor (n) /flɔː/
forgive (v) /fəˈgɪv/
front (n) /frʌnt/
fun (n) /fʌn/
gambler (n) /ˈgæmblə/
gang (n) /gæŋ/
get into trouble (v) /ˌget ɪntə ˈtrʌbəl/
grandmother (n) /ˈgrænˌmʌðə/
guess (v) /ges/
hairdresser (n) /ˈheəˌdresə/
hard-working (adj) /ˌhɑːd ˈwɜːkɪŋ/
heavy (adj) /ˈhevi/
hippie (n) /ˈhɪpi/
horrible (adj) /ˈhɒrɪbəl/
hysterical (adj) /hɪˈsterɪkəl/
ice cream (n) /ˌaɪs ˈkriːm/
ignore (v) /ɪgˈnɔː/
immediately (adv) /ɪˈmiːdiətli/
instrument (n) /ˈɪnstrəmənt/
interview (n and v) /ˈɪntəvjuː/
join (v) /dʒɔɪn/
journey (n) /ˈdʒɜːni/
key (n) /kiː/
killer (n) /ˈkɪlə/
kind (adj) /kaɪnd/
label (n) /ˈleɪbəl/
later (adv) /ˈleɪtə/
library (n) /ˈlaɪbrəri, -bri/
light (adj and v) /laɪt/
lock (v) /lɒk/
look after (v) /lʊk ˈɑːftə/
meal (n) /miːl/
memory (n) /ˈmeməri/
miss (v) /mɪs/
mostly (adv) /ˈməʊstli/
move (v) /muːv/
murder (n) /ˈmɜːdə/
mystery (n) /ˈmɪstəri/
neighbourhood (n) /ˈneɪbəhʊd/
non-fiction (n) /ˌnɒn ˈfɪkʃən/
organization (n) /ˌɔːgənaɪˈzeɪʃən/
paint (v) /peɪnt/
party (n) /ˈpɑːti/
pass (v) /pɑːs/

payment (n) /ˈpeɪmənt/
pick up (v) /ˌpɪk ˈʌp/
pipe (n) /paɪp/
politics (n) /ˈpɒlɪtɪks/
pour (v) /pɔː/
prefer (v) /prɪˈfɜː/
pretty (adj) /ˈprɪti/
programme (n) /ˈprəʊgræm/
promote (v) /prəˈməʊt/
pronounce (v) /prəˈnaʊns/
public relations company (n) /ˌpʌblɪk
    rɪˈleɪʃənz ˌkʌmpəni/
put down (v) /ˌpʊt ˈdaʊn/
run away (v) /ˌrʌn əˈweɪ/
rebel (n) /ˈrebəl/
record (v) /rɪˈkɔːd/
relax (v) /rɪˈlæks/
remember (v) /rɪˈmembə/
retired (adj) /rɪˈtaɪəd/
revolution (n) /ˌrevəˈluːʃən/
revolutionary (n & adj) /ˌrevəˈluːʃənəri/
romantic (adj) /rəʊˈmæntɪk, rə-/
sad (adj) /sæd/
science fiction (n) /ˌsaɪəns ˈfɪkʃən/
sentence (n) /ˈsentəns/
serious (adj) /ˈsɪəriəs/
sex (n) /seks/
shirt (n) /ʃɜːt/
shorts (n, plural) /ʃɔːts/
single (adj) /ˈsɪŋgəl/
slum (n) /slʌm/
smile (n) /smaɪl/
solve (v) /sɒlv/
spiritual (adj) /ˈspɪrɪtʃuəl/
spy (n) /spaɪ/
stick (v) /stɪk/
suburban (adj) /səˈbɜːbən/
sweetheart (n) /ˈswiːthɑːt/
teenager (n) /ˈtiːneɪdʒə/
theatre (n) /ˈθɪətə/
thriller (n) /ˈθrɪlə/
title (n) /ˈtaɪtl/
together (adj) /təˈgeðə/
top (adj) /tɒp/
train (n) /treɪn/
translation (n) /trænsˈleɪʃən, trænz-/
trousers (n, plural) /ˈtraʊzəz/
village (n) /ˈvɪlɪdʒ/
visit (n and v) /ˈvɪzɪt/
wait [for] (v) /weɪt /fə, fɔː/
war (n) /wɔː/
wedding (n) /ˈwedɪŋ/
whisky (n) /ˈwɪski/
wild (adj) /waɪld/
worried (adj) /ˈwʌrid/

Unit 4 Hooray for Hollywood!
accident (n) /ˈæksɪdənt/
acting (n) /ˈæktɪŋ/
action film (n) /ˈækʃən fɪlm/
actress (n) /ˈæktrɪs/
affair (n) /əˈfeə/
angry (adj) /ˈæŋgri/
answerphone (n) /ˈɑːnsəfəʊn/
assistant (n) /əˈsɪstənt/
attack (v) /əˈtæk/
ban (v) /bæn/
beauty contest (n) /ˈbjuːti ˌkɒntest/
bite (v) /baɪt/
blockbuster (n) /ˈblɒkˌbʌstə/
boyfriend (n) /ˈbɔɪfrend/
break down (v) /ˌbreɪk ˈdaʊn/
brilliant (adj) /ˈbrɪljənt/
brother (n) /ˈbrʌðə/
burning (adj) /ˈbɜːnɪŋ/
care (v) /keə/
channel (n) /ˈtʃænl/
cliff (n) /klɪf/
comedy (n) /ˈkɒmədi/
commercial (n) /kəˈmɜːʃəl/
communicate (v) /kəˈmjuːnɪkeɪt/
complain (v) /kəmˈpleɪn/
cook (v and n) /kʊk/
dancing (n) /ˈdɑːnsɪŋ/
danger (n) /ˈdeɪndʒə/
depressing (adj) /dɪˈpresɪŋ/
diet (n) /ˈdaɪət/
dinner (n) /ˈdɪnə/
direct (v) /dɪˈrekt, daɪ-/
drama (n) /ˈdrɑːmə/
drive (v) /draɪv/
exactly (adv) /ɪgˈzæktli/
excited (adj) /ɪkˈsaɪtɪd/
experience (n) /ɪkˈspɪəriəns/
fabulous (adj) /ˈfæbjʊləs/
fair (n) /feə/
field (n) /fiːld/
fight (v) /faɪt/
flower (n) /ˈflaʊə/
football (n) /ˈfʊtbɔːl/
forget (v) /fəˈget/
frightening (adj) /ˈfraɪtn-ɪŋ/
funny (adj) /ˈfʌni/
gun (n) /gʌn/
halfway (adv) /ˌhɑːfˈweɪ/
helicopter (n) /ˈhelɪkɒptə/
horror film (n) /ˈhɒrə fɪlm/
horse (n) /hɔːs/
immigrant (n) /ˈɪmɪgrənt/
interactivity (n) /ˌɪntərækˈtɪvəti/
jump (v) /dʒʌmp/

kilometre (n) /ˈkɪləˌmiːtə, kɪˈlɒmɪtə/
last (adj) /lɑːst/
mainly (adv) /ˈmeɪnli/
make-up (n) /ˈmeɪk ʌp/
message (n) /ˈmesɪdʒ/
mobile (n) /ˈməʊbaɪl/
modelling (n) /ˈmɒdl-ɪŋ/
motorbike (n) /ˈməʊtəbaɪk/
nothing (pron) /ˈnʌθɪŋ/
parachute (n and v) /ˈpærəʃuːt/
part (n) /pɑːt/
plan (v) /plæn/
pleasure (n) /ˈpleʒə/
pop (n) /pɒp/
prize (n) /praɪz/
producer (n) /prəˈdjuːsə/
ready (adj) /ˈredi/
right (n) /raɪt/
scene (n) /siːn/
shark (n) /ʃɑːk/
sink (v) /sɪŋk/
special effects (n) /ˌspeʃəl ɪˈfekts/
spring (n) /sprɪŋ/
studio (n) /ˈstjuːdiəʊ/
stunt (n) /stʌnt/
technician (n) /tekˈnɪʃən/
terrible (adj) /ˈterɪbəl/
through (prep) /θruː/
typical (adj) /ˈtɪpɪkəl/
valuable (adj) /ˈvæljuəbəl, -jəbəl/
vampire (n) /ˈvæmpaɪə/
violent (adj) /ˈvaɪələnt/
western (n) /ˈwestən/
wonderful (adj) /ˈwʌndəfəl/

Unit 5 Playing by the rules

accommodation (n) /əˌkɒməˈdeɪʃən/
activity (n) /ækˈtɪvəti/
air (n) /eə/
army (n) /ˈɑːmi/
aunt (n) /ɑːnt/
bossy (adj) /ˈbɒsi/
break (v) /breɪk/
breakfast (n) /ˈbrekfəst/
clean (adj) /kliːn/
climb (v) /klaɪm/
cookery (n) /ˈkʊkəri/
countryside (n) /ˈkʌntrisaɪd/
cruise (n) /kruːz/
daily (adj) /ˈdeɪli/
day off (n) /ˌdeɪ ˈɒf/
dirty (adj) /ˈdɜːti/
echo (n) /ˈekəʊ/
excitement (n) /ɪkˈsaɪtmənt/
facility (n) /fəˈsɪləti/
farm (n) /fɑːm/

fasten (v) /ˈfɑːsən/
fortunately (adv) /ˈfɔːtʃənətli/
fresh (adj) /freʃ/
fruit (n) /fruːt/
have to (v) /ˈhæv tə, tʊ/
health club (n) /ˈhelθ klʌb/
ID (n) /aɪ ˈdiː/
jeans (n, plural) /dʒiːnz/
let (v) /let/
location (n) /ləʊˈkeɪʃən/
marry (v) /ˈmæri/
middle (n) /ˈmɪdl/
millionaire (n) /ˌmɪljəˈneə/
mosquito (n) /məˈskiːtəʊ/
mountain (n) /ˈmaʊntən/
nightmare (n) /ˈnaɪtmeə/
obey (v) /əʊˈbeɪ, ə-/
obligation (n) /ˌɒblɪˈgeɪʃən/
organiser (n) /ˈɔːgənaɪzə/
outdoor (adj) /ˈaʊtdɔː/
owner (n) /ˈəʊnə/
parent (n) /ˈpeərənt/
peace (n) /piːs/
penalty fare (n) /ˈpenlti feə/
permission (n) /pəˈmɪʃən/
personal (adj) /ˈpɜːsənəl/
pet (n) /pet/
pick (v) /pɪk/
prove (v) /pruːv/
regulation (n) /ˌregjʊˈleɪʃən/
relationship (n) /rɪˈleɪʃənʃɪp/
relaxed (adj) /rɪˈlækst/
ridiculous (adj) /rɪˈdɪkjʊləs/
routine (n) /ruːˈtiːn/
rule (n) /ruːl/
rush hour (n) /ˈrʌʃ aʊə/
seatbelt (n) /ˈsiːtbelt/
shout (v) /ʃaʊt/
sign (v) /saɪn/
single (n) /ˈsɪŋgəl/
speed limit (n) /ˈspiːd ˌlɪmɪt/
stay (v) /steɪ/
strict (adj) /strɪkt/
suit (n) /suːt, sjuːt/
summer camp (n) /ˈsʌmə ˌkæmp/
summer (n) /ˈsʌmə/
swim (v) /swɪm/
tidy (adj) /ˈtaɪdi/
tie (n) /taɪ/
trainer (n) /ˈtreɪnə/
truthful (adj) /ˈtruːθfəl/
[the] Underground (n) /ðɪ ˈʌndəgraʊnd/
valid (adj) /ˈvælɪd/
van (n) /væn/
variety (n) /vəˈraɪəti/
wodding (n) /ˈwedɪŋ/

whereabouts (adv) /ˌweərəˈbaʊts/
wind-surfing (n) /ˈwɪnd ˌsɜːfɪŋ/

Unit 6 Where on earth?

airport (n) /ˈeəpɔːt/
along (prep) /əˈlɒŋ/
architecture (n) /ˈɑːkɪtektʃə/
arrangement (n) /əˈreɪndʒmənt/
art gallery (n) /ˈɑːt ˌgæləri/
basically (adv) /ˈbeɪsɪkli/
boiling (adj) /ˈbɔɪlɪŋ/
changeable (adj) /ˈtʃeɪndʒəbəl/
chemist (n) /ˈkemɪst/
climate (n) /ˈklaɪmət/
close (v) /kləʊz/
cloudy (adj) /ˈklaʊdi/
coach (n) /kəʊtʃ/
[the] coast (n) /ðə ˈkəʊst/
corner (n) /ˈkɔːnə/
cry (v) /kraɪ/
damp (adj) /dæmp/
definitely (adv) /ˈdefɪnətli, ˈdefənətli/
direct (adj) /dɪˈrekt, daɪ-/
dive (v) /daɪv/
dramatic (adj) /drəˈmætɪk/
drop (v) /drɒp/
earth (n) /ɜːθ/
east (n) /iːst/
far (adj) /fɑː/
ferry (n) /ˈferi/
flat (adj) /flæt/
flight attendant (n) /ˈflaɪt əˌtendənt/
forest (n) /ˈfɒrɪst/
freezing (adj) /ˈfriːzɪŋ/
further (adj) /ˈfɜːðə/
gentle (adj) /ˈdʒentl/
green (adj) /griːn/
guy (n) /gaɪ/
hand out (v) /ˌhænd ˈaʊt/
hand over (v) /ˌhænd ˈəʊvə/
hill (n) /hɪl/
hilly (adj) /ˈhɪli/
humid (adj) /ˈhjuːmɪd/
image (n) /ˈɪmɪdʒ/
inland (adj) /ˈɪnlənd/
intention (n) /ɪnˈtenʃən/
landing card (n) /ˈlændɪŋ kɑːd/
laugh (v) /lɑːf/
left (adv) /left/
library (n) /ˈlaɪbrəri, -bri/
lie (v) /laɪ/
map (n) /mæp/
mild (adj) /maɪld/
moor (n) /mʊə/
mountainous (adj) /ˈmaʊntənəs/
near (prep) /nɪə/

next to (adv) /ˈnekst tə, tʊ/
north (n) /nɔːθ/
northerner (n) /ˈnɔːðənə/
official (n) /əˈfɪʃəl/
package holiday (n) /ˈpækɪdʒ ˌhɒlɪdi/
package tour (n) /ˈpækɪdʒ tʊə/
park (n) /pɑːk/
passport (n) /ˈpɑːspɔːt/
perfect (adj) /ˈpɜːfɪkt/
pillow (n) /ˈpɪləʊ/
plan (n) /plæn/
possibility (n) /ˌpɒsɪˈbɪləti/
post office (n) /ˈpəʊst ɒfɪs/
rainy (adj) /ˈreɪni/
reserved (adj) /rɪˈzɜːvd/
right (adv) /raɪt/
river (n) /ˈrɪvə/
rocky (adj) /ˈrɒki/
[on] Safari (n) /ɒn səˈfɑːri/
[the] sea (n) /siː/
setting (n) /ˈsetɪŋ/
shopping (n) /ˈʃɒpɪŋ/
sightseeing (n) /ˈsaɪtˌsiːɪŋ/
snowy (adj) /ˈsnəʊi/
south (n) /saʊθ/
southerner (n) /ˈsʌðənə/
straight (adj) /streɪt/
street (n) /striːt/
sunbathe (v) /ˈsʌnbeɪð/
sunny (adj) /ˈsʌni/
suntan (n) /ˈsʌntæn/
supermarket (n) /ˈsuːpəmɑːkɪt, ˈsjuː-/
surprised (adj) /səˈpraɪzd/
take it easy (v) /ˌteɪk ɪt ˈiːzi/
turning (n) /ˈtɜːnɪŋ/
unfriendly (adj) /ʌnˈfrendli/
unusual (adj) /ʌnˈjuːʒuəl, -ʒəl/
upset (adj) /ʌpˈset/
usual (adj)) /ˈjuːʒuəl, -ʒəl/
vineyard (n) /ˈvɪnjɑːd/
visa (n) /ˈviːzə/
vitamin (n) /ˈvɪtəmɪn/
walk (n) /wɔːk/
warm (adj) /wɔːm/
water ski (v) /ˈwɔːtə skiː/
waterfall (n) /ˈwɔːtəfɔːl/
west (n) /west/
wet (adj) /wet/
whose (det) /huːz/
windy (adj) /ˈwɪndi/

Unit 7 The cruel heart

adult (adj) /ˈædʌlt, əˈdʌlt/
advertise (v) /ˈædvətaɪz/
alcohol (n) /ˈælkəhɒl/
alone (adj) /əˈləʊn/

anything (pron) /ˈeniθɪŋ/
anywhere (pron) /ˈeniweə/
artificial additive (n) /ˌɑːtɪfɪʃəl ˈædɪtɪv/
average (adj) /ˈævərɪdʒ/
banana (n) /bəˈnɑːnə/
barbecue (n) /ˈbɑːbɪkjuː/
blackmailer (n) /ˈblækmeɪlə/
calorie (n) /ˈkæləri/
career (n) /kəˈrɪə/
catch (v) /kætʃ/
certainly (adv) /ˈsɜːtnli/
character (n) /ˈkærɪktə/
[go] clubbing (v) /gəʊ ˈklʌbɪŋ/
cocktail (n) /ˈkɒkteɪl/
consumer (n) /kənˈsjuːmə/
contract (n) /ˈkɒntrækt/
cruel (adj) /ˈkruːəl/
darling (n) /ˈdɑːlɪŋ/
deal (n) /diːl/
delicious (adj) /dɪˈlɪʃəs/
destroy (v) /dɪˈstrɔɪ/
elegant (adj) /ˈelɪgənt/
empty (adj) /ˈempti/
engagement ring (n) /ɪnˈgeɪdʒmənt rɪŋ/
entertain (v) /ˌentəˈteɪn/
environmentally friendly (adj)
    /ɪnˌvaɪərənmentl-i ˈfrendli/
everyone (pron) /ˈevriwʌn/
everywhere (pron) /ˈevriweə/
evidence (n) /ˈevɪdəns/
fire (n and v) /faɪə/
fizzy (adj) /ˈfɪzi/
fool (n and v) /fuːl/
gender (n) /ˈdʒendə/
get married (v) /get ˈmærid/
girlfriend (n) /ˈgɜːlfrend/
glamour (n) /ˈglæmə/
grape (n) /greɪp/
grow up (v) /ˌgrəʊ ˈʌp/
handsome (adj) /ˈhænsəm/
health (n) /helθ/
healthy (adj) /ˈhelθi/
heart (n) /hɑːt/
ideal (adj) /aɪˈdɪəl/
idiot (n) /ˈɪdiət/
instructor (n) /ɪnˈstrʌktə/
jealous (adj) /ˈdʒeləs/
kill (v) /kɪl/
large (adj) /lɑːdʒ/
low (adj) /ləʊ/
mango (n) /ˈmæŋgəʊ/
mansion (n) /ˈmænʃən/
match (n) /mætʃ/
middle-aged (adj) /ˌmɪdl ˈeɪdʒd/
mother (n) /ˈmʌðə/
negotiate (v) /nɪˈgəʊʃieɪt/

no-one (pron) /ˈnəʊ wʌn/
non-fattening (adj) /ˌnɒn ˈfætn-ɪŋ/
nothing (pron) /ˈnʌθɪŋ/
occasion (n) /əˈkeɪʒən/
old (adj) /əʊld/
orange (n) /ˈɒrɪndʒ/
packaging (n) /ˈpækədʒɪŋ/
papaya (n) /pəˈpaɪə/
pathetic (adj) /pəˈθetɪk/
pineapple (n) /ˈpaɪnæpəl/
police (n) /pəˈliːs/
politician (n) /ˌpɒlɪˈtɪʃən/
product file (n) /ˈprɒdʌkt faɪl/
real (adj) /rɪəl/
recyclable (adj) /riːˈsaɪkləbəl/
regret (v) /rɪˈgret/
ruthless (adj) /ˈruːθlɪs/
secret (n) /ˈsiːkrɪt/
someone (pron) /ˈsʌmwʌn/
somewhere (pron) /ˈsʌmweə/
sophisticated (adj) /səˈfɪstɪkeɪtɪd/
sporty (adj) /ˈspɔːti/
strawberry (n) /ˈstrɔːbəri/
succeed (v) /səkˈsiːd/
sugar (n) /ˈʃʊgə/
tape (n) /teɪp/
target market (n) /ˈtɑːgɪt ˈmɑːkɪt/
tasty (adj) /ˈteɪsti/
treat (n) /triːt/
wheat (n) /wiːt/
workout (n) /ˈwɜːkaʊt/

Unit 8 Future dreams or nightmares?

accept (n) /əkˈsept/
angrily (adv) /ˈæŋgrɪli/
argument (n) /ˈɑːgjʊmənt/
ask [someone] out (v) /ˌɑːsk ˈaʊt/
attitude (n) /ˈætɪtjuːd/
badly (adv) /ˈbædli/
bookstore (n) /ˈbʊkstɔː/
briefcase (n) /ˈbriːfkeɪs/
bright (adj) /braɪt/
calm (adj) /kɑːm/
calmly (adv) /ˈkɑːmli/
certain (adj) /ˈsɜːtn/
charity (n) /ˈtʃærəti/
cloud (n) /klaʊd/
clue (n) /kluː/
coldly (adv) /ˈkəʊldli/
crowd (n) /kraʊd/
dangerously (adv) /ˈdeɪndʒərəsli/
earring (n) /ˈɪərɪŋ/
edge (n) /edʒ/
efficient (adj) /ɪˈfɪʃənt/
efficiently (adv) /ɪˈfɪʃəntli/

electricity (n) /ɪˌlekˈtrɪsəti, ˌelɪk-/
excellent (adj) /ˈeksələnt/
experiment (n) /ɪkˈsperɪmənt/
fantastic (adj) /fænˈtæstɪk/
fast (adj and adv) /fɑːst/
garage (n) /ˈgærɑːʒ, -ɪdʒ/
good-looking (adj) /ˌgʊd ˈlʊkɪŋ/
guide (n) /gaɪd/
happily (adv) /ˈhæpɪli/
identity (n) /aɪˈdentəti/
impression (n) /ɪmˈpreʃən/
injury (n) /ˈɪndʒəri/
intelligent (adj) /ɪnˈtelɪdʒənt/
invite (v) /ɪnˈvaɪt/
jump (n) /dʒʌmp/
laugh (n) /lɑːf/
maniac (n) /ˈmeɪniæk/
might (v) /maɪt/
moon (n) /muːn/
nervous (adj) /ˈnɜːvəs/
optimist (n) /ˈɒptɪmɪst/
organise (v) /ˈɔːgənaɪz/
own (v) /əʊn/
owner (n) /ˈəʊnə/
package (n) /ˈpækɪdʒ/
parapet (n) /ˈpærəpɪt, -pet/
passionate (adj) /ˈpæʃənɪt/
passionately (adv) /ˈpæʃənɪtli/
patiently (adv) /ˈpeɪʃəntli/
pay rise (n) /ˈpeɪ raɪz/
pessimist (n) /ˈpesɪmɪst/
philosophy (n) /fɪˈlɒsəfi/
pleasant (adj) /ˈplezənt/
pleasantly (adv) /ˈplezəntli/
point (v) /pɔɪnt/
prediction (n) /prɪˈdɪkʃən/
private (adj) /ˈpraɪvət/
probably (adv) /ˈprɒbəbli/
promotion (n) /prəˈməʊʃən/
public transport (n) /ˌpʌblɪk ˈtrænspɔːt/
qualification (n) /ˌkwɒlɪfɪˈkeɪʃən/
quick (adj) /kwɪk/
quickly (adv) /ˈkwɪkli/
quietly (adv) /ˈkwaɪətli/
race (n) /reɪs/
rain (v) /reɪn/
react (v) /riˈækt/
realistic (adj) /rɪəˈlɪstɪk/
recently (adv) /ˈriːsəntli/
retire (v) /rɪˈtaɪə/
scientific (adj) /ˌsaɪənˈtɪfɪk/
sculptor (n) /ˈskʌlptə/
secretary (n) /ˈsekrətəri/
selfish (adj) /ˈselfɪʃ/
seriously (adv) /ˈsɪəriəsli/

sexily (adv) /ˈseksɪli/
sexy (adj) /ˈseksi/
shoe (n) /ʃuː/
silver (n) /ˈsɪlvə/
[the] sky (n) /skaɪ/
slow (adj) /sləʊ/
slowly (adv) /ˈsləʊli/
smile (v) /smaɪl/
soon (adv) /suːn/
sports car (n) /ˈspɔːts kɑː/
square (n) /skweə/
stairs (n, plural) /steəz/
standard (n) /ˈstændəd/
star (n) /stɑː/
strange (adj) /streɪndʒ/
stranger (n) /ˈstreɪndʒə/
sunshine (n) /ˈsʌnʃaɪn/
tattoo (n) /təˈtuː, tæˈtuː/
terrace (n) /ˈterəs/
terrified (adj) /ˈterɪfaɪd/
top (n) /tɒp/
unemployed (adj) /ˌʌnɪmˈplɔɪd/
warmly (adv) /ˈwɔːmli/
wrong (adj) /rɒŋ/

Unit 9 My place
ambition (n) /æmˈbɪʃən/
antique (n and adj) /ænˈtiːk/
architect (n) /ˈɑːkɪtekt/
artist (n) /ˈɑːtɪst/
bed (n) /bed/
beige (adj) /beɪʒ/
blanket (n) /ˈblæŋkɪt/
break up (v) /ˌbreɪk ˈʌp/
caller (n) /ˈkɔːlə/
carpet (n) /ˈkɑːpɪt/
CD (n) /ˌsiː ˈdiː/
centre (n) /ˈsentə/
chair (n) /tʃeə/
character (n) /ˈkærɪktə/
chest of drawers (n) /ˌtʃest əv ˈdrɔːz/
clock (n) /klɒk/
colourful (adj) /ˈkʌləfəl/
comfortable (adj) /ˈkʌmftəbəl/
cooker (n) /ˈkʊkə/
cosy (adj) /ˈkəʊzi/
cupboard (n) /ˈkʌbəd/
curtain (n) /ˈkɜːtn/
cushion (n) /ˈkʊʃən/
dark (adj) /dɑːk/
decorate (v) /ˈdekəreɪt/
delay (n) /dɪˈleɪ/
designer (n) /dɪˈzaɪnə/
dishwasher (n) /ˈdɪʃˌwɒʃə/
duvet (n) /ˈduːveɪ/

extension (n) /ɪkˈstenʃən/
finally (adv) /ˈfaɪnəl-i/
financial (adj) /fɪˈnænʃəl, faɪ-/
fridge (n) /frɪdʒ/
furniture (n) /ˈfɜːnɪtʃə/
garden (n) /ˈgɑːdn/
grandfather (n) /ˈgrænd,fɑːðə/
hi /haɪ/
hold the line (v) /ˌhəʊld ðə ˈlaɪn/
investment (n) /ɪnˈvestmənt/
jazz club (n) /ˈdʒæz klʌb/
kitchen (n) /ˈkɪtʃən/
lamp (n) /læmp/
line (n) /laɪn/
litre (n) /ˈliːtə/
living room (n) /ˈlɪvɪŋ ruːm, rʊm/
main (adj) /meɪn/
member (n) /ˈmembə/
mess (n) /mes/
message pad (n) /ˈmesɪdʒ pæd/
microwave (n) /ˈmaɪkrəweɪv/
mirror (n) /ˈmɪrə/
mobile phone (n) /ˌməʊbaɪl ˈfəʊn/
news (n) /njuːz/
pass on (v) /ˌpɑːs ˈɒn/
pillow (n) /ˈpɪləʊ/
pink (adj) /pɪŋk/
plant pot (n) /ˈplɑːnt pɒt/
present (n and adj) /ˈprezənt/
psychological (adj) /ˌsaɪkəˈlɒdʒɪkəl/
receptionist (n) /rɪˈsepʃənɪst/
romance (n) /rəʊˈmæns, ˈrəʊmæns/
rug (n) /rʌg/
sample (v) /ˈsɑːmpəl/
second-hand (adj) /ˌsekənd ˈhænd/
set (n) /set/
sheet (n) /ʃiːt/
shelf (n) /ʃelf/
similar (adj) /ˈsɪmɪlə/
since (prep) /sɪns/
sink (n) /sɪŋk/
sofa (n) /ˈsəʊfə/
stereo (n) /ˈsteriəʊ/
table (n) /ˈteɪbəl/
throw (v) /θrəʊ/
traditional (adj) /trəˈdɪʃənəl/
untidy (adj) /ʌnˈtaɪdi/
vase (n) /vɑːz/
view (n) /vjuː/
wall (n) /wɔːl/
wardrobe (n) /ˈwɔːdrəʊb/
washing machine (n) /ˈwɒʃɪŋ məˌʃiːn/
window (n) /ˈwɪndəʊ/
winter (n) /ˈwɪntə/
wooden (adj) /ˈwʊdn/
wrong number (n) /ˌrɒŋ ˈnʌmbə/

Unit 10 He loves me, he loves me not . . .

act (v) /ækt/
afterwards (adv) /ˈɑːftəwədz/
assistant manager (n) /əˌsɪstənt ˈmænɪdʒə/
audience (n) /ˈɔːdiəns/
bake (v) /beɪk/
beer (n) /bɪə/
behave (v) /bɪˈheɪv/
believe (v) /bɪˈliːv/
blond[e] (adj) /blɒnd/
candle-lit (adj) /ˈkændl lɪt/
chat show (n) /ˈtʃæt ʃəʊ/
chat [someone] up (v) /ˌtʃæt ˈʌp/
cheat (v) /tʃiːt/
chocolate (n) /ˈtʃɒklɪt/
convince (v) /kənˈvɪns/
cottage (n) /ˈkɒtɪdʒ/
court (n) /kɔːt/
crash (n) /kræʃ/
cup (n) /kʌp/
damage (v) /ˈdæmɪdʒ/
drive [someone] crazy (v) /ˌdraɪv ˈkreɪzi/
engaged (adj) /ɪnˈgeɪdʒd/
fall in love (v) /ˌfɔːl ɪn ˈlʌv/
fancy (v) /ˈfænsi/
fed up (adj) /ˌfed ˈʌp/
free (adj) /friː/
general (n) /ˈdʒenərəl/
get on [someone's] nerves (n) /ˌget ɒn ˈnɜːvz/
get [your] own back (v) /ˌget jər ˈəʊn ˈbæk/
go off [someone] (v) /ˌgəʊ ˈɒf/
go out [with someone] (v) /ˌgəʊ ˈaʊt/
grandma (n) /ˈgrænmɑː/
have a lot in common [with someone] (v) /ˌhæv ə ˌlɒt ɪn ˈkɒmən/
hell (n) /hel/
helping (n) /ˈhelpɪŋ/
honeymoon (n) /ˈhʌnimuːn/
hospital (n) /ˈhɒspɪtl/
host (n) /həʊst/
instant (adj) /ˈɪnstənt/
irritate (v) /ˈɪrɪteɪt/
jealousy (n) /ˈdʒeləsi/
keep (v) /kiːp/
love at first sight (n) /ˌlʌv ət fɜːst ˈsaɪt/
lover (n) /ˈlʌvə/
nurse (n) /nɜːs/
pie chart (n) /ˈpaɪ ˌtʃɑːt/
play (n) /pleɪ/
playwright (n) /ˈpleɪraɪt/
poet (n) /ˈpəʊɪt/

pregnant (adj) /ˈpregnənt/
pretend (v) /prɪˈtend/
psychotherapist (n) /ˌsaɪkəʊˈθerəpɪst/
put [someone] through (v) /ˌpʊt ˈθruː/
retire (v) /rɪˈtaɪə/
return (v) /rɪˈtɜːn/
revenge (n) /rɪˈvendʒ/
ring (v) /rɪŋ/
secret (adj and n) /ˈsiːkrɪt/
separate (v) /ˈsepəreɪt/
serve (v) /sɜːv/
show (n) /ʃəʊ/
sick (adj) /sɪk/
soldier (n) /ˈsəʊldʒə/
split up /splɪt ˈʌp/
take revenge [on someone] (v) /ˌteɪk rɪˈvendʒ/
throw [someone] out (v) /ˌθrəʊ ˈaʊt/
tin (n) /tɪn/
tragedy (n) /ˈtrædʒədi/
unfaithful (adj) /ʌnˈfeɪθfəl/
viewer (n) /ˈvjuːə/

Unit 11 If . . .

advice (n) /ədˈvaɪs/
bother (v) /ˈbɒðə/
bottle (n) /ˈbɒtl/
can't stand (v) /ˌkɑːnt ˈstænd/
cycle (v) /ˈsaɪkəl/
explain (v) /ɪkˈspleɪn/
gadget (n) /ˈgædʒɪt/
hairdryer (n) /ˈheədraɪə/
hunt (v) /hʌnt/
invention (n) /ɪnˈvenʃən/
jacket (n) /ˈdʒækɪt/
laptop (n) /ˈlæptɒp/
lifesaver (n) /ˈlaɪfseɪvə/
marketing (n) /ˈmɑːkətɪŋ/
penknife (n) /ˈpen-naɪf/
pop in (v) /ˌpɒp ˈɪn/
queen (n) /kwiːn/
reject (v) /rɪˈdʒekt/
soap (n) /səʊp/
socialise (v) /ˈsəʊʃəl-aɪz/
someone (pron) /ˈsʌmwʌn/
space shuttle (n) /ˈspeɪs ʃʌtl/
stone (n) /stəʊn/
television (n) /ˈtelɪˌvɪʒən, ˌtelɪˈvɪʒən/
time off (n) /ˌtaɪm ˈɒf/
travel iron (n) /ˈtrævəl aɪən/
turn on (v) /ˌtɜːn ˈɒn/
umbrella (n) /ʌmˈbrelə/
unfair (adj) /ʌnˈfeə/
wheel (n) /wiːl/
wine (n) /waɪn/

Unit 12 Love me, love my car

almost (adv) /ˈɔːlməʊst/
angel (n) /ˈeɪndʒəl/
anxious (adj) /ˈæŋkʃəs/
Arrivals (n, plural) /əˈraɪvəlz/
astrological (adj) /ˌæstrəˈlɒdʒɪkəl/
astrology (n) /əˈstrɒlədʒi/
atlas (n) /ˈætləs/
automobile (n) /ˈɔːtəməbiːl/
bar (n) /bɑː/
budge (v) /bʌdʒ/
captain (n) /ˈkæptɪn/
cassette (n) /kəˈset/
casual (adj) /ˈkæʒuəl/
cautious (adj) /ˈkɔːʃəs/
cautiously (adv) /ˈkɔːʃəsli/
caviar (n) /ˈkæviɑː/
cell phone (n) /ˈsel fəʊn/
champagne (n) /ʃæmˈpeɪn/
chauffeur (n) /ˈʃəʊfə, ʃəʊˈfɜː/
city (n) /ˈsɪti/
creative (adj) /kriˈeɪtɪv/
cruise (v) /kruːz/
cuddle (v) /ˈkʌdl/
curiosity (n) /ˌkjʊəriˈɒsəti/
curious (adj) /ˈkjʊəriəs/
cyclist (n) /ˈsaɪklɪst/
degree (n) /dɪˈgriː/
depend [on] (v) /dɪˈpend/
descent (n) /dɪˈsent/
driving instructor (n) /ˈdraɪvɪŋ ɪnˌstrʌktə/
ejector seat (n) /ɪˈdʒektə ˌsiːt/
elegance (n) /ˈelɪgəns/
engine (n) /ˈendʒɪn/
expect (v) /ɪkˈspekt/
fantasy (adj) /ˈfæntəsi/
fast lane (n) /ˈfɑːst leɪn/
file (n) /faɪl/
gentleman (n) /ˈdʒentlmən/
get drunk (v) /ˌget ˈdrʌŋk/
glasses (n, plural) /ˈglɑːsɪz/
grudge (n) /grʌdʒ/
hit (v) /hɪt/
imagine (v) /ɪˈmædʒɪn/
independent (adj) /ˌɪndɪˈpendənt/
jet (n) /dʒet/
kiss (v) /kɪs/
lady (n) /ˈleɪdi/
lean (v) /liːn/
licence (n) /ˈlaɪsəns/
lie (n) /laɪ/
lively (adj) /ˈlaɪvli/
local (adj) /ˈləʊkəl/
loose (adj) /luːs/
madam (n) /ˈmædəm/

mile (n) /maɪl/
mood (n) /muːd/
moody (adj) /ˈmuːdi/
music system (n) /ˈmjuːzɪk ˌsɪstəm/
New Year's Eve (n) /ˌnjuː jɪəz ˈiːv/
next-door (adj) /ˌnekst ˈdɔː/
no entry sign (n) /ˌnəʊ ˈentri saɪn/
one-way street (n) /ˌwʌn weɪ ˈstriːt/
order (n) /ˈɔːdə/
park (v) /pɑːk/
particular (adj) /pəˈtɪkjʊlə/
passenger (n) /ˈpæsɪndʒə/
periscope (n) /ˈperɪskəʊp/
privacy (n) /ˈprɪvəsi, ˈpraɪ-/
proud (ad) /praʊd/
pull out (v) /ˌpʊl ˈaʊt/
push (v) /pʊʃ/
radio (n) /ˈreɪdiəʊ/
reliable (adj) /rɪˈlaɪəbəl/
reverse (v) /rɪˈvɜːs/
scream (v) /skriːm/
shut down (v) /ˌʃʌt ˈdaʊn/
sincere (adj) /sɪnˈsɪə/
slow down (v) /ˌsləʊ ˈdaʊn/
softly (adv) /ˈsɒftli/
song (n) /sɒŋ/
speed (n) /spiːd/
spontaneous (adj) /spɒnˈteɪniəs/
stand (v) /stænd/
status (n) /ˈsteɪtəs/
steal (v) /stiːl/
stroll (v and n) /strəʊl/
strong (adj) /strɒŋ/
style (n) /staɪl/
swear (v) /sweə/
swimming pool (n) /ˈswɪmɪŋ puːl/
tinted (adj) /ˈtɪntɪd/
unfasten (v) /ʌnˈfɑːsn/
until (prep) /ʌnˈtɪl, ən-/
whisper (v) /ˈwɪspə/
windscreen wiper (n) /ˈwɪndskriːn ˌwaɪpə/
wish (n and v) /wɪʃ/
zodiac (n) /ˈzəʊdiæk/

Unit 13 What a holiday!

aerobics (n) /eəˈrəʊbɪks/
air conditioning (n) /ˈeə kənˌdɪʃənɪŋ/
airline (n) /ˈeəlaɪn/
bathroom (n) /ˈbɑːθruːm, -rʊm/
behind (adv) /bɪˈhaɪnd/
blind (n) /blaɪnd/
brilliant (adj) /ˈbrɪljənt/
bull (n) /bʊl/
deal [with] (v) /diːl/
diary (n) /ˈdaɪəri/
diving board (n) /ˈdaɪvɪŋ bɔːd/

fall (v) /fɔːl/
guest (n) /gest/
holiday resort (n) /ˈhɒlɪdi rɪˌzɔːt/
huge (adj) /hjuːdʒ/
hurry up (v) /ˌhʌri ˈʌp/
jet skiing (n) /ˈdʒet skiːɪŋ/
light (n) /laɪt/
lots [of] (n, plural) /lɒts/
luggage (n) /ˈlʌgɪdʒ/
mini-bar (n) /ˈmɪni bɑː/
noisy (adj) /ˈnɔɪzi/
noticeboard (n) /ˈnəʊtɪsbɔːd/
paragliding (n) /ˈpærəglaɪdɪŋ/
reception (n) /rɪˈsepʃən/
repair man (n) /rɪˈpeə mæn/
rock (n) /rɒk/
a lot [of] (n) /ə ˈlɒt/
straightaway (adv) /ˌstreɪt əˈweɪ/
toilet paper (n) /ˈtɔɪlɪt ˌpeɪpə/
towel (n) /ˈtaʊəl/
unsuccessful (adj) /ˌʌnsəkˈsesfəl/
water skiing (n) /ˈwɔːtə ˌskiːɪŋ/
wind-surfing (n) /ˈwɪnd ˌsɜːfɪŋ/
yet (adv) /jet/

Unit 14 Crime doesn't pay!

across (prep) /əˈkrɒs/
age (n) /eɪdʒ/
ambulance (n) /ˈæmbjʊləns/
arrest (v) /əˈrest/
bank robber (n) /ˈbæŋk rɒbə/
bath (n) /bɑːθ/
beard (n) /bɪəd/
blow (v) /bləʊ/
brave (adj) /breɪv/
break into (v) /ˌbreɪk ˈɪntə, ˈɪntʊ/
brick (n) /brɪk/
brown (adj) /braʊn/
bubble bath (n) /ˈbʌbəl bɑːθ/
burglar (n) /ˈbɜːglə/
bus stop (n) /ˈbʌs stɒp/
carry (v) /ˈkæri/
cell (n) /sel/
charge [someone with something] (v) /tʃɑːdʒ/
cheek (n) /tʃiːk/
clean shaven (adj) /ˌkliːn ˈʃeɪvən/
concert (n) /ˈkɒnsət/
criminal (n) /ˈkrɪmɪnəl/
death (n) /deθ/
desperately (adv) /ˈdespərətli/
discover (v) /dɪsˈkʌvə/
emergency services (n) /ɪˌmɜːdʒənsi ˈsɜːvɪsɪz/
frame (v) /freɪm/
glove (n) /glʌv/

ground (n) /graʊnd/
guilty (adj) /ˈgɪlti/
handbag (n) /ˈhændbæg/
heavily (adv) /ˈhevɪli/
hold (v) /həʊld/
in front [of] (prep) /ɪn ˈfrʌnt/
innocent (adj) /ˈɪnəsənt/
investigation (n) /ɪnˌvestɪˈgeɪʃən/
jeweller (n) /ˈdʒuːələ/
jewellery (n) /ˈdʒuːəlri/
jump bail (v) /ˌdʒʌmp ˈbeɪl/
knife (n) /naɪf/
melon (n) /ˈmelən/
mug (v) /mʌg/
mugger (n) /ˈmʌgə/
murder (v) /ˈmɜːdə/
murderer (n) /ˈmɜːdərə/
notice (v) /ˈnəʊtɪs/
officer (n) /ˈɒfɪsə/
operation (n) /ˌɒpəˈreɪʃən/
opposite (prep) /ˈɒpəzɪt/
out of (prep) /ˈaʊt əv, ɒv/
overweight (adj) /ˌəʊvəˈweɪt/
past (prep) /pɑːst/
pickpocket (n) /ˈpɪkˌpɒkɪt/
plead (v) /pliːd/
pony tail (n) /ˈpəʊni teɪl/
prison (n) /ˈprɪzən/
pulse (n) /pʌls/
regularly (adv) /ˈregjʊləli/
release on bail (v) /rɪˌliːs ɒn ˈbeɪl/
rob (v) /rɒb/
rush (v) /rʌʃ/
scar (n) /skɑː/
shampoo (n) /ʃæmˈpuː/
shock (n) /ʃɒk/
shoplifter (n) /ˈʃɒplɪftə/
short cut (n) /ˈʃɔːt kʌt/
stiff [drink] (n) /ˌstɪf/
still (adv) /stɪl/
suddenly (adv) /ˈsʌdnli/
suspicious (adj) /səˈspɪʃəs/
T-shirt (n) /ˈtiː ʃɜːt/
tall (adj) /tɔːl/
thief (n) /θiːf/
torch (n) /tɔːtʃ/
towards (prep) /təˈwɔːdz/
under (prep) /ˈʌndə/
upstairs (n, plural) /ʌpˈsteəz/
victim (n) /ˈvɪktɪm/
wallet (n) /ˈwɒlɪt/
washing powder (n) /ˈwɒʃɪŋ ˌpaʊdə/
witness (n) /ˈwɪtnɪs/
[be] worth (v) /wɜːθ/
youngish (adj) /ˈjʌŋɪʃ/

Unit 15 What are you talking about?

ashtray (n) / 'æʃtreɪ/
boxer (n) / 'bɒksə/
burn (v) /bɜːn/
calendar (n) / 'kæləndə/
chilli powder (n) / 'tʃɪli ˌpaʊdə/
close (adj) /kləʊs/
conditioner (n) /kən'dɪʃənə/
corkscrew (n) / 'kɔːkskruː/
customer (n) / 'kʌstəmə/
date (n) /deɪt/
dentist (n) / 'dentɪst/
dry (adj) /draɪ/
ex-wife (n) /ˌeks 'waɪf/
goggles (n, plural) / 'gɒgəlz/
heel (n) /hiːl/
insect repellent (n) / 'ɪnsekt rɪˌpelənt/
journalist (n) / 'dʒɜːnəl-ɪst/
lawyer (n) / 'lɔːjə/
pepper (n) / 'pepə/
purple (adj) / 'pɜːpəl/

scissors (n, plural) / 'sɪzəz/
sensitive (adj) / 'sensɪtɪv/
share (v) /ʃeə/
size (n) /saɪz/
snobbish (adj) / 'snɒbɪʃ/
stuff (n) /stʌf/
sunglasses (n, plural) / 'sʌnˌglɑːsɪz/
suntan lotion (n) / 'sʌntæn ˌləʊʃən/

Unit 16 The strangest thing happened to me . . .

abduct (v) /əb'dʌkt/
alien (n) / 'eɪliən/
amazing (adj) /ə'meɪzɪŋ/
bench (n) /bentʃ/
body-building equipment (n) / 'bɒdi bɪldɪŋ ɪˌkwɪpmənt/
changing room (n) / 'tʃeɪndʒɪŋ ruːm, rʊm/
chaos (n) / 'keɪ-ɒs/
client (n) / 'klaɪənt/
close-up (n) / 'kləʊs ʌp/
coincidence (n) /kəʊ'ɪnsɪdəns/
colleague (n) / 'kɒliːg/

conference (n) / 'kɒnfərəns/
empire (n) / 'empaɪə/
exclusive (adj) /ɪk'skluːsɪv/
familiar (adj) /fə'mɪljə/
get off (v) /gət 'ɒf/
incredible (adj) /ɪn'kredɪbəl/
locker (n) / 'lɒkə/
massage room (n) / 'mæsɑːʒ ruːm, rʊm/
[the] media (n) / 'miːdiə/
mistake (v) /mɪ'steɪk/
panic (v) / 'pænɪk/
realise (v) / 'rɪəlaɪz/
recognise (v) / 'rekəgnaɪz, 'rekən-/
rescue (v) / 'reskjuː/
sauna (n) / 'sɔːnə/
several (adj) / 'sevərəl/
squash court (n) / 'skwɒʃ kɔːt/
stage (n) /steɪdʒ/
[on] strike (n) / 'straɪk/
such (det) /sʌtʃ/
video monitor (n) / 'vɪdiəʊ ˌmɒnɪtə/
weight (n) /weɪt/
zoom button (n) / 'zuːm ˌbʌtn/

Recording scripts

Recording 1

SUE: So, you're doing an advanced computing course?
DAVE: Yes, I need it for my job.
S: Oh, right. What do you do?
D: I'm a maths teacher.
S: My son loves maths. Where do you work?
D: At the university, but I'd like to do something different.
S: Yeah . . . What job would you like to do?
D: My wife thinks I'm crazy, but I'd like to be a writer.
S: A writer . . . So you're married. Do you have any children?
D: Yes . . . a son and a daughter. They're both at university now. Well . . . er . . . nice talking to you. It's time for the lesson.

Recording 8

NINA: What's the matter?
STEVE: Well, I'm a bit stressed. It's my first day . . . and everything's going wrong.
N: Well, can I help you? Would you like me to post those letters for you?
S: Yes, please. That's really nice of you.

N: That's all right.
S: Um . . . he wants me to get him a ham sandwich too.
N: Mmm . . . I bet, that's Bill. Don't worry! I'll get his sandwich.
S: Oh, thanks a lot.
N: That's OK. Look, it's almost lunchtime. Shall I get you something?
S: No, it's OK. Thanks anyway. I'm not really hungry.
N: All right. Erm . . . what's this?
S: Oh, someone wants me to take it to Room 101.
N: Oh, that's John Kent's office. I'll take it.
S: Oh, don't worry. I'll do it.
N: Are you sure?
S: Oh, yeah. Thanks for your help.

Recording 17

LARRY: Well, Monica, your family moved to California when you were a baby but you weren't born there. Where were you born?
MONICA: That's right. I was born in Chicago in 1954.
L: Who looked after you when you were a child?

M: My grandmother. I really loved her, she was so sweet and kind. She looked after me. My mother and father were always very busy, you know, work, parties, you know. I didn't see them very much. When we moved to California my grandmother came with us, but she died when I was six.
L: So, did you have a happy childhood?
M: Yeah, I did. It was very happy, really. We were very rich. California is a beautiful place. I had a lot of friends at school – they were the children of film directors, writers, actors, musicians. Of course I was very sad when my grandmother died . . . and I didn't like school very much. But there was one teacher who was really nice to me, I really liked her.
L: . . . and here is that teacher. You last saw her in 1967 . . .
MRS MOORE: I was her art teacher . . . Monica loved art and she was very good. She could paint very well.
M: Oh! Mrs Moore!
L: What did you do when you left school?
M: I didn't finish school. I left home when I was sixteen. I ran away actually . . .

L: . . . and you became a hippie. You joined a commune in San Francisco. And that's where you met Brian, your first husband. Where did you get married?

M: On a beach in India . . . I was nineteen and Brian was twenty-one. It was very romantic. It was a very exciting time. Brian talked to me about revolutionary politics and I became a revolutionary. We lived in Latin America. We were there for five years.

L: Then you got divorced in 1978. Why did you get divorced?

M: Well, Brian wasn't interested in me. He was only interested in politics and revolutions. And we were poor . . . I missed my friends and I wanted to go back to California. So I did. My father bought me a lovely little juice bar in Los Angeles, a lot of famous people came in . . .

Recording 18

LARRY: . . . That's where you met this man.

CHUCK: The first time I saw Monica, I remember thinking "I want a woman like that". She was beautiful, clever and very ambitious. We got married two weeks later in Las Vegas and we're still together. That was fifteen years ago.

L: Your husband, Chuck Masters.

MONICA: Oh! Chucky!

L: So, you started a business together and in the 1980s and you made a lot of money. Why did you sell your business?

M: Well, we needed a change. We wanted something more spiritual.

L: And, why did you move to Scotland?

C: Oh, it's so beautiful and wild. Life in the USA was too stressful . . . and dangerous. And we wanted a family, children, you know . . .

L: When did you move there?

M: We moved in 1992 and our first baby was born in 1993. We have five children now . . . two boys and three girls.

L: So, are you happy with your life now?

C: Very happy . . .

M: . . . er . . . yes . . . very happy . . .

Recording 22

1 WOMAN 1: My first memory? I don't remember my early childhood very well, but I remember falling off my bike when I was about six. There was blood everywhere . . . my mum was hysterical . . . and I had to go to hospital in an ambulance.

2 W 2: I don't know if this is my first memory but, anyway . . . when I was little I had this doll with beautiful, long, yellow hair. I used to spend hours brushing it. Anyway, one day my brother wanted to play hairdresser's and he cut all her hair off. He said it was fashionable. I remember crying and crying.

3 MAN: What's my first memory? Er . . . That's difficult, oh yeah, maybe it was my first day at school. I was about four. I didn't like it very much at first, but then they gave us ice cream for lunch. I remember eating the ice cream and thinking "School's really fun!". Every day after that I waited for the ice cream but we never had it again.

Recording 23

1 FEMALE FRIEND: What kind of things do you usually read?

DENIS: Well, I think I read the newspaper mostly.

FF: Why?

D: Well, I like to know what's happening in the world . . . and I don't really like the TV or radio news. The newspapers erm . . . give more information about the stories.

FF: Uh huh . . .

D: But, I always start with the sports page, the most important page.

FF: Oh yeah . . .

D: So, I always read the paper from the back to the front.

FF: Do you ever read books?

D: Oh yeah, if I have time . . . but I like non-fiction more than fiction. I'm reading a biography at the moment about this man . . . er . . . he was a spy in France in the Second World War. It's really good.

2 MALE FRIEND: What kind of things do you like to read?

ANN: Well, I don't read as much as I used to because I used to have a really long train journey to work. And that's when I do most of my reading . . . on the train.

MF: Right . . .

A: But I read all sorts of things really. My job's really busy and sometimes it's quite stressful. I just like to relax when I read. Um . . . I don't like books that are too "heavy" and serious. I read lots of best-sellers. You know politics, sex, beautiful people. I love those kinds of books. They're light. It's easy to pick them up and put them down.

3 MALE FRIEND: So what kind of things do you read?

MAGDA: Well, um . . . it's a bit different in Polish and English. Er . . . in my language I read a lot . . . fiction . . . novels. I love reading. But . . . it's difficult in English.

MF: Oh, so you don't read . . .

M: No, no I do. It's good . . . er . . . for my vocabulary, you see a word again and again and then maybe you remember it.

MF: Yeah, maybe . . .

M: I read simple books . . . er, you know . . . for English students . . . I really like . . . detective stories . . . um . . . American stories about private detectives . . . things like that . . . They're great . . . because you want to know who the killer is . . . so you always finish the book.

MF: Yeah . . .

M: And I love . . . English murder mysteries . . .

MF: Do you mean Agatha Christie? Things like that?

M: Yeah, you know a sweet little village . . . and then . . . there's a horrible murder. There's always a body in the library . . . and then . . . an old lady solves the crime and then everyone has tea! I love those.

Recording 25

1 HANS: Sometimes I write words in groups . . . you know like clothes . . . shirt, trousers, shorts. Sometimes I write words on labels and stick them on things in my house. For example, yesterday I wrote "wardrobe" on a label and stuck it on the wardrobe. Now when I go to get my clothes, I read the label and remember the word.

2 MARIA: I need to hear words . . . um . . . and I want to know how to pronounce them. I record new words I've learnt on my cassette recorder. Then I can play the cassette in my car.

3 STELIOS: I use an address book because it has the letters of the alphabet, then I write er . . . new words on the correct page. Sometimes with a translation, maybe a sentence. It's like my own little dictionary.

4 MAGDA: I write new words in sentences. That helps me with prepositions too. Like "He got into the car . . . I'll see you on Friday". Sometimes I write erm . . . adjectives, nouns, verbs, prepositions in different colours too. It's good, it helps me remember.

Recording 27

MIKE: Lara, come in, sit down.

LARA: Hi, Mike. Nice to meet you, thanks . . .

M: So, uh, you're interested in the part.

L: Yeah. It looks great! I'm really excited.

M: It's not a big part, you know.

L: Oh yeah, but that's OK. You're one of my favourite directors. I loved *White Death*. It was a brilliant action film!

M: Oh . . . Well, er, thank you . . . but anyway why don't you tell me a bit about yourself? How did you end up in Hollywood?

L: Well, I won a beauty contest. I was Miss Montana . . . I'm from Montana. And the prize was a trip to Hollywood and a film test at a Hollywood studio. That was a few years ago and well, Hollywood was just so exciting, I never went home!

M: Oh yeah, I see. Well, now can you tell me a bit about your acting experience?

Recording 29

MIKE: Well, it er, sounds very interesting but look er, I'm really sorry, I have to go. You know . . . things are a bit busy at the moment with the new film and everything.

LARA: Oh yeah, don't worry. No problem.

M: But er, look, er . . . what are you doing this evening? What about discussing this a bit more over dinner?

Recording 30

MAN: Oh, Julie Andrews, she's great! I loved her in *Mary Poppins*. *Mary Poppins* is the best film I've ever seen.

WOMAN: *Mary Poppins*! You're joking! It's awful. It's so sweet. It's a children's film! How old are you?

M: OK, OK. So, what's the best film you've ever seen?

W: Um . . . I don't really know but one of my favourites is *Psycho*. I loved it! It was so frightening! I saw it when I was about sixteen, I couldn't sleep for a week! Have you ever seen it?

M: No, I haven't. I don't like violent films – I think the worst film I've ever seen is *Predator*.

W: Oh yeah, Arnold Schwarzenegger.

M: Yeah, it was disgusting. I hated it. What about you? What's the worst film you've ever seen?

W: Ugh . . . *Titanic*! It was so long, so slow, so boring. I saw it with my boyfriend. He only wanted to see the special effects. He went out for a cigarette every five minutes and every time he came back he asked "Is it sinking?". It was awful.

Recording 32

HARRY: Sorry, I'm late. The traffic was terrible!

LOUISE: Well, why didn't you leave earlier? It's typical of you.

H: OK, OK, I'm sorry. What more can I say?

L: Nothing . . .

H: You used to be so sweet.

L: What did you say?

H: Nothing, I . . .

WAITER: Are you ready to order, sir?

H: Er . . . No, not yet . . . What's wrong with you these days? You're always angry about something.

L: Yeah? Well you're not exactly "Mr Wonderful".

H: What do you mean?

L: You know what I mean. We haven't been to a restaurant for three months and you're late.

H: I said I'm sorry.

L: You used to take me to restaurants all the time. You used to buy me flowers.

W: Would you like to order now?

H: No, we're not really ready . . .

W: Of course, sir.

L: When was the last time you bought me flowers?

H: Oh, don't start.

L: You're always out with your friends these days. And when you are at home all you do is watch football. You used to talk to me. You never talk to me now.

H: Well, you used to be more fun. You used to cook nice meals. Now you're always on a diet.

L: Well, I want to look nice for you – but I don't know why. You don't care. You don't even remember my birthday any more. You didn't use to forget my birthday.

H: Oh, not that again. And you didn't use to complain all the time.

L: Well, I . . .

W: Can I get you something to drink?

H: Look! We're really not . . .

Recording 33

JUDY: Thank you for coming in, Karl.

KARL: It's a pleasure, Judy.

J: So, have you ever done any stunt work?

K: Oh, yes. I've done a lot of action films, you see.

J: Oh really? And, what's the most dangerous thing you've ever done?

K: Er, maybe when I parachuted from a helicopter into a group of sharks. They weren't too friendly. One of them attacked me.

J: Oh no, what happened?

K: Well, it was really frightening but I fought it off.

J: Gosh.

K: I've driven cars off cliffs at 250 kilometres an hour. Um . . . I've ridden a motorbike through a burning village. I burnt my hair in that one.

J: Why do you do it?

K: Well, it's fun. I love danger.

J: Have you had many accidents?

K: One or two.

J: What are you working on at the moment?

K: It's an action film called *Air disaster*. I'm going to jump from a plane without a parachute. I've never done it before, but I'm not worried. It's my job and I love it.

J: I see . . . well, have you done any television work?

K: Oh well, I was in *Crazy Love* . . . on Channel 7.

J: Oh, that was great.

K: Yeah, I played the boyfriend of . . .

Recording 37

A WOMAN: Oh hi, are you here for the interview?

MAN: Yeah, it seems like a friendly company, very informal.

W: Yeah, it's quite relaxed here. You can work the hours you want. I don't like driving in the rush hour so I usually come a bit later and stay a bit later. But my friend Carol works different hours because she's got kids. And as you can see, you can wear jeans . . . or what you like really. You don't have to wear a suit and tie.

B BOUNCER: Oi! Wait a minute. How old are you?

GIRL: Twenty-one. Why?

B: Have you got anything to prove it? Have you got any ID?

G: No.

B: Well . . . you can't come in here then.

G: But I am twenty-one.

B: Yeah . . . and I'm Leonardo DiCaprio! Come back later, with your ID!

C INSPECTOR: May I see your ticket, madam?

WOMAN: Um . . . well . . . I . . . I can't find it. I know I bought a single to Piccadilly Circus but . . . er . . . I don't know . . . it's not here.

I: I'm afraid you have to have a valid ticket when you travel on the Underground, madam. There's a £10 penalty fare if you don't have a ticket.

W: What?! That's ridiculous! It's here somewhere! I just can't er . . .

Recording 42

1 MALE FRIEND: So, where are you from in South Africa, Cheryl?

CHERYL: I'm from the Cape, which is in the south of the country . . . on the south coast.

MF: And what's it like around there?

C: Well, Cape Town is in a lovely setting. The mountains drop right down to the sea so you have the city nestled between the sea and the mountains. And . . . there's some lovely architecture and some lovely places to go.

MF: And what's the countryside around Cape Town like?

C: Oh the countryside around is . . . very hilly, very green. About an hour's drive from Cape Town you, you reach the vineyards. It's very Mediterranean.

MF: Oh, so quite hilly, not . . .

C: No, it's very mountainous actually, quite high mountains.

MF: Right, and do you have a favourite place to go round there?

C: Oh, one of my favourite places is the top of Table Mountain. Whenever I go back there I climb up to the top . . . and it's quite flat at the top . . . with beautiful wild flowers . . . and views all around the coast.

MF: Right . . . and what are the beaches like?

C: The beaches are lovely, pure white sand, wonderful long beaches with waves. Surfing's very popular.

MF: What are the people like?

C: Well, they're great fun, they go out a lot – people do things in groups a lot . . . more than in London . . . maybe it's because the weather's so good and sunny. We have barbecues and things like that . . . I miss that.

2 **FEMALE FRIEND:** You're from the north of England, aren't you?

MARCUS: Yeah.

FF: Whereabouts?

M: I'm from Manchester. It's er, quite a big city . . . in the north-west.

FF: And what's it like round there?

M: Well, it's . . . the countryside near there is quite hilly . . . and green. Er, but there are a lot of moors too.

FF: They're quite wild, aren't they?

M: Yeah . . . very open . . . and wild . . . no trees . . . very dramatic!

FF: Hmm . . . is that your favourite place?

M: Well, actually my favourite place is the Lake District. It's further north . . . about an hour's drive from Manchester. There are a lot of mountains . . . lakes . . . and some beautiful waterfalls. It's great for walking.

FF: It sounds great.

M: Oh yeah . . . I go there a lot with friends.

FF: What about the people? Northerners are quite different from southerners, aren't they?

M: Yeah, definitely! Um . . . Northerners are warm and very friendly and welcoming.

FF: They're quite direct, too, aren't they?

M: Oh yeah . . . my dad's a good example of that. He always says exactly what he thinks. Maybe that's not always a good idea but . . . northerners are like that. That's one of the things I like about them.

FF: Right. But that's different from the usual image of reserved English people.

M: Yeah.

Recording 43

1 **MALE FRIEND:** So . . . what's the weather like . . . what's the climate like?

CHERYL: Cape Town has a lovely climate. The summers are very warm . . . not humid at all and the winters are wet, very rainy but not too cold, so it's . . . it's a perfect climate.

MF: When's the best time to go?

C: Our summers start around October . . . from October to March . . . so I'd say round October, November or February, March are the best times to go.

2 **FEMALE FRIEND:** So, what's the weather like in the north?

MARCUS: Not very good. Um . . . like all of England it's very changeable . . . it rains a lot . . . but er, I think it's colder in the north . . . it can be very cold in the winter . . . and very damp.

FF: When's the best time to go there then, do you think?

M: Well, I think the best time to visit is probably the summer er . . . between June . . . and September.

FF: So, it won't rain then?

M: Well, I didn't say that . . . but er, it can be quite warm . . . and sunny . . . on a good day.

Recording 44

WENDY: Have you booked your holiday?

JULIA: Yeah, I'm going to Kerala. I'm flying on Saturday.

W: Oh, that sounds nice. It's got beautiful beaches, hasn't it?

J: I hope so.

W: Where is it exactly?

J: In the south-west of India.

W: That's a long way for just one week, isn't it? How long's the flight?

J: Oh . . . I don't know. About eleven hours I think. But I just want to get away and have a real break.

W: So where are you staying?

J: Well, I've booked a package holiday, I'm staying at a hotel on the beach. I don't know exactly where.

W: Are you going to travel around or just lie on the beach?

J: Oh, I don't know. Maybe I'll visit one other place. I don't like planning these things. I'm going to take it easy. Perhaps I'll just sleep for a week . . . on the beach of course!

Recording 45

IAN: . . . Yeah! India's great. Have you ever been there?

JULIA: Yeah, I've been twice – sort of. The first time I went for a month and the second time I went for about . . . forty-five minutes.

I: Forty-five minutes!?

J: Yeah, forty-five minutes.

I: What do you mean forty-five minutes?

J: Well, it was supposed to be a one-week package tour in Kerala, in the south of India. And I booked it by phone and paid for it with my credit card and I thought everything was fine and I asked about a visa and the guy said I could get one when I arrived at the airport in Kerala. So I flew to Kerala . . . and I was on the plane . . . and they handed out the landing cards. And I took mine and started to fill it in. One of the questions was "What's the number on your visa?" – but I didn't have a visa. I started to get a bit worried. So I asked the people on the plane, the . . . flight attendants. They didn't know anything. I got to the airport and handed my passport over and one guy – as a joke said "Um . . . you haven't got a visa. You'll have to go back to London". They all started laughing so I thought it was OK. And then they told me to go to a different place in the airport. Then this er . . . man came over and said I didn't have a visa so I couldn't come into the country and there was no way I could get a visa in the airport. So, I started crying. The other Indians were upset, but the man still said "No".

I: You're joking! He was serious then?

J: He was absolutely serious. There was nothing I could do because the plane was waiting for me. It was the plane that I came on. And I had to . . . basically just get back on the plane . . . and fly for another eleven hours – straight back to London.

I: What?! You had to go back? They didn't let you stay?

J: No, they didn't let me stay at all. So, I had a . . . four-day holiday in London.

Recording 49

Scene 2

LOVER: Let's get married and go to Mexico. I can get work there.

MOM: But what about Joe?

L: Look, I've told you. I don't like kids. If that kid comes, I won't marry you.

Scene 3

TROY: I'm going to miss you and Nancy when I go to Harvard.

JOE: Yeah . . . you and Nancy are the only real friends I've ever had. Nancy's parents were so kind when Mom left. They gave me a home when I had nothing.

T: Yeah, they're good people.

J: You've got Harvard . . . and Nancy. You're so lucky. You've always had everything.

T: Well . . . I guess I am pretty lucky. Life's really good at the moment. Do you think Nancy will like her engagement ring?
J: Yeah, it's beautiful.
T: If she says "Yes", I'll be so happy. Joe, can you do me a favour? Can you look after her for me when I'm at college?
J: Yeah, Troy. Sure.

Scene 4
NANCY: Joe? Dad wants to talk to you about something.
JOE: Yes, sir?
DAD: Well, Joe. Now that you're going to marry our daughter, we need to think about your future career. How do you feel about Springfield Business College? It's a very good school.
J: Well, thank you, sir . . . but I've thought a lot about this. I want to succeed and I know I can do it – but I need the best college – and that's Harvard.
D: Harvard?! I see . . .
J: If you help me, sir, you won't regret it.
N: Oh, Dad! I know Joe can do it!

Scene 5
JOE: It's just not going to work, Nancy. Things are different now. I'm going to be a success and I need people like the Vanderbergs.
NANCY: What do you mean, Joe?
J: I'm marrying Tania Vanderberg.
N: Oh, Joe.
J: Forget me. Find someone else. Troy still loves you.
N: But I love you, Joe – I'll always love you . . . If you ever need me, I'll be here.

Scene 6
TROY: Are you crazy?! How can you do this to Mr Vanderberg?!
JOE: Vanderberg's an old fool. He lives in the past.
T: But he's given you everything! If you do this, you'll destroy him!
J: Listen. I'm going to do it and no-one's going to stop me – no-one!
T: Well, I won't help you!
J: If you don't help me, I'll fire you!
T: You don't have to fire me! I'm leaving! You don't care about anyone but yourself!
J: Fine! Go!

Scene 7
TANIA: First you destroy my family – and now you want to destroy me! How can you do this?
JOE: Shut up. I've told you. I'm leaving you.
T: If you leave me, I'll kill myself!
J: God! Look at you! You're pathetic! I've given you money. What more do you want?!
T: But Joe! I love you!
J: Sorry, I've got a plane to catch.

Recording 51

1 MAN: Here you are.
WOMAN: Hmm . . . Cheers! Happy New Year!
M: And something with your drink?
W: Oh thank you. Mmm . . . These are delicious . . . and so elegant. What are they?
M: Savoury Delights. A special treat – for a sophisticated woman.
VOICE OVER. Savoury Delights . . . for that special occasion.
2 KID 1: Savoury Delights! Give me some?
KID 2: No. Hmm . . . tasty.
K1: Ah come on. I'll lend you my Mega Ray gun.
K2: Hmm . . .
K1: OK . . . you can borrow all of my Neutron Destroyer computer games!
K2: Hmm . . . and the Mega Ray gun?
K1: Yeah, all right.
K2: Cool . . . Here!
K1: Hey! It's empty!
3 GIRL 1: Whew! What a workout! That new instructor's really tough.
GIRL 2: All I can think about now is food. I'm so hungry.
G1: Oh . . . I've got these.
G2: Uh-uh. My diet.
G1: No, don't worry. They're really low in calories.
G2: What are they?
G1: Savoury Delights.
G2: They don't look low in calories.
G1: I know. But I'm telling you . . . they are! Go on . . . try one.
G2: Hmm . . . they're nice!
G1: Yeah . . . and they're good for you. Whole grain wheat and vitamin B!
G2: You sound like an advert.
G1: Well, they are good for you.
G2: So, now we'll be beautiful and healthy.

Recording 52

JENNY: Guess what Ken and I are going to do this summer? We're going round Europe on the bike! For two months!
MANDY: That sounds great!
DAN: On the motorbike! But it might rain every day!
M: They'll have great weather. It'll be nicer there than here!
D: Two months is a long time. What'll you do if you have an argument?
M: Oh come on. I'm sure you'll have a great time, Jenny. And you'll probably meet some really nice people.
D: Yeah, you might but you won't understand them. Do you speak any languages? What'll you do if the bike breaks down?
M: If the bike breaks down, they'll take it to a garage. It's Europe, not the moon!

You'll have some great food and you'll both get fantastic suntans.
D: Maybe, but . . .

Recording 54

1 KATE: Hi, Todd? It's Kate.
TODD: Hi, where have you been? I haven't heard from you for ages! How's London?
K: Great. I've been very busy. I've moved.
T: Not again.
K: Yeah, I wanted to be nearer the centre. My other flat was too far out.
T: Yeah, it was a bit far out. So when did you move?
K: About two months ago. I've been here since August.
T: And what's the flat like?
K: Oh . . . It's great. I love it. The guy who lived here before decorated it just the way I like it. This room's very simple, you know, white walls . . . It's quite large and really light. It's got lovely wooden floors.
T: Sounds nice.
K: Yeah. So when are you coming over?
T: Well, if you pay my flight, I'll be there next week.
K: Yeah, right.
2 JOAN: I love your house, Liz. How long have you been here?
LIZ: Ooh, we've lived in this house for eight . . . no . . . nine years.
J: It's lovely. This room's so welcoming and cosy.
L: Yeah, I like it a lot. This is where we spend most of our time. It's a real family room. We sit round the table talking, eating. I've had this table for ages, it's really old. My parents gave it to us when we got married. When friends come round we always sit in here, too.
J: Well, it's really comfortable . . . and relaxing.
L: Yeah . . . and untidy. It's always a mess because everybody lives in here. But it's nice though because I can cook and talk to the kids, listen to all their news.
J: You've got a great view!
L: Yeah, that's one of my favourite things about this room. I sit here in winter and look out at the garden . . . and in summer we have the doors open all the time.
3 NICK: Come on in. Do you want a coffee before we start?
LOUISE: Yeah, thanks . . . that sounds good. I hate doing these reports.
N: Yeah, so do I.
L: You're flat's nice, Nick. It's so bright and colourful.
N: Well, all the walls were sort of beige, when I first moved here, really boring. My girlfriend hated it. So, I finally painted it and bought some things . . . about six months ago.

L: How long have you lived here?

N: Hmm . . . for about a year.

L: Right . . . Oh, wow! Great sofa. It's really comfortable.

N: Yeah, my dog loves it.

L: Oh, right. Nice cushions.

N: Hmm . . . My girlfriend bought those. Right . . .

Recording 55

1 FRIEND: Oh, this rug is beautiful. Where did you get it?

KATE: In Turkey. I've had it for about seven years. It's travelled to all my different flats with me.

2 FRIEND: How long have you had this clock?

LIZ: We've had it since we got married. My grandfather gave it to us as a wedding present.

F: Is it an antique?

L: Yes, it's quite valuable.

3 FRIEND: What's this?

NICK: What do you mean?

F: This chair?

N: Be careful. I love that chair.

F: How long have you had it?

N: Oh, I've had it for ages. I bought it in a second-hand shop. I just can't throw it out.

Recording 57

MAN: Hello.

PATSY: Um . . . is that Mann Interior Design?

M: Er . . . No . . . you've got the wrong number.

P: Oh, sorry.

M: That's OK.

P: Bye.

M: Bye.

Recording 58

RECEPTIONIST: Mann Interior Design.

PATSY: Hello. Can I speak to Jason Lombard, please?

R: One moment. Who's calling, please?

P: It's Patsy Wright.

R: Yes, can you spell that?

P: Yes, W - R - I - G - H - T.

R: Is there a company name?

P: No.

R: Right. Hold the line, please, Ms Wright . . . I'm afraid he's in a meeting. Can I take a message?

P: Um . . . Do you know when he'll be free?

R: I'm afraid not. He's been in the meeting since nine o'clock this morning.

P: I see. Could you ask him to phone me? I'd like to talk about the plans for my flat.

R: Certainly. May I take your number?

P: Yes, it's 01713 586 4770. Extension 615.

R: Right. I'll give him the message.

P: Thank you very much.

R: Goodbye.

P: Goodbye.

Recording 60

PATSY: . . . the walls are going to be pink! And he's ordered me a fantastic sofa in Valentine Red.

BOB: It sounds wild, I can't wait to see it.

P: So, anyway, that's my news. How's everything with you?

B: Fine. Guess what! I saw [Tom Jackson] last week.

P: Sorry, I've got a bad line. Who did you see?

B: Tom Jackson.

P: Oh yeah?

B: Well, anyway we went to [a jazz club].

P: Where did you go?

B: A jazz club.

P: Oh, right.

B: Anyway, he asked for your [phone number].

P: Oh! Sorry? What did he ask for?

B: Your phone number! He's away for a few days but he's going to call you on [Friday].

P: Oh! This line is terrible! When is he going to call?

B: On Friday! Oh, this is stupid. Call me later when you've got a better line.

P: No! Don't go! What else did he say? Bob? Bob?

Recording 63

ROGER: Tell me, Mandy, why did you get engaged to Charles?

MANDY: Well, I fell in love with him . . . Er . . . he was very romantic . . . He made a lot of money in his job and we did lots of fun things . . .

R: Why did you get married?

M: I don't know . . . I had lots of boyfriends . . . but I wanted something more . . . And my best friend got married . . .

R: And, why did you get pregnant?

M: I love children . . . I wanted a little girl . . .

R: Why did you have an affair?

M: I was bored. We had money but, Charles was always working. We never had any fun together . . .

R: Why did you and Charles separate?

M: He was jealous . . . He was angry about the affair . . .

R: And, why did you get divorced?

M: Well, Charles fell in love with a woman in his company. He wanted to marry her . . .

Recording 65

1 COLLEAGUE: Oh, Jean! Could you just get the phone for me. I'm a bit busy here. Thanks.

JEAN: Smith and Son. Good morning. OK, I'll just put you through! It really irritates me when she does that. She never does any work. She just stands around telling stupid stories and chatting the assistant manager up!

BRIAN: Oh, I know what you mean. She gets on my nerves too.

2 WIFE: Oh, thanks. A drink. That's just what I need.

HUSBAND: Oh, me too. What a day. It was crazy at the office.

SON: Hello, Grandma!

GRANDMA: Hello, my darling!

H/W: Oh, no!

W: Your mother! She never rings before she comes. She makes me so angry.

H: I know.

G: Hi, kids.

H/W: Hello, Mum . . .

S: Look what Grandma bought me!

H: More chocolate!

G: Oh, it's nothing . . . and I know he loves his chocolate!

H: Yes, Mum.

G: I'll just go and make everybody a cup of tea. Come and talk to Grandma, Nikkie.

W: It drives me crazy when she does that. She knows we don't want Nick to have chocolate!

H: I know!

Recording 66

TERRY: Well . . . Helloooooo! We've got a wild audience, haven't we! I love ya! Welcome to my show. I'm Terry Stinger. Well thank you! We've got a good one for you tonight! Couples! Do you drive each other crazy? Are you heading for the divorce courts?! Are you miserable? Are you . . . "The Couple From Hell"?! Yes, folks. That's the subject of our show tonight, "Couples from Hell". But first, let me introduce you to our first very unhappy couple. From Chicago, please welcome, Eileen and Harold Dumpster!

Recording 68

1 WOMAN: I honestly don't know what I'd do if I didn't have one! I mean . . . we've got the five kids! Nigel's brother and his wife are always coming round to eat. And we have lots of dinner parties, you know, entertaining Nigel's business contacts. Nigel just breaks everything, so he's no help. And I hate washing-up all those dirty plates. This is so easy. I just pop them in, turn it on, and that's it!

2 MAN 1: Well, I've had it since I was ten. My uncle gave it to me. I took it all round Europe with me. It's opened a lot of bottles of wine I can tell you. Um, you can use it for anything. I even cut my hair with it the other day! I don't know what I'd do, if I didn't have it. It's like my best friend!

3 M2: I know they irritate some people but I don't know what I'd do if I didn't have mine! I mean, my life's so busy! I hardly see my family . . . but I keep in touch with them this way! I can phone them from the train, taxis, the supermarket! It's a lifesaver!

Recording 69

RICHARD: Did you get it?

SAM: No.

R: Oh! You didn't! Who got it?

S: This new guy, Duncan. He's only been there for six months. It's his first job in marketing and now he's Assistant Marketing Manager!

EMMA: You're joking? Why?

S: Don't ask me! It's this new manager, Sarah. I don't know why – but she just doesn't like me. She never says anything good about my work. When I asked for one day off to go to a friend's wedding she said it was "difficult". Then, when somebody else wanted two days off it was OK! It's ridiculous!

R: Have you thought about talking to her?

S: Yeah, but she always says she's busy.

R: Well, maybe she is busy. Does she ever have a drink with the people from the office? Why don't you ask her about it then?

S: No, she never goes for a drink with us.

E: Look! This is unfair. I think you should complain. If I were you, I'd go above her – to the boss.

S: Look, life is already difficult. If I did that, she'd make my life hell.

R: Yeah . . . I agree. I don't think you should go above her. It's too dangerous . . .

E: Yeah, but you've been there for a long time . . . and she isn't going to change. If I were you, I'd look for another job.

S: Well . . . jobs aren't easy to find at the moment . . .

Recording 71

RON: Good morning, Mrs White. I'm Ron, your new driving instructor.

MRS WHITE: Oh . . . er . . . Nice to meet you . . . . What happened to my old driving instructor?

R: Er . . . I'm afraid, Mr Grey had to go away. . . Anyway, er, could you show me your licence, please?

MW: Oh, right. Um . . . here it is . . . oh . . . no, it's not . . . Er . . . Ah . . . got it!

R: Thank you. That's fine. Now, let's get into the car. Right . . . now, start the car. Er . . . That's fine. But . . . er . . . could you turn the windscreen wipers off? It's not raining.

MW: Oh . . . sure . . . sorry. I'm a bit nervous.

R: Of course you are. I'm nervous too.

MW: Are you?

R: No, no, no, of course not. I'm only joking. Right . . . now . . . check your mirrors . . . and then pull out. Uh . . . Can you slow down Mrs White? Mrs White . . . slow down! No! Don't stop in the middle of the road! Just slow down!

MW: Please don't shout.

R: I'm sorry.

CYCLIST: Get off the road! You idiot!

MW: Oh yeah??!!

R: Mrs White! Don't worry about the cyclist, Mrs White. Now, start the car again and just drive straight along this road. OK . . . now could you turn left, please? Mrs White . . . I . . .

MW: You told me to turn right!

R: I told you to turn left! This is a one-way street! Now stop the car and reverse slowly! Now what?

MAN: Oi! That's my Mercedes you idiot!

R: Please, don't get so excited.

M: Excited?! Get out of the car.

MW: Oh . . . please, don't hit him!

POLICEMAN: 'Ello! 'Ello! Having some problems?

MW: Well, um . . . you see officer . . . he, er, he told me to . . .

P: Excuse me, madam. Could you wait in the car? I'd like to speak to your instructor for a moment. Now Mr . . . Hello? Hello? Oh dear, what's happened to him?

Recording 72

POLICEMAN: So . . . What happened?

MAN: Well, this idiot!

P: Just a moment, sir.

MRS WHITE: Well, it was horrible! Just horrible!

P: Yes, Mrs White. Just give me the details.

MW: Well, first he er . . .

P: Who?

MW: Mr Johnson . . . my driving instructor . . . I don't think he's had a lot of experience . . . Well, anyway . . . he asked me to show him my licence . . . so I did. Then he told me to start the car. Oh . . . he asked me to turn off the windscreen wipers. You see I was a bit nervous . . .

P: Yes, Mrs White . . . can you just give me the important details.

MW: Oh . . . of course. Er . . . Well . . . I checked my mirrors and pulled out . . . just like he told me. And then he told me to stop – right in the middle of the road! I don't know why! And then the cyclist hit us and he just started shouting.

P: Who started shouting?

MW: Mr Johnson! I asked him not to shout. I was really nervous!

P: I see . . .

MW: And the cyclist was shouting too! He told me to get off the road. Such a rude boy!

P: Yes, Mrs White . . . and then?

MW: Well, Mr Johnson told me not to worry about the cyclist. He was a bit calmer then. But then everything went wrong again . . . He asked me to turn right . . . but it was a one-way street! . . . And the man told Mr Johnson to get out of the car . . . and . . .

P: What man!?

MW: That man!

P: Oh . . .

MW: And I asked him not to hit Mr Johnson . . . and then . . . you came   and . . .

Recording 74

No Particular Place To Go

Ridin' along in my automobile
My baby beside me at the wheel.
I stole a kiss at the turn of a mile,
My curiosity runnin' wild
Cruisin' and playin' the radio,
With no particular place to go.

Ridin' along in my automobile
I'm anxious to tell her the way I feel,
So I told her softly and sincere,
And she leaned and whispered in my ear
Cuddlin' more and drivin' slow,
With no particular place to go.

No particular place to go,
So we parked way out on the Kokomo
The night was young and the moon was bold
So we both decided to take a stroll
Can you imagine the way I felt?
I couldn't unfasten her safety belt!

Ridin' along in my calaboose
Still tryin' to get her belt unloose
All the way home I held a grudge,
But the safety belt, it wouldn't budge
Cruisin' and playin' the radio
With no particular place to go.

Recording 75

MAN: At about five minutes to twelve, I went out into the garden – to look for my girlfriend, Lisa. I saw a man and a woman. I wasn't wearing my glasses so I couldn't see who they were at first. They were standing by the swimming pool. He was kissing her and she was laughing. I knew the laugh. It was Lisa. She was with Brad, my best friend – anyway, I thought he was my best friend. I don't know why, but I just ran up to them and pushed them both into the swimming pool. Lisa screamed and Brad swore.

Then I started to laugh. I don't know what happened to them after that. I left the party and went to a bar and got very drunk. I haven't seen them since – and I don't want to!

Recording 76

WOMAN: Oh, that was so special for me. My husband, Johnny, and I were at a party. Johnny was my boyfriend then. We didn't want to be with other people at midnight so we went out into the garden. It was a beautiful night. Everyone was enjoying themselves and so was I. I was standing in Johnny's arms and he was kissing me when a complete stranger ran up to us and pushed us both into the swimming pool! I screamed and Johnny swore. Then the man ran off and started laughing. I don't know who he was. I've never seen him since. Anyway, that night Johnny asked me to marry him and I said, "Yes". Johnny still thinks that man was pushing us together. Maybe he was some kind of angel of love.

Recording 80

ANN: Look at that idiot!
MAGGIE: Who? Where?
A: That guy over there . . . on the jet ski.
M: Oh, no. He's going to crash into that boat! No . . . it's OK . . . he's not.
A: Look at that huge wave behind them!
M: They're going to fall into the water! Oh, I can't look!
A: Well, that's it. I'm staying on the beach. It's safer . . .

Recording 81

1 MAGGIE: Oh, look! He's going to crash into the rocks.
2 MAGGIE: Look at that! He's going to drop her.
3 ANN: Oh! Look over there!
MAGGIE: Where?
ANN: There! That bull's going to attack her!
MAGGIE: Oh, my God. Hey!
4 ANN: Oh, no. Look at her.
MAGGIE: Poor woman. She's going to fall off.

Recording 82

RAY: Ann!
ANN: Oh . . . Ray . . . hi. How's it going?
R: Great! I've just been paragliding. It's brilliant! Have you tried it?
A: No, I haven't. But it sounds fun.
R: It is . . . It's great here! It's my first time at Club Torso and I love it. I've been jet skiing . . . water skiing. I've booked a dancing lesson for tomorrow morning . . . then, in the afternoon, I'm going horse-riding.

A: Are you?! You're active! Aren't you tired?
R: No, it's great! So, what about you? What have you done?
A: Well . . . not much, really. Er, I've done an aerobics class.
R: You can do aerobics anywhere . . . Have you been wind-surfing yet?
A: No, not yet. But I'm going tomorrow. I hope I like it.
R: Oh, you'll love it. It's good fun. I really enjoyed it. You fall off a lot, but it's all right it's only water. Oh, hi, Simon. How are you?
A: Simon. What's the matter? What happened?
SIMON: Well, I went jet skiing yesterday. I was having a great time when I suddenly saw this rock. I crashed into it and broke my arm.
A: Oh . . .

Recording 84

GUEST: Look . . . I was here about an hour ago about the light in my bathroom.
RECEPTIONIST: The light in your bathroom?
G: Yes, I spoke to you and you were going to see to it straightaway but it's been an hour!
R: Well, I'm afraid there's nothing I can do at the moment – our repair man's at lunch.
G: Well, when does he get back? This is ridiculous. Can I speak to the manager, please?
R: Look. We're very busy. We'll see to it as soon as possible. OK?
G: I'd like to speak to the manager.
MANAGER: Is there a problem?
G: Yes, the light in my bathroom doesn't work.
M: Oh, I am sorry, sir. I'll get someone to look at it straightaway.

Recording 85

1 MAN 1: Well, I was looking out of this window when I saw the burglar. He was climbing into the Smiths' house. They're away on holiday at the moment. He was wearing a black and white T-shirt. I think his jacket was black, too. Oh, yes . . . and he had a beard. He looked about thirty – thirty-five – he was very tall. Anyway I called the police straight away.
2 WOMAN 1: Well, I was on the Underground and the pickpocket was standing next to a tall man in a suit. He looked a bit suspicious. He was youngish too, maybe in his twenties? Er . . . he had short, black hair and um . . . a beard. He was wearing a jacket . . . it was a dark colour . . . Oh! And he had a scar on his . . . . right cheek. He was looking at the man's wallet – he was really quick – he just took it and got off at the next

station. That was when the man started shouting about his wallet. He was really angry.
3 M2: Yes, I first saw him when I was walking across the street. The car park's opposite the bank, you see. He was walking past the chemist's – going towards the bank. I noticed him because he was carrying a very large bag – and he was wearing gloves! He looked just like a bank robber! You know. He was about forty, short, overweight and he had long brown hair . . . in a pony tail! Can you believe it – at his age! Anyway . . . he was wearing jeans . . . a red T shirt . . . and orange trainers . . . awful!
4 W2: I saw him when I was standing at the bus stop. He was just standing in front of the jeweller's. A bit strange because it was 10 o'clock in the evening. He had something in his hand. He was quite tall and he had short, blonde hair. He was wearing a white T-shirt, black trousers and a black jacket . . . oh, yes . . . and he had a moustache. There was a big black bag I think. It was on the ground, next to him.

Recording 87

CHARLIE DIXON: Well, first I was arrested – I was with my girlfriend at the time. Then I was taken to the police station. In the police station I was questioned for about an hour, so was my girlfriend! Then I was charged with robbery – there were witnesses, you see. I was sent to court and tried. I was found guilty and then I was sentenced to five years. I was sent straight to Pentonville Prison. Finally after five years I was released. It wasn't that bad, I suppose. And maybe something good will come of it. I'm going to write a book about my life of crime and my prison experiences! My mum will be so proud of me, I just know it. But . . . I don't want to go back to prison. No, once was enough!

Recording 89

1 KIM: Roger . . . Roger . . . What do you think about this blue one?
ROGER: Very nice, Kim. Now can we go?
K: Yeah, but do you think it makes me look a bit fat?
R: No! It looks very nice.
K: It does, it makes me look fat. Oh, what am I going to wear?
R: Well, I thought the black one was nice and um . . .
K: What? The one which didn't fit? Anyway, it was too expensive . . .
R: Well, get the . . . er . . . white one. That was OK.

K: Do you mean the one that was in the window? It was all right. But, if I get the white one, I'll need a new pair of shoes.

R: Why?

K: Oh, you don't understand anything. Oh, those red ones look OK. Can you go and get them?

R: Which ones?

K: The red ones, over there, on that shelf. The ones that have really high heels. Go on. Please.

R: Kim! These?

K: Yeah, yeah. Are they size 6?

R: Yes. Now, can we go?

K: Oh, I don't know if I like them.

2 WOMAN: Nice dress, Kim.

KIM: Oh . . . I bought it this afternoon. I went with Roger. It was a nightmare. He hates shopping.

W: Where is Roger?

K: Oh, he hates parties. I'm here on my own. Anyway, who's that man in the armchair? He looks interesting. He looks like a journalist or a writer. Do you know him?

W: No, but I think he's a friend of my husband's.

K: Oh, right.

W: See that woman over there?

K: Which one?

W: The one with black hair.

K: Do you mean the one that's talking to Edward? Poor thing . . .

W: No, the other one. The one in the red dress.

K: Yeah . . .

W: Well, she's the one who's having an affair with the new Marketing Manager.

K: What? Isn't he married?

W: Yeah. That's his wife. The one who's dancing.

K: Sshh. She's coming over.

Recording 91

CLARE: She looks nice.

EDWARD: Hmm . . . that's my ex-wife. Yeah, I thought she looked nice when I first met her, but, well she never really understood me.

C: Oh, I see. She looks like a fashion model. You know, she looks glamorous and sophisticated.

E: She's certainly glamorous. Actually she's a TV producer.

C: And who's this other woman?

E: She's my sister.

C: Oh, right . . . and is this your daughter?

E: Yes, that's Camilla.

C: She's lovely and she looks very sweet.

E: Oh, she is. She's a lovely girl.

C: She looks a bit like her mother.

E: Yeah, maybe but she's not like her at all. She's very sweet . . . kind . . .

generous. My mother says she's more like me. We're very close. My other daughter, Priscilla, is more like her mother. She's very ambitious, a bit hard. We don't really get on.

C: Do you have any other children?

E: Yes, Robert – my youngest child. This is him with his friend Henry.

C: Ah . . . they look like angels. Is this one Robert?

F: Yes, how did you know?

C: Well . . . he looks like you. He looks very sensitive and intelligent. Is he?

E: Well, actually he is . . .

Recording 94

HELGA: Would you like some wine?

MIKE: Yeah, that sounds nice.

H: Can you pass that, er, thing? The thing that you use to open the bottle.

M: Oh . . . the corkscrew.

H: Yeah . . . How do you say it?

M: Corkscrew.

H: Corkscrew . . . hmm . . . Now . . . have some of my special ice cream.

M: Thank you. Hmm . . . This is interesting.

H: Really? Good! I put in the stuff that makes it hot.

M: What? Pepper?

H: No, um, it's different. It looks like pepper, but it's red.

M: Chilli powder?

H: Ah . . . chilli . . . yes! I call it "Spicy ice cream".

M: Oh, lovely. Er, could I have a glass of water, please?

H: Yes, is it too hot?

M: Oh no, no it's lovely, really . . .

Recording 95

LAURA: How was the trip to Paris?

CHARLES: I don't want to talk about the trip there. It was a nightmare. I was with the strangest people – the journey back to London was fine. Oh, guess what? I met this man on the train who knows you.

L: Did you? Who was it?

C: Um . . . just a second. I've got his card somewhere. Where is it? Well, anyway . . . he knows you. He asked about you.

L: What do you mean?

C: Well, you know, we started talking about work and I said I was in advertising. He asked me where I worked and when I told him, he asked me if I knew you.

L: Hmm . . . so, does he work in advertising?

C: No, he said he worked in publishing and that was why he was coming to London. He said he was going to a conference.

L: Hmm . . . I can't think who it is. Did he say anything else?

C: He asked if you still lived in North London.

L: Oh, I . . .

C: Ah . . . here's his card, er . . . Joe Evans.

L: Oh, Joe Evans. What a coincidence. My brother and I were just talking about him last night. They used to go to college together. The three of us used to go out a lot. He's really nice. I haven't seen him for ages. So what else did he say?

C: Well, he said he was married . . .

Recording 97

JUDITH: Who's that?

ANN: Which one?

J: The guy with the moustache. The one with dark hair . . .

A: That's Alex. Alex is the one who rescued me when I went wind-surfing.

J: Oh, and this one? The woman with blonde hair? She looks like a fashion model.

A: Oh, that's Debbie. She's the one who fell in love with Martin, the waiter.

J: So, which one's Martin?

A: The one with the pony tail and the sun tan.

J: He's looks nice.

A: Yeah. He's the one who brought us breakfast in bed every morning.

J: Oh, very nice . . . and who's this the one with the scar?

A: Show me . . . oh . . . that's Damian and the one holding the drink is Sheila. They're the ones who got married on the beach.

Recording 98

HELEN: The other day I met Carlo, an Italian who lives and works in London. I asked him where he was from and he said he was from Salerno. I asked him what he thought about London and he said he thought it was OK, but he didn't like the food. I asked him if he missed Italy and he said he didn't. The only things he missed were the weather and his mum's cooking. He told me his mum was a great cook and she was coming to London. He wanted to take her to some restaurants but he didn't know where to go. He said the food in London looked nice, but it didn't have any taste.

Unit 14, Exercise 1b), page 84

ALL STUDENTS

a) These are the nineteen things Sheila has stolen. Look at the picture for one minute. How many things can you remember?

b) When you finish, go back to Exercise 1c), page 84.

Unit 8, Exercise 1b), page 48

ALL STUDENTS

Check your partner's answers and fill in his / her score.

Are you an optimist or a pessimist?

	3 points	2 points	1 point
1	b	c	a
2	a	c	b
3	c	a	b
4	a	—	b
5	b	a	c
6	a	c	b
7	a	c	b
8	a	c	b
9	a	b	c
10	b	c	a

My partner's score: ☐

24–30 You're an optimist. You see the best in people and in life. When things go wrong you don't worry. You feel lucky most of the time and you usually look on the bright side of life!

9–23 You're realistic about life. You know that sometimes good things happen and sometimes bad things happen. You worry sometimes – but not a lot because your philosophy is "That's life!". You think that if something bad happens today, something good will probably happen next week.

1–8 You probably think you're a realist – and maybe you are. You usually think the worst will happen and life can be quite difficult for you sometimes. Try and see the positive side of a situation as well as the negative. The next time you want to jump off a very tall building, remember – every cloud has a silver lining!

Unit 1 Day to day English, Exercise 6, page 11

STUDENTS A, B AND C

In groups of three. Look at the pictures (1–3). What are the people saying? Take it in turns to be the boss, the temp and the helpful colleague. Act out your conversations.

1

Student A is the temp, Student B is the boss, Student C is the helpful colleague.

2

Student A is the boss, Student B is the helpful colleague, Student C is the temp.

3

Student A is the helpful colleague, Student B is the temp, Student C is the boss.

Unit 13, Exercise 7a), page 81

STUDENT A

You're the water skier. You had this accident on Wednesday.

Unit 5, Exercise 7b), page 33

STUDENT A

a) You're at a very strict health club. Write five sentences about the trainers in the club. Use *make / don't make* and *let / don't let*.

b) Read your sentences to the group. They have to guess who you're talking about.

Unit 6 Day to day English, Exercise 4, page 41

STUDENT A

a) You begin. Ask Student B for directions to a supermarket, a bookshop and a café. Label these places on your map.

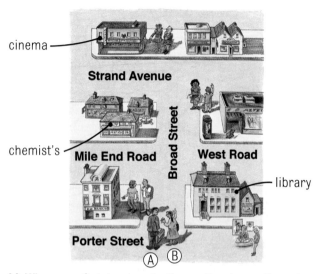

b) When you finish, change these direct questions to indirect questions. Ask Student B your questions and make notes on his / her answers.

1 (supermarket) When does it close?
2 (bookshop) Do they sell maps?
3 (café) Is it very expensive?

c) Give Student B directions to the three places on your map. Use the information below to answer his / her questions about the places.

1 The library opens at 9 a.m. but it's closed on Sundays.
2 They sell vitamins at the chemist's.
3 Tickets are £10 at the cinema.

Unit 13, Exercise 7a), page 81

STUDENT D

You're one of the dancers. You had this accident on Tuesday.

Unit 4 *Do you remember?* 1–4, Exercise 3c), page 28

ACTORS / ACTRESSES

a) You really need a job because you're broke. A small film company is planning to make a new action film. They're looking for experienced actors / actresses. In groups. Talk about the work you've done. Use the questions to help you.

1 What films have you been in? What parts did you play? What stunts did you do?
2 What directors have you worked with?
3 What other work have you done? TV (including adverts)? modelling? pop videos?

b) In groups of four. Two directors interview two actors / actresses and make notes.

c) In groups of actors / actresses. Talk about the interviews. Compare the directors and their films. Who would you like to work with and why?

Unit 7, Exercise 7a), page 45

BLACKMAILERS

a) You know something about a well-known, successful politician. This will end his / her career if people find out about it. You want to use this information to get things for yourself or for your town. Talk about these questions.

1 What do you know about the politician?
2 What evidence do you have? (e.g. a video, a photograph, a taped conversation)
3 What do you want the politician to do for you / your town?
4 What will you do with your evidence if the politician won't give you what you want?

b) When you finish, go back to Exercise 7b), page 45.

Unit 9 Conversations, Exercise 5, page 59

STUDENT B

a) Read your conversation and fill in the gaps with places, people, times and things that happened.

B: Guess what! I'm going to .... !

A: ?

B: I'm leaving next ....

A: ?

B: And .... is going with me.

A: ?

B: .... isn't / aren't happy about it.

A: ?

B: We've got lots of money to take with us because I ....

A: ?

b) Student A will phone you. You can't hear some things, so you have to ask Student A questions to make him / her repeat the information you missed.

Example: <u>Where</u> did you go?

c) When you finish, phone Student A to tell him / her your story. When you come to the information in the gaps speak very quickly or quietly, so Student A can't understand what you're saying. Student A has to ask questions to make you repeat the information he / she missed.

Unit 10, Exercise 7b), page 63

ALL STUDENTS

Check your ideas.

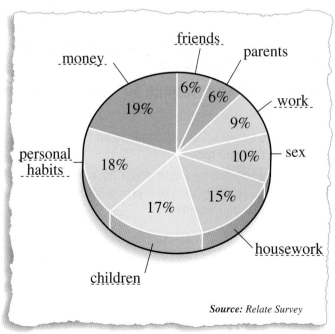

Source: Relate Survey

Unit 8 *Do you remember?* 5–8, Exercise 2a), page 52

GROUP A

a) You're a very kind person. You always help people and you love animals. What are you going to do with the money? Fill in the table.

Plans	Possible ideas (*Maybe / Perhaps I'll . . .*)	Future arrangements
I'm going to buy a farm so I can give a home to lost animals.	Maybe I'll take all of you on holiday with my family.	I'm taking all my family on holiday to Hawaii.
1	1	1 ....
2	2	2 ....

b) When you finish, go back to Exercise 2b), page 52.

Unit 10, Exercise 8b), page 63

CHAT SHOW HOSTS

a) You're going to interview the couples on your show. You have to find out as much as you can about their relationship – from the beginning to now. Use these questions to help you.

1 How did they feel about each other in the beginning?
2 Why did they get married?
3 What problems do they have and when did the problems start? On their honeymoon? After a few years?
4 Why do they drive each other crazy – or make each other unhappy? Have they had affairs? Do they have irritating habits?
5 What do they have rows about?

• Before the interview prepare ten questions to ask the couples.

Examples: How long have you been together?
How did you first meet?
What did you think of him / her at first?

• In the interview introduce the show and your couple.

Example: Hello, welcome to my show. Tonight I'm interviewing John and Mary.

• Remember to finish off at the end.

Example: Well, thank you for coming. I hope things get better.

b) When you finish, go back to Exercise 8c), page 63.

Unit 5, Exercise 7b), page 33

STUDENT B

a) You go to a very relaxed school. Write five sentences about the teachers. Use *make / don't make* and *let / don't let*.

b) Read your sentences to the group. They have to guess who you're talking about.

Unit 6, Exercise 7, page 39

STUDENT C

Read about your holiday. Then write questions for the table below. In groups of four, take it in turns to ask and answer questions about your holidays and fill in the table. Whose holiday sounds the most exciting?

You've won a two-week holiday in Tahiti and you have a ticket for Thursday. You really want to relax and get a nice suntan. You love good food and good conversation and you've always wanted to learn to water ski.

	Where?	When?	How long?	What are you going to do? (possible ideas / definite plans)
A				
B				
C				
D				

Unit 8 *Do you remember?* 5–8, Exercise 2a), page 52

GROUP B

a) You're a very adventurous person. You love exciting, dangerous sports and travel. What are you going to do with the money? Fill in the table.

Plans	Possible ideas (*Maybe / Perhaps I'll . . .*)	Future arrangements
I'm going to organise an expedition to the North Pole.	Maybe I'll buy a hot-air balloon and fly round the world.	I'm flying to Timbuktu next month.
1	1	1 ....
2	2	2 ....

b) When you finish, go back to Exercise 2b), page 52.

Unit 7, Exercise 7a), page 45

POLITICIANS

a) You are a well-known, successful politician but you have some dark secrets too. A blackmailer knows something about you. This will end your career if people find out about it. What are you going to do? Talk about these questions.

1 What do you think the blackmailer knows about you?
2 What evidence do you think he / she has? (e.g. a video, a photograph, a taped conversation)
3 What will you offer the blackmailer to get the evidence?
4 What will you do if the blackmailer isn't happy with your offer?

b) When you finish, go back to Exercise 7b), page 45.

Unit 8, Exercise 4a), page 50

GROUP A

a) Read this information and think about the good and bad things that will happen.

You're going to work as a tour guide for a coach tour company. You're going to take a group of foreign tourists round your country.

b) When you finish, go back to Exercise 4b), page 50.

Unit 15, Exercise 4, page 92

STUDENT A

a) You begin. Ask Student B about:

1 the man who was sitting on the sofa.
2 the woman who was dancing.
3 the man who was singing.
4 the cat that was sleeping on the sofa.

Example. A. Where's the man who was sitting on the sofa? What's he doing?
B: The man who was sitting on the sofa is . . .

b) When you finish, look at your picture and answer Student B's questions.

Unit 5 Conversations, Exercise 4b), page 35

TEAM B

a) Work together and fill in the gaps in these sentences. Then write an echo question and an extra sentence or question for each of the sentences (1–10).

Example: A: I went to Paris at the weekend.
B: Did you? Can you speak French?

1 My uncle has a house near ....
2 I've climbed Mount Everest .... times.
3 .... has just married a millionaire.
4 .... have coffee and a cigarette for breakfast every day.
5 .... is a spy.
6 I had a terrible dream about .... last night.
7 My sister is doing .... at the moment.
8 I was in the film ....
9 I went to ....'s wedding last week.
10 I play the .... in a band.

b) Play the echo game. Team A begins.

Unit 14, Exercise 4b), page 86

STUDENT B

a) A tourist was walking along the High Street taking photographs when the mugging happened. Look at the picture of the mugging. What really happened? Did Reginald Kramer commit the crime? Answer the questions.

1 What was the witness, Josie Robinson, doing when she saw the crime?
2 What was the man holding?
3 What was the old woman holding?
4 What was the man wearing?
5 What did the man look like?
6 What did the old woman do when the man tried to take her handbag?

b) Now listen to Student A's newspaper article. The article has ten mistakes in it because Josie Robinson wasn't a very good witness. Why do you think she wasn't a very good witness? In pairs. Ask and answer questions to find the ten differences (2–10) between the article and the picture.

Example: In the article	In the picture
1 Josie was going into a café.	No, she wasn't. She was coming out of a pub.

135

Unit 8 *Do you remember?* 5–8, Exercise 2a), page 52

GROUP C

a) You're a very selfish person. What are you going to do with the money? Fill in the table.

Plans	Possible ideas (*Maybe / Perhaps I'll . . .*)	Future arrangements
I'm not going to buy anything for my friends / family.	Maybe I won't give any money to charity.	I'm flying to Bali on holiday next month. My wife / husband doesn't like the sun but I don't care. I'm leaving him / her at home.
1	1	1 ....
2	2	2 ....

b) When you finish, go back to Exercise 2b), page 52.

Unit 14, Exercise 9a), page 87

STUDENT B

a) Your house has been burgled. You're at the police station and a police officer is going to interview you. Look at the Crime Report that the police officer will fill in about you. Plan what you will say.

CRIME REPORT

Victim's name: ....
Crime: ....
Time: ....
Place: ....
Details of crime (what exactly happened): ....
....
....
What has been stolen: ....
....
....
Description of criminals: ....
....
....

b) Student A is the police officer. Answer his / her questions.

c) Now you're the police officer. Ask Student A questions and fill in the Crime Report.

d) When you finish, go back to Exercise 9b), page 87.

Unit 9 Conversations, Exercise 3, page 59

STUDENT B

a) Have a conversation like the one in Exercise 1c). Student A is the receptionist at Mann Interior Design. You are a caller. Student A begins.

Conversation 1

B: Ask to speak to Jason Lombard.

B: Give your name (Sam Collins) and your company's name (Planet Earth Furniture).

B: Leave your message: the sofa and chairs that he ordered in Valentine Red have arrived. You want him to phone you.

B: Give your phone number – 013962 765976.

B: Say thank you and goodbye.

b) Now change roles and have a new conversation. This time you are the receptionist and take the message. Student A is a caller. You begin.

Conversation 2

B: Answer the phone. Say the name of the company.

B: Ask who's calling.

B: Ask the caller to hold the line while you check. Tell the caller that Jason Lombard is out of the office and offer to take a message.

B: Write the message. Ask for the caller's phone number.

B: Say you will give Jason Lombard the message.

B: Say goodbye.

mann interior **design**

Message for: Jason Lombard ....
Caller's name: ....
Company: ....
Phone number: ....
Message: ....
....
....
....
....

Unit 6, Exercise 7, page 39

STUDENT B

Read about your holiday. Then write questions for the table below. In groups of four, take it in turns to ask and answer questions about your holidays and fill in the table. Whose holiday sounds the most exciting?

You and your partner have won a four-day shopping and sightseeing holiday at a luxury hotel in London. It's near the museums, shops and theatres and that's what you want. Your partner loves English pubs and food. You leave on Wednesday.

	Where?	When?	How long?	What are you going to do? (possible ideas / definite plans)
A				
B				
C				
D				

Unit 15, Exercise 4, page 92

STUDENT B

a) Look at your picture and answer Student A's questions.

b) When you finish, ask Student A about:

1 the woman who was sitting in front of the picture.
2 the man who was playing the piano.
3 the cat that was sitting on the piano.
4 the man who was wearing glasses.

Example: A: Where's the woman who was talking about the picture? What's she doing?

B: The woman who was talking about the picture is . . .

Unit 5, Exercise 7b), page 33

STUDENT C

a) You're a dog and you love your owners. They're very easy-going and relaxed. Write five sentences about your owners. Use *make / don't make* and *let / don't let*.

b) Read your sentences to the group. They have to guess who you're talking about.

Unit 8, Exercise 4a), page 50

GROUP C

a) Read this information and think about the good and bad things that will happen.

You're going to take part in a scientific experiment where you and six other people that you don't know, have to live the "natural life" in the mountains for two months. You won't have any electricity or modern conveniences.

b) When you finish, go back to Exercise 4b), page 50.

Unit 5 Conversations, Exercise 4b), page 35

TEAM A

a) Work together and fill in the gaps in these sentences. Then write an echo question and an extra sentence or question for each of the sentences (1–10).

Example: A: I went to Paris at the weekend.
B: Did you? Can you speak French?

1 I practise speaking English for .... hours every evening.
2 I've met a famous ....
3 .... has bought a motorbike.
4 My brother is a ....
5 .... is studying French cookery.
6 My aunt gave me .... for my last birthday.
7 .... owns a five-star hotel on the French Riviera.
8 I have two pets – a dog and a ....
9 I was afraid of .... when I was a child.
10 We went to .... last summer.

b) Play the echo game. Your team begins.

Unit 9 Conversations, Exercise 3, page 59

STUDENT A

a) Have a conversation like the one in Exercise 1c). You are the receptionist at Mann Interior Design and take the message. Student B is a caller. You begin.

Conversation 1

A: Answer the phone. Say the name of the company.

A: Ask who's calling.

A: Ask the caller to hold the line while you check. Tell the caller Jason Lombard is out of the office and offer to take a message.

A: Write the message. Ask for the caller's phone number.

A: Say you will give Jason Lombard the message.

A: Say goodbye.

mann interior **design**

Message for: Jason Lombard ....

Caller's name: ....

Company: ....

Phone number: ....

Message: ....

....

....

....

....

....

b) Now change roles and have a new conversation. This time Student B is the receptionist and you are a caller. Student B begins.

Conversation 2

A: Ask to speak to Jason Lombard.

A: Give your name (Helen Murray) and your company's name (House of Colours).

A: Leave your message: you have the paint he wanted, ten litres of paint in Poodle Pink. You want him to phone you.

A: Give your phone number – 0081 336 6681.

A: Say thank you and goodbye.

Unit 8, Exercise 4a), page 50

GROUP B

a) Read this information and think about the good and bad things that will happen.

You want to be an artist. (Decide what type of artist. A painter? A sculptor?) You're going to give up your job / studies and move to Paris.

b) When you finish, go back to Exercise 4b), page 50.

Unit 6, Exercise 7, page 39

STUDENT A

Read about your holiday. Then write questions for the table below. In groups of four, take it in turns to ask and answer questions about your holidays and fill in the table. Whose holiday sounds the most exciting?

You've won a two-week holiday for two in Kenya. Your flight is on Saturday. You can spend part of your holiday on safari and part of the holiday on the beach. You're very tired at the moment so you don't want to do too much. Your friend is coming with you and he loves sunbathing and diving.

	Where?	When?	How long?	What are you going to do? (possible ideas / definite plans)
A				
B				
C				
D				

Unit 9 Conversations, Exercise 5, page 59

STUDENT A

a) Read your conversation and fill in the gaps with places, people, times and things that happened.

A: I went to .... last night.

B: ?

A: I saw .... there. He / She looked great!

B: ?

A: I did a really stupid thing. I ....

B: ?

A: And then he / she .... I was so surprised!

B: ?

A: Then we ....

B: ?

A: I didn't get home until .... o'clock.

B: ?

b) Phone Student B to tell him / her your story. When you come to the information in the gaps speak very quickly or quietly, so Student B can't understand what you're saying. Student B has to ask questions to make you repeat the information he / she missed.

c) When you finish, Student B will phone you. You can't hear some things, so you have to ask Student B questions to make him / her repeat the information you missed.

Example: Where are you going?

Unit 13, Exercise 7a), page 81

STUDENT B

You had this accident on Sunday – the first day of your holiday!

Unit 10, Exercise 8b), page 63

COUPLES FROM HELL

a) The show's host is going to interview you about your relationship. You've had a lot of problems and you want a divorce! Prepare your "story" (the details of your relationship from the beginning to now). Use these questions to help you. Make your story as interesting as possible.

1 How long have you been together?
2 How / Where did you meet?
3 What did you think of him / her at first?
4 Why did you get married?
5 When did your problems start? On your honeymoon? After a few years?
6 Why did you go off him / her?
7 Has your husband / wife changed? What did he / she used to be like?
8 What do you have rows about? Money / children friends / irritating habits / housework?
9 Has your husband / wife ever had an affair? What happened?
10 Why do you want a divorce?

b) When you finish, go back to Exercise 8c), page 63.

Unit 12, Exercise 3c), page 72

ALL STUDENTS

Did you choose the right description?

a = Libra (24th September – 22nd October)
b = Taurus (22nd April – 22nd May)
c = Aries (22nd March – 21st April)
d = Leo (24th July – 23rd August)
e = Cancer (23rd June – 23rd July)
f = Scorpio (23rd October – 22nd November)
g = Pisces (21st February – 21st March)
h = Gemini (23rd May – 22nd June)
i = Sagittarius (23rd November – 22nd December)
j = Virgo (24th August – 23rd September)
k = Capricorn (23rd December – 20th January)
l = Aquarius (21st January – 20th February)

Unit 14, Exercise 4b), page 86

STUDENT A

a) Did Reginald Kramer commit the crime? Read the newspaper article and answer the questions.

Josie Robinson, a witness, told our reporters about the crime. "I was going into a café when I saw it. A young man was holding a knife and pointing it at an old woman. She was holding a walking stick in one hand and her handbag in the other. She looked very frightened. He was wearing a black leather jacket and jeans. He was blonde, clean shaven and he had a scar on his left cheek. He told the woman not to scream. Then he told her to give him her handbag. She gave it to him, of course. She was terrified."

1 What was Josie doing when she saw the crime?
2 What was the man holding?
3 What was the old woman holding?
4 What was the man wearing?
5 What did he look like?
6 What did the old woman do when the man tried to take her handbag?

b) Now read the article to Student B. The article has ten mistakes in it because Josie Robinson wasn't a very good witness. Why do you think she wasn't a very good witness? In pairs. Ask and answer questions to find the differences (2–10) between the article and the picture.

Example: In the article	In the picture
1 Josie was going into a café.	No, she wasn't. She was coming out of a pub.

Unit 6 Day to day English, Exercise 4, page 41

STUDENT B

a) Give Student A directions to the three places on your map. Use the information below to answer his / her questions about the places.

1 The supermarket closes at 8 p.m. in the week and 10 p.m. at the weekend.
2 They don't sell maps in the book shop.
3 The café isn't very expensive.

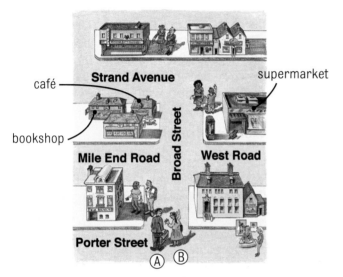

b) Ask Student A for directions to a library, a chemist's and a cinema. Label these places on your map.

c) When you finish, change these direct questions to indirect questions. Ask Student A your questions and make notes on his / her answers.

1 (library) When does it open?
2 (chemist's) Do they sell vitamins?
3 (cinema) How much does it cost?

Unit 13, Exercise 7a), page 81

STUDENT C

You're the horse-rider. You had this accident on Monday.

Unit 6, Exercise 7, page 39

STUDENT D

Read about your holiday. Then write questions for the table below. In groups of four, take it in turns to ask and answer questions about your holidays and fill in the table. Whose holiday sounds the most exciting?

You love clothes and you've won a one-week trip to Paris. Your flight is on Tuesday. You've never been to Paris before so you want to see as much as you can – the Eiffel Tower, museums, art galleries – and you want to buy some clothes too.

	Where?	When?	How long?	What are you going to do? (possible ideas / definite plans)
A				
B				
C				
D				

Unit 14, Exercise 9a), page 87

STUDENT A

a) Your car has been stolen. You're at the police station and a police officer is going to interview you. Look at the Crime Report that the police officer will fill in about you. Plan what you will say.

CRIME REPORT

Victim's name: ....
Crime: ....
Time: ....
Place: ....
Details of crime (what exactly happened): ....
....
....
What has been stolen: ....
....
....
Description of criminals: ....
....
....

b) Now you're the police officer. Ask Student B questions and fill in the Crime Report.

c) Student B is the police officer. Answer his / her questions.

d) When you finish, go back to Exercise 9b), page 87.

Unit 5, Exercise 7b), page 33

STUDENT D

a) You're a teenager. Your parents are very strict. They're driving you crazy! Write five sentences about your parents. Use *make / don't make* and *let / don't let.*

b) Read your sentences to the group. They have to guess who you're talking about.

Unit 10 Skills, Exercise 1b), page 64

ALL STUDENTS

Check your answers.

William Shakespeare (pronounced /ˈʃeɪkspɪə/) is England's most famous playwright and poet. He was born in Stratford-upon-Avon in 1564. In 1582 he married Anne Hathaway and they had three children. What happened in Shakespeare's early life is still a mystery. In 1590 he was writing and acting in plays in London. He wrote more than thirty plays between 1590 and 1613. These include *Romeo and Juliet, Othello, King Lear, Macbeth* and *Hamlet. Hamlet* is the longest play and contains the famous line "To be, or not to be – that is the question". In 1613 Shakespeare retired and returned to his family in Stratford-upon-Avon. He died in 1616.

Unit 8 *Do you remember?* 5–8, Exercise 2a), page 52

GROUP D

a) You're a very boring person. What are you going to do with the money? Fill in the table.

Plans	Possible ideas (*Maybe / Perhaps I'll . . .*)	Future arrangements
I'm not going to leave my job at Hamburger Palace because the people are so nice.	Maybe I'll buy a new English Language dictionary.	I've bought a new tent and I'm going camping. I'm leaving on Saturday.
1	1	1 ....
2	2	2 ....

b) When you finish, go back to Exercise 2b), page 52.

Unit 4 *Do you remember?* 1–4, Exercise 3c), page 28

DIRECTORS

a) A film company is planning to make a new action film. They are a small company so they can't afford big Hollywood stars. They've asked you to think of ideas for the film and to interview actors and actresses who can do stunt work. Prepare eight questions to ask the actors / actresses.

Think about these things:

1 What is your film about? Where does it happen?
2 What stunt work do you want the actors / actresses to do?
3 What experience have the actors / actresses had in film, TV (including adverts), stunt work, etc? What directors have they worked with?

b) In groups of four. Two directors interview two actors / actresses and make notes.

c) In groups of directors. Talk about the interviews. Compare the actors / actresses. Choose two for your film. Then tell the class who you've chosen and why.

Key to Grammar and vocabulary puzzles

Puzzle 1 (Units 1–4)

ACROSS

2 divorced
6 suburban
8 fiction
10 are
12 were
13 you
14 did not
16 technology
17 ever

DOWN

1 used
2 did
3 vegetarian
4 hardly
5 salary
7 birthday
9 need
11 hasn't
15 the

Puzzle 2 (Units 5–8)

ACROSS

3 whereabouts
7 invite
8 will
11 after
13 efficient
17 promotion
20 all
21 single
22 Prime
23 have to
24 did
25 son

DOWN

1 fit
2 it's
4 relationship
5 be
6 seen
9 let
10 if
12 reputation
14 complain
15 do
16 success
18 might
19 toe
21 stay

Puzzle 3 (Units 9–12)

ACROSS

1 be
3 the wrong number
7 near
8 traditional
10 was playing
15 for
17 won
20 driving instructor
21 were

DOWN

2 ever
3 turn
4 were speaking
5 get
6 man
9 cupboard
10 would
11 am
12 new
13 honeymoon
14 invention
16 told
18 since
19 clock

Puzzle 4 (Units 13–16)

ACROSS

5 mystery
7 abroad
9 be
10 by
11 emergency
13 bad
14 not to
15 ID
17 air conditioning
18 dad

DOWN

1 noticeboard
2 was murdered
3 broke into
4 cab
5 mugger
6 try
8 dear
10 back
12 going to
16 so

Irregular verb list and Guide to pronunciation

Verb	Past Simple	Past Participle	Verb	Past Simple	Past Participle
be	was / were	been	sink	sank	sunk
become	became	become	sit	sat	sat
begin	began	begun	sleep	slept	slept
bite	bit	bitten	speak	spoke	spoken
blow	blew	blown	spell	spelt / spelled	spelt / spelled
break	broke	broken	spend	spent	spent
bring	brought	brought	split	split	split
burn	burned / burnt	burned / burnt	stand	stood	stood
buy	bought	bought	steal	stole	stolen
catch	caught	caught	stick	stuck	stuck
choose	chose	chosen	swear	swore	sworn
come	came	come	swim	swam	swum
cost	cost	cost	take	took	taken
cut	cut	cut	teach	taught	taught
do	did	done	tell	told	told
dream	dreamed / dreamt	dreamed / dreamt	think	thought	thought
drink	drank	drunk	throw	threw	thrown
drive	drove	driven	understand	understood	understood
eat	ate	eaten	wear	wore	worn
fall	fell	fallen	win	won	won
feel	felt	felt	write	wrote	written
fight	fought	fought			
find	found	found			
fly	flew	flown			
forget	forgot	forgotten			
forgive	forgave	forgiven			
get	got	got			
give	gave	given			
go	went	gone / been			
grow	grew	grown			
have	had	had			
hear	heard	heard			
hit	hit	hit			
hold	held	held			
keep	kept	kept			
know	knew	known			
learn	learned / learnt	learned / learnt			
leave	left	left			
lend	lent	lent			
let	let	let			
lose	lost	lost			
make	made	made			
mean	meant	meant			
meet	met	met			
pay	paid	paid			
put	put	put			
read	read	read			
ride	rode	ridden			
ring	rang	rung			
run	ran	run			
say	said	said			
see	saw	seen			
sell	sold	sold			
send	sent	sent			
show	showed	shown / showed			
shut	shut	shut			
sing	sang	sung			

Guide to pronunciation

Vowels

/ə/	again, doctor, finally, seven
/æ/	cat, glad
/ʌ/	mum, run
/ɑː/	half, arm
/e/	red, any
/ɪ/	miss, ill
/iː/	seat, see
/ɒ/	boss, on
/ɔː/	forty, awful
/ɜː/	bird, early
/ʊ/	put, good
/uː/	food, true
/ɪə/	beer, year
/ʊə/	cure, tourist
/eə/	hair, care
/eɪ/	plane, play
/ɔɪ/	join, boy
/aɪ/	wife, eye
/əʊ/	go, boat
/aʊ/	out, town

Consonants

/p/	pop, shop
/b/	bike, job
/f/	five, cough
/v/	video, wave
/t/	time, sit
/d/	dad, read
/θ/	thing, healthy
/ð/	then, weather
/tʃ/	church, question
/dʒ/	jar, agent
/s/	soft, rice
/z/	magazine, noise
/ʃ/	shut, ambition
/ʒ/	television, pleasure
/k/	coast, black
/g/	girl, bag
/m/	make, home
/n/	name, fun
/ŋ/	sing, long
/h/	hot, who
/l/	live, level
/r/	rock, married
/w/	wet, away
/j/	yellow, use

Pearson Education Limited,
Edinburgh Gate
Harlow
Essex CM20 2JE
England
and Associated Companies throughout the World.

www.longman-elt.com

First published 2000
Fourth impression 2001

Set in 11.5/13pt Bulldog

Printed in Spain by Graficas Estella

ISBN 0 582 30546 2

Illustrated by: Matt Buckley, Phil Healey, Jelly (Folio), Kevin Jones
Associates, Tim Kahane, Peter Richardson, Mark Shattock (The Art
Market), Kim Smith (Eastwing), Kath Walker.

Cover illustration by Tim Kahane.

Acknowledgements

The authors and publishers would like to thank the following teachers
for piloting and / or reporting on the manuscript:

In **Argentina**, Patricia Nélida López (Academia Cultural Inglesa Villa
Devoto, Buenos Aires); in **Brazil**, Márcia Araújo Pinto (Cultura Inglesa,
Belo Horizonte), Stephanie Bradley (Cultura Inglesa, Maceió), Adriana
da Cruz Romanini (Cultura Inglesa, São Carlos), Lara Danon (Cultura
Inglesa, Jundiaí), Sérgio Gabriel (Cultura Inglesa, São Paulo), Katia
Lomar (Cultura Inglesa, Rio de Janeiro), Elisabete de Lemos Fulco
Cosato (Cultura Inglesa, Rio de Janeiro), Elvira Nunes (Cultura Inglesa,
Rio de Janeiro), Marilisa Shimazumi (Cultura Inglesa, São Paulo), Anna
Szabó (Cultura Inglesa, São Carlos); in **Colombia**, Josephine Taylor
(Universidad de los Andes, Bogotá); in the **Czech Republic**, Jiřina
Babáková (VOŠE a OA Mladá Boleslav); in **Hungary**, Valéria Arva (Eötvös
Loránd University, Budapest); in **Italy**, Fiona Campbell (Teach-in, Rome),
Monica Martino (Upter - Universitá Popolare di Roma), Giuseppe
Ruggieri (International House, Rome), Sophie Salaman (Centro
Linguistico dell Ateneo, University of Siena); in **Poland**, Ludmiła Hano-
Nawrot (Politechnika Śląska, Gliwice), Anna Hilgier (Polish Foundation
for Science Advancement, Warsaw), Elizabeth Laws (International
House, Łódź), Zofia Lebiedzka (Politechnika Śląska, Gliwice), Joanna
Leszkiewicz (Wrocław University of Technology), Magda Markiewicz
(International House, Kraków), Chris Rich (International House, Łódź),
Krystyna Wrońska-Sawin (Polish Foundation for Science Advancement,
Warsaw); in **Slovakia** Paul Stocks, Mark Walker (British Council,
Bratislava); in **Spain**, Fernando Alba Navarro (Escuela Oficial de
Idiomas de Valdemoro), Fiona Baird (Language Centre, University of
Granada), Francisco Bazaga Calderón (Escuela Oficial de Idiomas,
Jesús Maestro, Madrid), Mike Carter (CLIC International House,
Seville), Margaret Curtis (Escuela Oficial de Idiomas, Alcorcón,
Madrid), Román Landajo Porta (Escola Oficial d'Idiomes de L'Hospitalet
de Llobregat), Maria Luz López Martinez (Escuela Oficial de Idiomas de
Bilbao), Francisco Martín Ordaz (Escuela Oficial de Idiomas, Jesús
Maestro, Madrid), Blanca Martinez López (Escuela Oficial de Idiomas
Las Rozas, Madrid), Lourdes Montoro (Escola Oficial d'Idiomes 2,
Barcelona), Diane Naughton (Language Centre, University of Granada),
Thomas Patterson (The English Centre, Madrid), Ben Rowdon (ESADE,
Barcelona), Russell Stannard (CLIC International House, Seville),
Amanda Stephenson (Language Centre, University of Granada), Emma
Thomas (CLIC International House, Seville), Imma Torregrosa Triviño
(Escola Oficial d'Idiomes de L'Hospitalet de Llobregat), Alejandro
Zarzalejos (Escuela Oficial de Idiomas, Las Rozas, Madrid); in **the UK**,
the staff and students of the Bell Language School (Saffron Walden),
Rolf Donald (Eastbourne School of English), Melanie Faulmann and the
staff and students at Greenhill College, Carolyn Jones (Bell School of
Languages, London), Denis Lyons (Communicaid Group, London), Katy
Mann (Crawley College), Martin, Sarah Nava (South Thames College,
London), Louise Sasada (Wimbledon School of English).

The Wavelength publishing team:

Judith King, (Publishing Manager), Sue Ullstein, (Senior Development
Editor), Sarah Crawford, (Senior Editor), Rose Wells, (Editorial
Assistant), Rob Briggs, (Senior Designer), Hilary Morgan, (Picture
Editor), Paul Katumba, (Production Controller).

Photo Acknowledgements

We are grateful to the following for permission to reproduce copyright
photographs:

Catherine Ashmore for 16 top; Britstock-IFA for 99 top (J Heron); J
Allan Cash Ltd for 21 bottom; Compaq Computers for 68(e); DFG for 56
top right; James Davis Travel Photography for 37 bottom;
DesignPoint/Andrew McCarten for 56 top left; Ronald Grant Archive for
21 middle right; Immediate PR for 68(d); Index Stock Photography for
32 right; The Kobal Collection for 96; Moviestore Collection for 21 top;
Pearson Television/Grundy for 57; Pictor International for 15 bottom
left, 27 top right, 27 middle, 37 top, 68(a) and 99 bottom; Retna/Jonnie
Miles for 75; Rex Features for 15 top right, 21 middle left, 27 bottom
left (Today), 56 bottom; 68 (b) and 68(c) (Paul Fievez/Times); Ann
Ronan Picture Library for 64; Spectrum Colour Library for 15 top left
and 47; Tony Stone Images/Dave Rosenberg for 15 bottom right, 16
middle, 27 top left, 27 bottom right and 36 bottom; Sygma for 16
bottom; Telegraph Colour Library/Guy Edwardes for 32 left; Travel Ink
Photo Library/Derek Allan for 32 middle and Simon Warner for 36 top.

All other photographs not acknowledged are © Pearson Education /
Peter Lake.

We are grateful to the following for their help with the location
photography: Bar Coast, Cambridge; Bell Language School, Saffron
Walden; Eurostar; Zoe Firebrace; Furlong Homes, Waltham Cross; Great
Hadham Golf Club; Highbury Park, London; Jack Kessler; Lisa Kovach;
Le Mercury, Islington; Alison McGowan; Nachos, Islington; Alan Ogden;
Cheryl Pelteret; The Pitcher and Piano, Holborn; Royal Holloway & New
Bedford College, Egham, Surrey; Saffron Walden Police Station; Graham
Shipley; Wilson Associates, Chelmsford.

The back cover photographs of the authors by Charles Yacoub.

We regret that we have been unable to trace the copyright holder of
the artwork on pages 63 and 133 and would welcome any information
enabling us to do so.

We are grateful to the following for permission to reproduce copyright
material:

Authors' agents A P Watt on behalf of The Lord Tweedsmuir and Jean,
Lady Tweedsmuir for an adapted extract from THE THIRTY NINE STEPS
by John Buchan; Express Newspapers plc for an extract from the
article "Lover's Dogfood Revenge" in THE DAILY EXPRESS 9.9.92 ©
Express Newspapers; Mautoglade Music Limited for lyrics to "No
Particular Place to Go" © 1964 Arc Music Corp., by kind permission of
Jewel Music Publishing.